# Learning Excel VBA for Beginners

## Understand the Basic and Build a Sample Project

Santhana Krishnan. V

# Table of Contents

Introduction ................................................................................. 7

1. Basics of Excel ....................................................................... 10
2. Over View of VBA ................................................................. 12
    Developer Tab .................................................................... 12
    VBA Elements ..................................................................... 14
    Macro .................................................................................. 15
        Create Macro ................................................................. 15
        Edit Macro ..................................................................... 17
        Macro Security warning ............................................... 18
    Visual Basic Editor(VBE) .................................................... 20
        Project Explorer ............................................................ 21
    Controls .............................................................................. 23
        Create Controls ............................................................. 24
3. Visual Basics ......................................................................... 27
    Procedure ........................................................................... 28
    Statement ........................................................................... 29
    Comments .......................................................................... 30
    Events ................................................................................. 30
4. Data Type and Variable ....................................................... 34
    Data Type ........................................................................... 34
    Variables ............................................................................ 35
        Constants Variable ....................................................... 36
        Method to Declare Variable ......................................... 37
        Variable Scope .............................................................. 38
5. VBA Excel Object Model ..................................................... 39
    Excel Objects ..................................................................... 40
        Application object ........................................................ 40

- Excel Workbook Object ............................................. 41
- **Set Keyword** .......................................................... 43
  - Worksheet ............................................................ 44
  - Ranges and Cells ................................................... 45
- **Testing Application: -1** ........................................ 48
  - Combo Box ........................................................... 49
  - Finding Last Row .................................................. 56
  - Finding Last Column ............................................. 58

## 6. Debugging ............................................................. 59
- Debugging the code ................................................. 60
- **Debug in Test Application-1** ................................ 67

## 7. Conditional check and Loops ............................. 70
- **Conditional statement** ........................................ 70
  - If else Statement .................................................. 70
  - Select Case statement .......................................... 71
- **Loop Statement** ................................................... 72
  - Do Loop ................................................................ 72
  - For Next Loop ....................................................... 73
  - For Each Loop ...................................................... 74
  - GoTo Statement ................................................... 75

## 8. VBA Operators .................................................... 77
- Arithmetic Operators .............................................. 77
- Comparison Operators ............................................ 77
- Logical Operators ................................................... 78
- Concatenation Operator ......................................... 78
- **Testing Application 1 - Continue** ........................ 80

## 9. VBA Procedure .................................................... 82
- **Subroutine(Sub)** .................................................. 82

Function .................................................................................... 83
    Parameter / Argument ........................................................ 84
    ByRef / ByVal parameter .................................................... 85
    Call sub procedure ............................................................... 87
    Function Return .................................................................. 88
    Exit Procedure ..................................................................... 90

# 10. Message and Input Box ............................................... 92

Message Box .......................................................................... 92
    Prompt ................................................................................. 92
    Buttons ................................................................................ 93
    Title ..................................................................................... 94
    HelpFile and Context ......................................................... 94

Input Message Box ................................................................ 95
    Default ................................................................................. 96
    XPOS .................................................................................. 96
    YPOS .................................................................................. 96

Testing Application 1 - Continue ........................................... 96

# 11. Arrays ........................................................................ 103

Static Array .......................................................................... 103
    Array Index Base ............................................................... 104
    LBound and UBound ........................................................ 104
    Multi-Dimensional Array .................................................. 107

Dynamic Array ..................................................................... 111
    Redim ................................................................................ 111

# 12. Data Manipulation by In-build function ................. 114

String .................................................................................... 115
    Left(), Right() and Mid() function ..................................... 115
    Len() function .................................................................... 115
    LTrim(), RTrim() and Trim() function ............................. 115

Lower(), Upper() and Proper() function ............................. 116

InStr() and InStrRev() function ........................................... 116

Chr() and Asc() function ...................................................... 117

Split() and Join() function .................................................... 117

Replace() function ................................................................ 118

## Date and Time ............................................................... 120

Date(), Time() and Now() function ..................................... 120

DateAdd() Function ............................................................. 121

DateDiff() Function .............................................................. 121

Day(), Month(), Year(), Weekday() Function ..................... 122

Hour(), Minute(), Second() Function ................................. 122

MonthName(), Function ...................................................... 122

WeekDay() function ............................................................. 123

WeekDayName() function ................................................... 123

DateSerial() , TimeSerial() function .................................... 123

DateValue(), TimeValue() function ..................................... 124

Comparing date    124

## Activity Function ........................................................... 124

Find function ........................................................................ 124

Offset function ..................................................................... 125

Sorting Method .................................................................... 126

Filter Method ........................................................................ 128

# 13. Error Handling ........................................................... 135

# 14. Project ......................................................................... 138

## Project Concept ............................................................... 139

## Project Building .............................................................. 142

Dashboard ............................................................................ 142

Reference Library ................................................................ 144

File Upload Script ................................................................ 145

- With....End with .................................................................. 149
- Category Form ................................................................... 149
  - Main Category ................................................................ 152
  - Sub Category .................................................................. 161
- Data Adding Form .............................................................. 173
  - Expenses Data Sheet ....................................................... 177
  - Extract Expenses Data .................................................... 181
  - Save Expenses ................................................................ 185
  - Bills Attachment .............................................................. 188
  - Upload Bills .................................................................... 192
- Report ............................................................................... 196

## Annexure - Project Application Codes ....................... 202
- Dash Board Sheet ............................................................ 202
- Expenses Sheet ............................................................... 209
- This Work Book ............................................................... 216
- Forms .............................................................................. 216
  - Bills ................................................................................ 216
  - Category form ................................................................ 219
- Module1 .......................................................................... 224

## Annexure – VBA Inbuilt function List ......................... 226

# Introduction

In our day to day activity, we use Microsoft Excel to perform a repetitive task. Excel VBA is an extremely helpful tool since it will help you to automate a big task by simple button click. Also we can build an application by VBA and Excel, to capture and monitoring the job with multiple user. VBA stands for Visual Basic for Applications, an event-driven programming language from Microsoft that is now predominantly used with Microsoft office applications such as MS-Excel, MS-Word, and MS-Access. Beyond Microsoft office application, VBA is also supported in other company's software like AutoCAD, ArcGIS, LibreOffice, CATIA, Word Perfect, Corel-Draw and solid Works.

VBA 5.0 was launched in 1997 along with MS Office 1997 products. Then next version VBA 6.0 and VBA 6.1 were launched in 1999, notably with support for COM, add-ins in Office 2000. VBA 6.5 was released with office 2007 and after that Microsoft stopped licensing VBA to other application. After development of .NET VB, Microsoft is not continuing the development of VBA, but it upgraded VBA version 7.1 is supported to all release of MS-office application from office 2013 to office 2021.

VB (Visual Basic) and VBA (Visual Basic for Applications) are use same programming language "Basic" and use "VISUAL" layer which allows developers to create user friendly user forms and controllers and act as a Integrated Development Envirinment (IDE) to help in Application development. However, VBA works within a 'host' application like Word or Excel or AutoCAD and it cannot work independently like a standalone application. But .Net VB can create DLL and EXE files and run as a Standalone application. This means that the programs can run independently like any other applications.

So please remember that VBA can't work as a standalone application, so we have to build any application using Excel or MS-Access. In this book we will learn Excel based application using VBA. VBA allows you to automate various activities in Excel such as generating reports, preparing charts & graphs, doing calculations, do repetitive task, etc. This book covers some basic information about VBA including the different data types and variables that you can use to automate processes and functions.

People use Excel VBA for multiple reasons like Creating budget, Data base, generating invoices, analyzing data, submit a Report, Developing Graphical charts using data and Forecasting. There are many applications available in the market developed by different vendors but it will not exactly match to your requirement. To use such application, you have to sacrifice some needs or you have to go around with different loop and achieve a task. So You can either tweak those applications or develop new applications using VBA. You can use these new applications to complete your work in a few minutes or less.

To build a small application, we have to follow some discipline and procedures. To understand the application building, I am going to explain a small application which is used to record Home Budget. The dash board of that project is shown below.

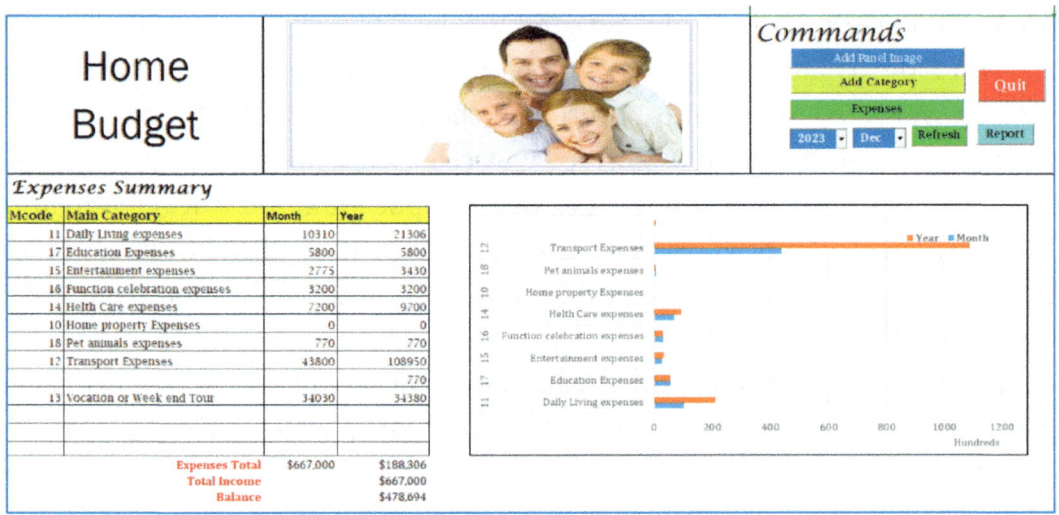

Learning any programing script, you have to test all the code in your system, so that we can familiarize the syntax and which is very helpful while debugging. Many examples have been given across the book that will help you to learn the concepts better. You should practice these examples before you write any new code. Since we are going to build an Excel application, you should have a latest version (2013 or Later) in your system. I am using Microsoft office 2016 on windows machine for demonstrating examples in this book. There is not much difference in the script code for 2013 to 2021 version, but some reference library file may differ.

# 1. Basics of Excel

Before learning the program code, first you have to learn the basic terminology used to specify the excel components. Any excel file is called **workbook** and its main role is to organize and create related data in a single place, categorized into different **worksheets** for simple and easy organization. It has one or many worksheets and user can add any number of sheets based on memory usage.

In opened Excel file, we may see three section like Menu ribbon (Top), Working Section (Middle) and **Sheets** (Bottom). The Middle section area is a work space used to enter our Data.

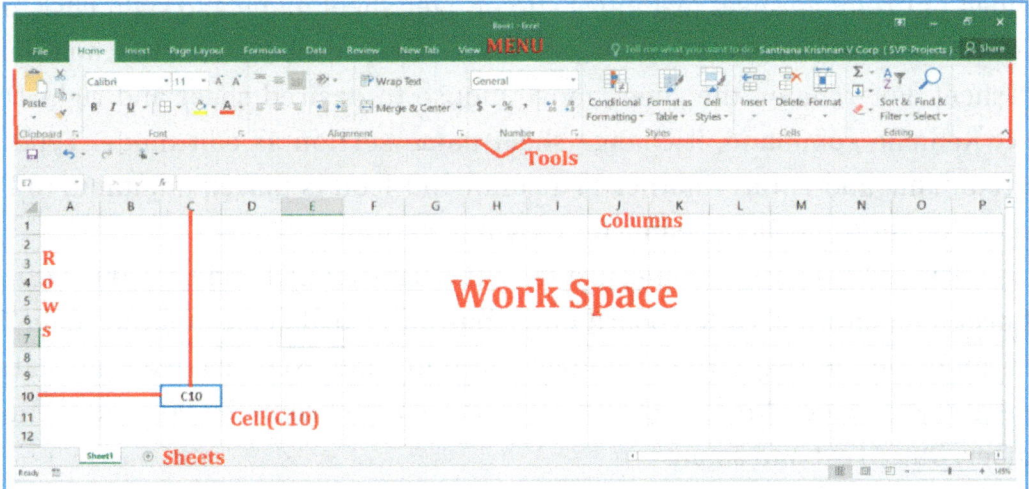

The Top section is just like other application **Menu** provides shortcuts to Excel sheets commands. A command is an action that allows you to make something like insert, Edit, Modify and save in that work sheet. The work space is having Grid Lines on vertical and horizontal direction and form a lot of rectangular boxes. This boxes are called Cell which can hold any type of data and formulas. The horizontal alignment of cells is called **Rows** and Vertical Alignment of Cells are called **Columns**. The Columns are classified with alphabetical labeling from A to Z and rows are numerically graduated from 1 to 1048576. There is no restriction for columns and Rows and it can be extended according to our file requirement.

The entire workspace is further broken down into smaller rectangles known as **Cells**. All our data are typed into the cells, which can be edited or deleted in any time. Other than data it can be formatted with different styles to improve the view presentation. The cells are referenced with row and column intersection value like C10, which indicate that the cell is on column "**C**" and row "**10**". This also referred in VBA as **Cells (10,3)**. Hear the first value is Row number and second value is count of column number(C=3).

The Bottom section contains various sheets name to save different groups of data in different sheets. It just like a Table in database. When you start a new file, it assigns one Sheet by default in the name of Sheet1. You can insert / create many sheets in a single workbook and you can add or remove any sheets. You can also change the Sheets name as you like which is help to easily change over the sheet and access the data easily by programs. For create a new sheet, just click the Plus sign, it adds a new sheet at right side and Name it as **Sheet** with a number. For remove sheet just move curser over sheet name and right click, then select **Delete** Command. If the work book has only one sheet, then we can't delete that sheet. For rename the sheet, move mouse to desired sheet and right click, select **Rename** command, it change sheet name section as edit mode. Type the desired name and enter. Another List command Icon is placed adjutants to Plus sign, which show all Sheets name for easy navigation.

Data entry is very simple, just click the Desired Cell and type the data and to finish data entry, click keyboard enter button or just select another Cell. This data can be either Text string, Number and Date, and excel make all this data as General Type data. We can change this data type from the format menu to number, Date, Text and so on.

## 2. Over View of VBA

Programs are a container that hold specific code that is used to perform some tasks. It can be written with any program language and we should follow a specific structure and syntax related to that programing language. To write any programing code, we have to use any one of editor either a Text editor or Powerful Integrated Development Environment (IDE). For VBA, Microsoft has developed a Visual Basic Editor (VBE) and VBE is a separate application come along with MS Office software and no need to install it separately. VBA is a visual programming environment and we can see how our program will look before we run it. Any project should build under a project folder and all related Procedure, Function, forms are stored in that folder. But in VBA there is no separate project folder and it will be in-build and stored in each workbook. To access excel VBA editor, we have to navigate through Developer Tab.

### Developer Tab

The Developer tab is a built-in tab in Excel, provides the features to develop any program code by Visual Basic or by a macro. The tab is disabled by default, because most of the users, use excel application as a simple spread sheet with minimum calculation by its in-build function. This files will not have any coding or Macro and saved in .XLSX file format. To add any Macro or VBA script, Developer Tab must be enabled first in the Options section and make it visible on the Excel menu bar. To enable developer menu, click File->Options and select customise ribbon on left side panel. Check the Developer option check box in the main Tabs ribbon. Then click Ok button. It creates a Developer Option in the menu bar and it has all VBA related function commands.

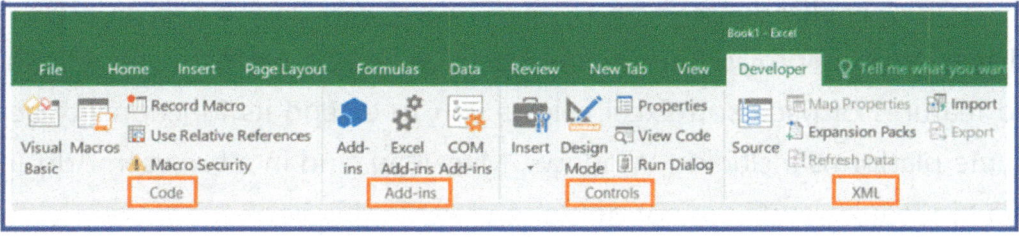

10

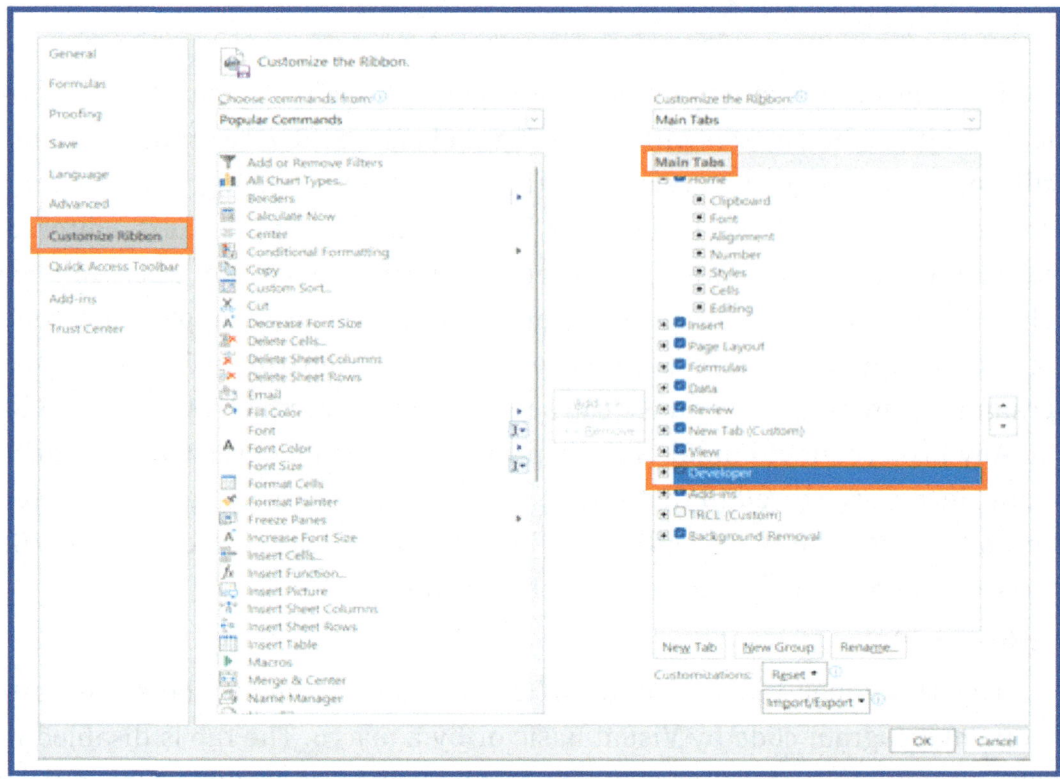

Developer tab has four groups: Code, Add-ins, Controls and XML.

**Code:** Excel supports basic programming to create powerful scripts and actions in Excel with Visual Basic and Excel Macro options. To open Visual Basic Editor, you have to click the Visual basic command and we can build our own programing code. Another simple way of coding is creating a macro, where you can make, record, and edit macros which can automate your repetitive or manual tasks in Office applications.

**Add-Ins**: Add-ins provide additional commands and features other than in-build features of Microsoft Excel, allows you to extend its functionality across multiple platforms including Windows, Mac, iPad, and in a browser. Add-Ins is also a big feature and I am not going to cover in this book.

**Controls**: There are two kinds of Controls Form Control and ActiveX control and both are almost similar for executing the function, but the appearance and its properties are vary. Form Controls are simple & easy to use in Excel. In contrast, ActiveX control is slightly advanced and provides a more flexible design, which is most commonly used in Excel VBA.

**XML**: Microsoft Excel makes it easy to import Extensible Markup Language (XML) data that is created from other databases and applications, to map XML elements from an XML schema to worksheet cells, and to export revised XML data for interaction with other databases and applications. XML is also a big feature and I am not going to cover in this book.

## VBA Elements

Every program, including a VBA program, consists of some building blocks, build with lot of elements. The important element of any program is procedure or functions. Procedure or function is a one block in application, which contain a code to complete a specific task and we have to build many procedure or function for different tasks. Each procedure has a starting and ending declaration and in between it has lot of statements which contains many program elements. They may be a variable, Condition statement, Loop statement, Arithmetic calculation, String Manipulation, comments and so on. The main agenda of this book is to learn about all elements of VBA, so we will see in detail in next chapter.

## Macro

Excel macro is an action or a set of actions that you can run as many times as you want. When you create a macro, you are recording your mouse clicks and keystrokes and save it in a name. You can call back that macro by its name and run it number of times. It will repeat all your mouse and key strokes whatever you recorded and do it instantly. After you create a macro, you can edit it to make minor changes to the way it works. Macros help you to save time on repetitive tasks involved in data manipulation and data reports that are required to be done frequently. We can write the Macro manually or by recording the actions and save it as a macro.

### Create Macro

We can learn the macro by a testing example as explained below. Open the excel file and click the **Developer** menu and click **record macro** command. It popup a dialogue box as shown below

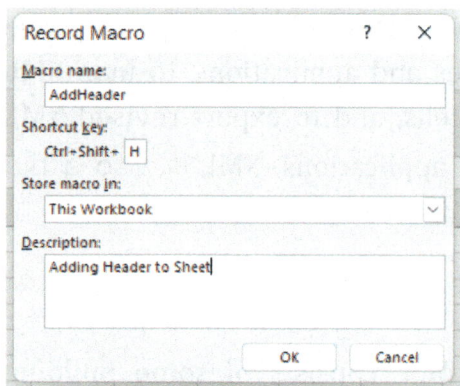

Here macro name is a meaning full name to easily understand the macro function. The shortcut Key is shortcut command with a Letter and control key combination. If you enter lower case letter, it adds Ctrl+ and if you enter Upper case letter it adds Ctrl+Shift. In this example, after completion of recording, Ctrl+Shift+H key strokes will run the macro and complete our task. The macro should be saved in some location for future use. Excel has three option in "Store macro in" drop down field.

1. **This workbook**- It is a default option and save the macro to current workbook.
2. **New Workbook** – It open a new workbook and save the macro in new workbook.
3. **Personel workbook** – It save the macro in a separate excel file in the name of personel.XLSB. Personel workbook is a common file to place a common macro which can be used in entire excel application of our system. So we run this macro from any excel workbook. This macro is available whenever you open existing workbook or a New workbook. This Personal.xlsb file is stored in the XLSTART folder in the location
C:\Users\User Name\AppData\Roaming\Microsoft\Excel\XLSTART

The Description column will explain the function in detail, which will help to understand the purpose of macro by other user or for future remembrance. Add the name and all other data as shown in the Image and click Ok button to save the macro. Now excel file is ready to record your action. Add Title at row one and add Some header in row two. Adjust and do format the Title and headers as shown in the Image.

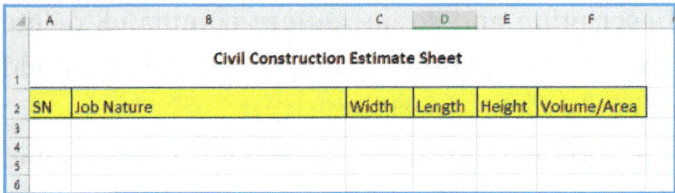

Once you completed all the above format, click the **Stop Recording** Command in Developer menu. Now your macro is ready and to run this macro select another sheet and press **Ctrl+Shift+H** keys. You will notice, in a fraction of second this macro creates an identical formatted header in sheet2. When you record a macro, Excel stores it all action in a VBA code. You can view this code in the VBA editor and you can modify that code if you have substantial knowledge of Excel VBA.

**Edit Macro**

To view or edit the macro, click the **Macros** command in **developer** menu. It popup a dialogue box as shown below and show all the macro name in the list box. You can select any one of the macro from list and it will be shown in Macro name field.

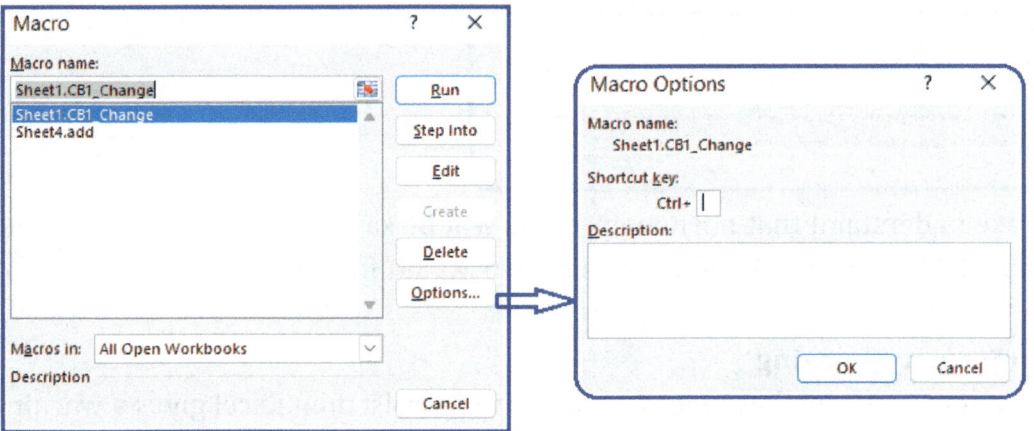

In general, all our macros codes are stored in "Module" object and some time we will also write some procedure in that module. The macro list shows all procedure with start declaration of **Sub** or **Public Sub** from all module. Just select any one macro and click **Run** command, it execute the macro. The **step into** command will run the code and stop at execution at first line in debug mode. **Edit** command open the relevant module and position the cursor at the selected macro code first line. **Create** will create a new macro and we have to fill all the data like Name, Short cut Key, Description and so on. **Delete** command, delete the selected macro. **Options** command open another dialogue box to edit or add the other options like Name, Short cut key and description.

The macro you recorded recently will be shown in "Module1" object and you may notice that a lot of code is written to make this task as shown below.

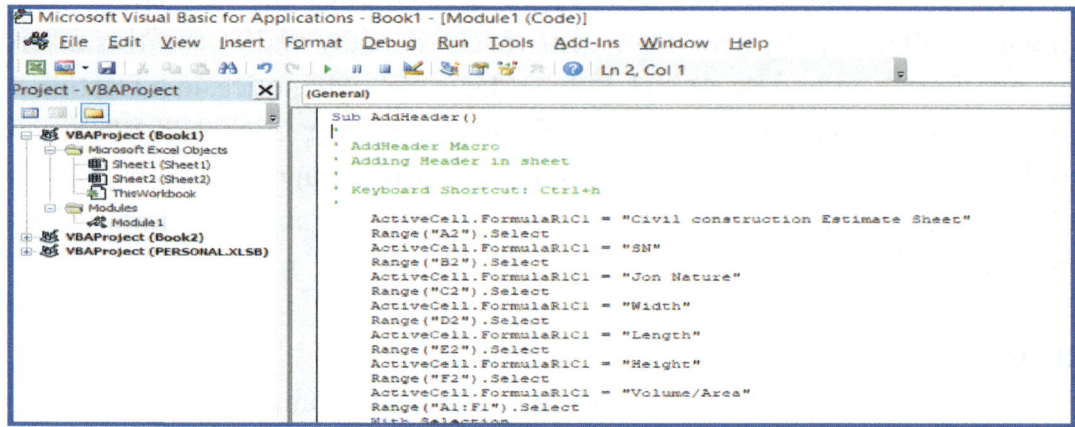

That's all now you have created a VBA script and test it in excel file. While Saving the excel file, it will pop up a message box, saying you have to select different file type to save the file with macro.

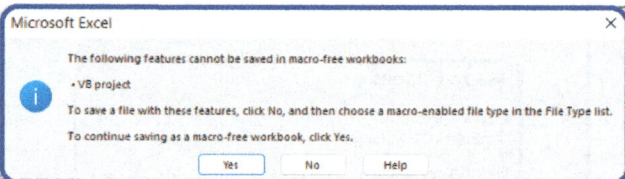

So please understand that normal excel file will be saved with **.XLSX** format and macro or VBA script excel file will be saved in **.XLSM** format.

### Macro Security warning

If the workbook has macro or ActiveX controls, then Excel gives a warning message at the time of opening. These warning messages are just to alert you about the potential problems. Some macros or ActiveX events will be triggered while activate a workbook or sheet, which may change or modify certain data or value. To safe guard the data always the macro and ActiveX controls are disabled. If you know the file source and the source is trusted, then we can enable the macro by clicking Enable Content otherwise no macro will be function.

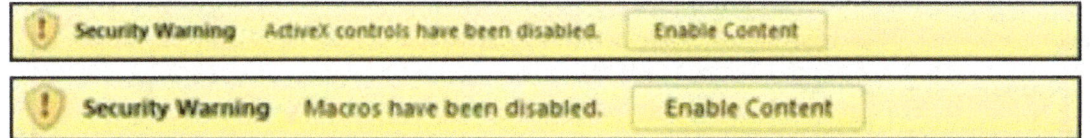

Instead of enable the macro every time while opening, we can fix that to change some settings in trust center.

1. Click on the "Macro Security" button on your "Developer" tab. You can see it in the image above. It has the icon of a yellow triangle with an exclamation mark inside it.
2. Once you click on this button, it will bring up a dialogue box called "Trust Center" and select "Macro Settings" option
3. Alternatively, you can navigate to File->Options->Trusted Center and click "Trust Center Settings" button, it will open the Trust center dialogue box and select the macro settings option.
4. In the main part of the dialogue box, you will see a menu that has two parts: "Macro Settings" and "Developer Macro Settings."
5. Select the "Enable all macros" option in macro settings and check "Trust access to the VBA project object model." Option.
6. IF the file has ActiveX controls, then change the option to ActiveX Settings in left side panel and click the option "Enable all controls without restrictions and without prompting"
7. Change the option to message Bar in left side panel and click the "Never show information about blocked content" option.

Please remember that, this setting is for Excel application and not for a specific excel file. So by changing this setting it will not generate any warning message for all excel file which have macros.

## Visual Basic Editor(VBE)

VBA Editor is a very powerful tool and it is an interface for creating scripts. Visual Basic Editor is a separate application and it is a part of Microsoft Office package. By default, it's hidden, and you have to activate to access it. To activate the VBE, in short cute Just click **Alt+F11** keys otherwise click Developer menu tab and click Visual Basic command. Another way to open VBE, just move the mouse curser over the sheet name and right click, then click View Code option. All the above command opens the VBA editor screen as shown below.

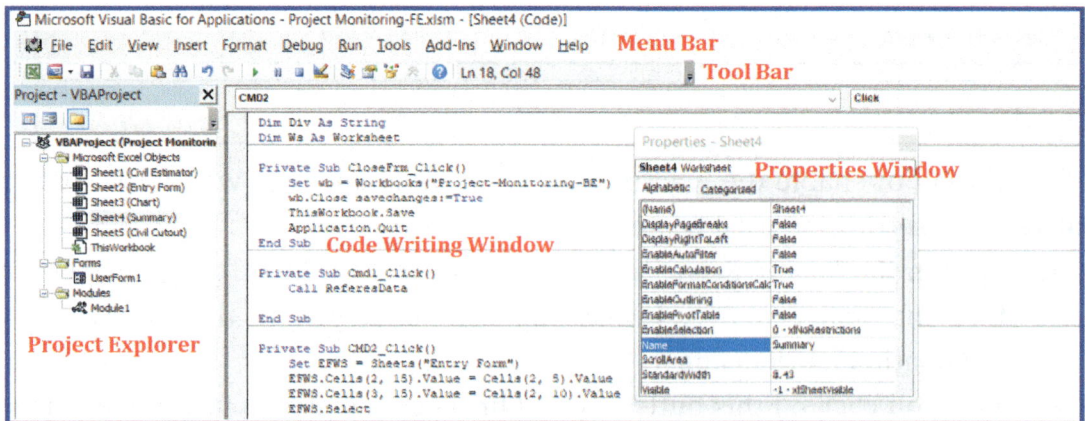

Menu bar and Tool bars are similar to other application; all commands can be executed from here. This editor is formed with multiple floatable windows like Project explorer, Properties window, Local window, Watch window, Immediate window, Object browser and tool box. We can hide or show all these window based on requirement. Also we can move and position all these window to any area. All the part of VBA is explained in detail in Debugging chapter.

The main part of VBE is code writing window, where we write all our script and develop user forms. The content of the code writing window, dynamically change based on selection of objects in project explorer panel located at left side.

**Project Explorer**

The Project Explorer Window is used to interact with different objects that make up the project. Every project is an individual file that hold all our program and this will be saved the Office document as a separate file. If the project explorer is not visible, then we can activate by a menu command View->Project Explorer.

When you're working with Excel, every workbook is considering as a separate project and will be shown in the project explorer. Each project has four objects like Microsoft Excel object, Forms, Module and Class Module. Here the Microsoft Excel object will be added automatically for all work book and other object we can add based on our requirement. VBA editor is not for a specific workbook and it always show all the projects of all workbook which is opened.

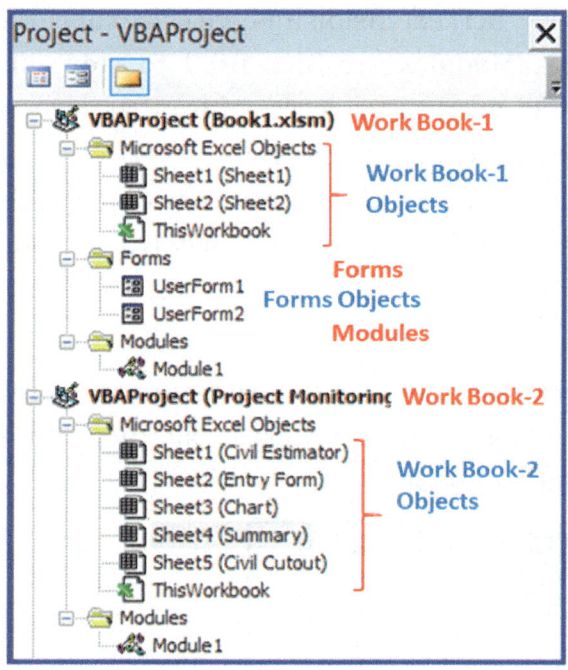

**Microsoft Excel Object**: - Excel Objects is refers to the entities that make up an Excel workbook, such as Worksheets, Rows, Columns, Cell Ranges, and the Excel Workbook itself (This workbook). Each object in Excel has a number of Properties, which are stored as a part of that object. For example, an Excel Worksheet's properties include the Worksheet's Name, Protection, Visible Property, Scroll Area, etc. The individual sheets in that work book will work as an individual module having the sheet name. All the procedure written in that sheets are stored in that module.

**Forms**: - Editing a longer data sheet in excel file is very difficult task. So we can overcome this by creating a user form or Data form and edit a filtered record. We can add any number forms in this object to do different data collection or data calculation. We can add a new user form by right click over the desired workbook in project explorer window and click Insert->User form or from Menu Insert->User form.

**Module**: - A module is a designated space within the VBA editor of Excel where you can write and store procedures and functions which can be either Private or Public and can be accessed either from within that module (Private) or from anywhere in the project (Public). In general, a common procedure like to check whether the file is open, Check the week day of given date. So Any procedure from Sheet or Form can access this module procedure and use that results. The module is maintained in a file with (. bcf) extension and we can export the entire module to any other work book. Modules are also used to store variables, constants and declarations that will need to be accessed from anywhere in the project. By default, macro codes are saved in the module.

**Class Module**: - Class modules allow you to create your own objects which can have their own properties and methods like any other object (range, worksheet, Excel).

## Controls

Controls in Excel are objects and that can be inserted in the spreadsheet to perform different types of actions. We can access all these tools from Developer Tab by clicking the Insert command.

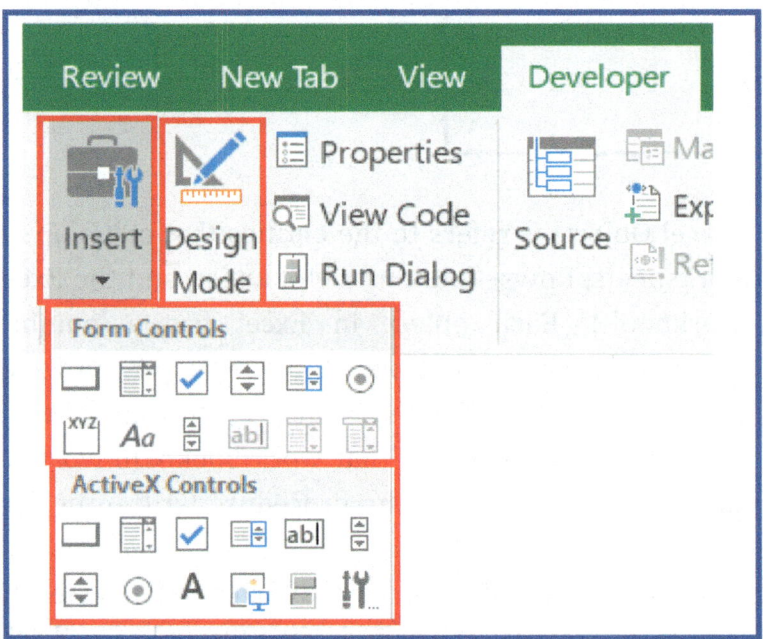

There are two types of Controls **Form** Control and **ActiveX** control. Both are mostly similar, but the appearance and its properties are varying between them. Both types of controls can be used on worksheets but only ActiveX controls can be used on **user forms**. Both types of controls can be created, modified and deleted from either the worksheet, or programmatically with VBA.

Form controls are almost fixed design with simple look and can't change its shapes color etc. Whereas ActiveX control have an elegant look and we can change all it appearance property. Form controls are not used as on object whereas ActiveX control will be act as on object. Form control don't have any properties settings, whereas ActiveX controls has more property settings and can be modified manually or by event. Both type has all frequent use controls like Command Button, Combo Box or Drop Down list, Spin button, List Box, Label, Text Box, Check box, Radio Button, Option button. Other than the above controls ActiveX controls has more controls. In this book only we are going to Deal ActiveX controls and learn each controls in details while doing the sample projects.

## Create Controls

Open any blank excel work book and enable the Developer Tab, if it is hidden. To insert any controls, you have to go Developer tab click the **Insert** sub menu and select the form control or ActiveX controls from the list. For example, select **command button** in **ActiveX** Controls, move the mouse and click any one location and press left key of mouse and Drag diagonally in right direction to size the controls and leave it. While doing this action you may notice that the Design Mode controls is automatically selected.

## Design Mode

The 'Design Mode' is a tool toggle the editing of controls. The design mode tab is useful only with excel containing macros or Visual basic controls. It is easy to toggle the design mode, just click over the Design mode button in Developer tab. If the Design mode is selected, then it will not allow to run any code and no events are executed.

To edit any control properties or events, first we have to turn on the Design mode and then edit the control. For example, to edit the recent inserted command button, turn on the Design mode and click the button. Now the button is selected and it shows some handles on all side. You can resize or change the position of button by drag the handles appear around the button.

To add event code or edit event code, just double click the button, it opens the VBA editor screen and locate the cursor at the first line of event. If no code is written previously, then it writes the starting and ending **sub** procedure declaration code and wait for adding further codes. Another way right clicks the button and select View Code command, it will open the events. Please remember that all editing on controls is only possible with **Design Mode** in on condition.

## Properties

We can set or change the properties of each controls in design mode, right-click a control and click Properties which will display the Properties window. Another way, Select the control click the properties button in Developer Tab to open the properties window. VBA is built with many objects to form an application and each object has more properties. Object properties are defined as a simple association between **name** and **value**. All properties have a name and value is one of the attributes linked with the property, which used to access that property.

In the property window, Property **names** are shown in the left column in the window, and property **values** are shown in the right column. The name of property is self-explanatory type and it convey its purpose straight away by its name. So I am not going to explain in detail about all the property name and its value. Also you can learn all this property by google search, whenever you required. So just You have to set a property value by entering the new value to the right of the property name. We can view the properties in two modes Alphabetic or Categorized. In alphabetic mode it sorts all property name in alphabetic and in Categorized mode, it groups all related properties in a group and show it under Group header.

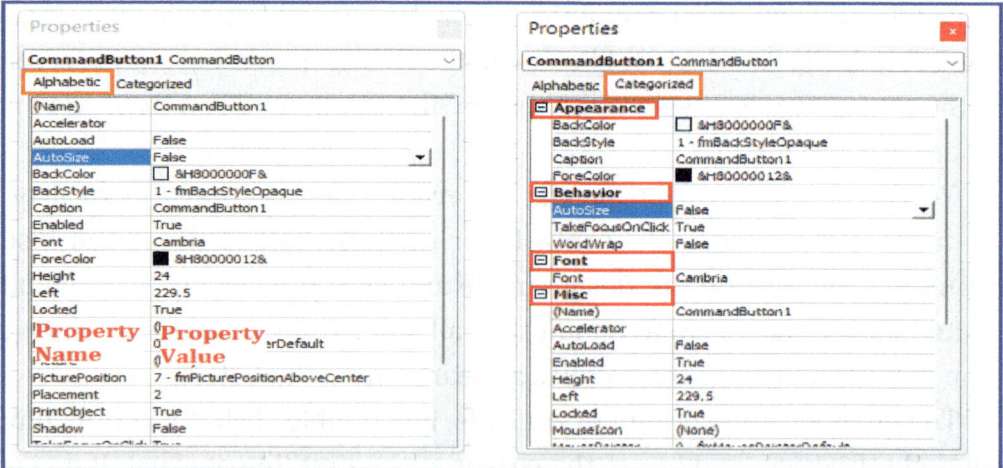

Here the main key property is the **name** of controls. Whenever we insert a controls, it automatically adds the name by its control type, but we can change this according to our function. We can change the Button Display text in caption properties. For our learning purpose Change, the name property from CommondButton1 to **"Find"** and caption from CommondButton1 to "Find". Caption property is a descriptive text that appears directly on or around a

21

control. Like we can change properties of font, Back color, Fore Color, width and height as you like.

## 3. Visual Basics

The **Basic** is a programming language developed by Microsoft for their windows operating system. The Basic is short form of **B**eginners **A**ll-Purpose **S**ymbolic **I**nstruction **C**ode. To Build program code, Microsoft developed an Editor which provides a graphical user interface (GUI) which allows programmers to modify code by simply dragging and dropping objects and defining their behavior and appearance. So they named the language to visual Basic and for next generation "Visual" is become their trade name and used for all their application. VBA uses simple English statements to write the instructions and easy to learn.

For any programing language we have to understand the main elements of script like code syntax, Key words, Procedure, Variables, Arithmetic and logical Operators, Condition and Loop statements, Data types and some in-build function to manipulate the Number, String and Images.

**Color code**

To differentiate all elements in code all code editor will show different color for each element. Same way, in this book also, I am used different color for different elements as shown below. This will help to visualize and understand the code easily.

1. VBA key words like Dim, Sub, Private, If, Else, for, Set, in-built function and methods etc.
2. Variable name used to hold string or integer value
3. Data type for variable like String, Integer, Long etc.
4. Object Variable name to hold object properties
5. Procedure name (sub or function)
6. Control names used for button, Combo box, Check box et.
7. All Comments
8. Parameter value or Input value
9. Already written codes

Please remember, Visual basic editor will not provide this much color code and it will be different than this.

## Procedure

A procedure is a block of statements that is enclosed by a particular start declaration and End declaration statements. All VBA instruction(Code) are generally written within the procedure. The main purpose of a procedure is to carry out a particular task or action. There are three types of procedure: Sub, Function and Property. The most common types of procedures are **Sub** procedures and **Function** procedures.

The **Sub** procedures will perform an **action** like write data to cell or Create a New Sheet in the excel workbook. In general **function** procedure are called from any one of Sub procedure at intermittent of program, pass some value (parameter) to function and the function procedure carry out certain calculation with that parameter and return the result value to Sub procedure. All macro recorder codes are written only in sub procedure, since it is an action you carried over in the excel workbook.

A property procedure is used to manipulate a custom property on a module, class, or structure of excel workbook. Usually property procedures are use Get and Set statements in pairs. By this we will get the settings value and set it to different one as we need.    For writing Sub procedure, it should start with declaration statement **Sub** (subroutine) and a Procedure name then Open and close Parentheses and end with declaration statement **End Sub**. This is minimum requirement and we can add other optional in the starting declaration statement.

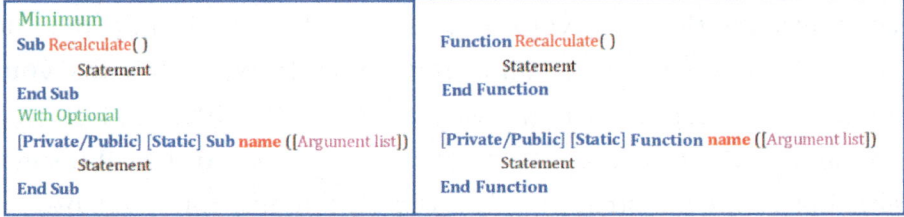

In any procedure it does all instruction written in between Sub – End Sub. We will learn the procedure in detail in chapter 9.

## Statement

A statement is a complete instruction written in many lines. It has many element like keywords, operators, variables, constants, and  expressions. Declaration statements are used to name a variable with data type. Also procedure use a starting and ending declaration statement with a procedure or event name. Assignment statements are used to assign a value or expression to a variable or constant. Executable statements are used to initiate the actions. These statements can execute a method or function, and they can loop or branch through blocks of code. Executable statements often contain mathematical or conditional operators.

A statement usually fits on one line, but you can continue a statement onto the next line by using a line-continuation character which is underscore character ( _ ).

```
Code written in single line
MsgBox Prompt:="Hello " & myVar, Title:="Greeting Box", Buttons:=vbExclamation
Code written in multi-line
MsgBox Prompt:="Hello " & myVar, _
Title:="Greeting Box", _
Buttons:=vbExclamation
```

We can write a small statement in a single line by adding Colon (:) at end of each statement.

X= "Krish"  :  Y =12  :  Z=23

## Comments

Always You should write the comments for important steps in the code. Comments can explain the purpose and function of that procedure or give some clarification instruction for particular line of code. It is useful to other developer who edit your code or some time it is very much help full to you to improve the application in later stage. Visual Basic ignores comments when it runs your procedures. Comment lines begin with an apostrophe (' ) or with Rem followed by a space. It can be added anywhere in a procedure and to add it in the same line of statement, insert an apostrophe after the statement, followed by the comment. By default, comments are displayed as green text.

'This is area calculation program
Rem This is area calculation program
Dim x As integer          'variable x is used for getting width value

## Events

An event is an action that can be triggered by any object, which will execute a specified task. For example, when you double-click on a cell, it's an event or click a button in that sheet, it's an event. There are many such events in VBA, as soon as an event occurs, the corresponding procedure will run the code and execute the desired task. There are different objects in Excel, such as Excel application, workbooks, worksheets, charts, Controls, on Timer and on key combination. Each of these objects can have various events associated with it. For example:

If you create a new workbook, it's an application level event.

If you add a new worksheet, it's a workbook level event.

If you change the value in a cell in a sheet, it's a worksheet level event.

If you click a button, It's a Control level event.

In general, all event procedure is named by its object name and event type with underscore (_).

> Sub workbook_Open()
> Sub Worksheet_Activate()
> Sub Button1_Click()

The object events are saved in their respective main object module. For example, if it's a worksheet related event whether a button or cell, then it should be saved in related sheet object. If it's workbook related, then it should be saved in This workbook object.

While opening the VBA editor, the project Explorer show all the objects of that workbook. Double click any one of sheet Object (Sheet1(Area)), it opens a code window for that sheet.

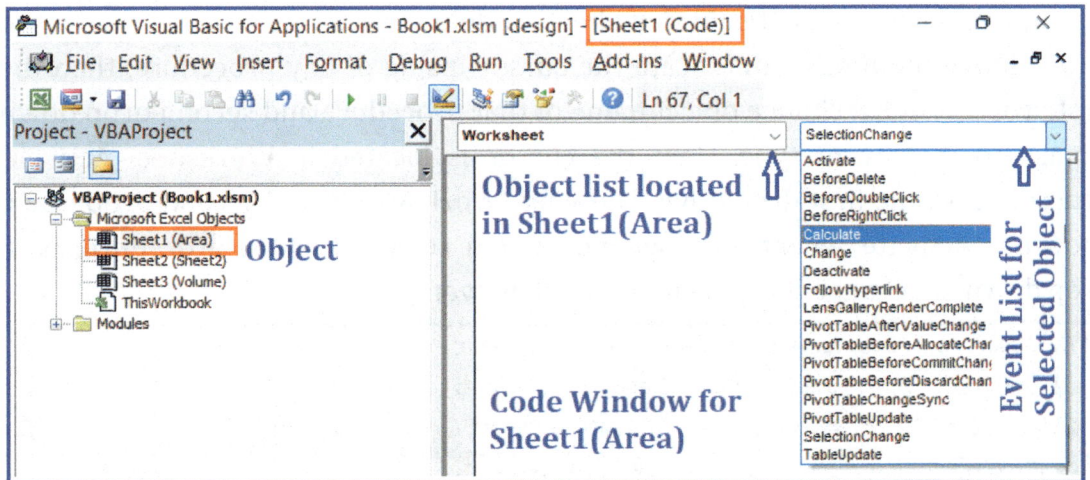

VBA editor provided two drop down list at top of code writing panel. The first drop down list is for object and it list all the object name located in the selected module (Sheet1(Area) module). It will show General, work sheet, Command buttons, Check box and so on. In the above picture worksheet object is selected. The second drop down list show all the events available for selected object. Here a big event list is shown for worksheet like Activate, Deactivate, Change, etc. So no need to mesmerize all the event to our mind, just by these two drop down list we can use any events for any objects. Also it is very help full to access or locate the existing code for any objects.

Select worksheet and select Activate in the event list, Excel automatically add the sub procedure as shown below. You may notice, the procedure name is written with the combination of Object and event name with Underscore. Also it adds the end declaration key word. So, we have write all our code in between the Sub and End sub and we should not change or modify this name. If we add any button in the work sheet, that button name also listed in object drop down list and we can select any event from the second drop down list.

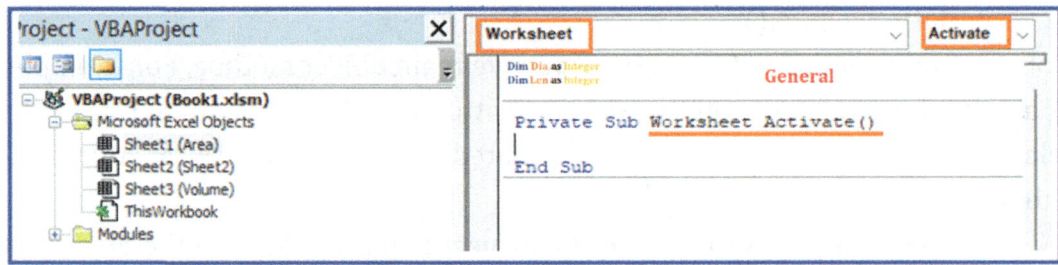

In the object list "General" is the first option which is top most part of window code and we can declare any common variables, which can be used to any other procedure written in that sheet module.

Move the mouse and locate the cursor inside of any procedure, then the first drop down list change object name of that procedure and second drop down change to that event type. Here the cursor is located in Worksheet_Activate procedure, so the first drop down showing "Work Sheet" and second drop down showing "Activate" event. Like whenever you select different procedure, both drop down list change its value to match that event.

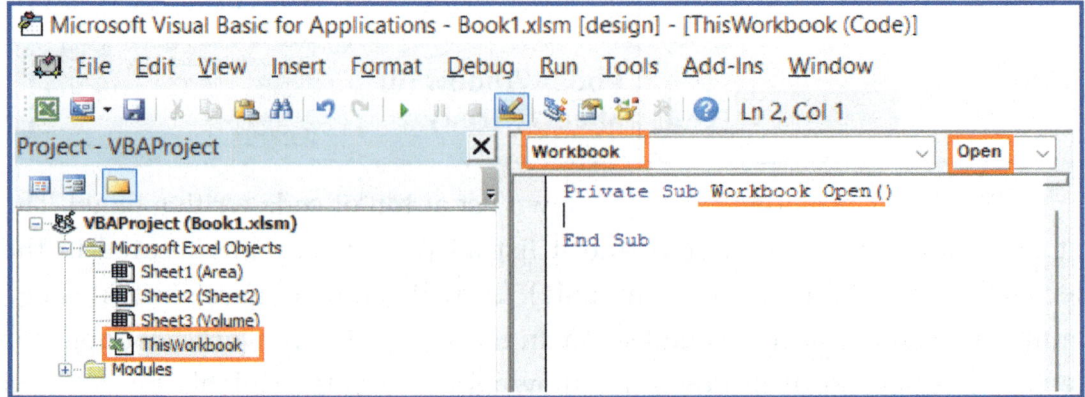

Please Note that each event procedure is stored in their respective worksheet module. So we can create a command button in two sheets with same name and different code, which will be executed based on the active sheet. So the code in Sheet1 module will work only, if the Sheet1 is selected or active. Just like worksheets, if you have a workbook level event code, you can place it in "This Workbook" module. All other events will be explained in later chapters.

## 4. Data Type and Variable

Variables and data types are almost used in every program to store and represent data. Similarly, Excel VBA also has variables and data types to store and represent data. When working with VBA, a variable is a location in your computer's memory where you can store data. The type of data you can store in a variable would depend on the data type of the variable. For example, if you want to store integers in a variable, your data type would be 'Integer' and if you want to store text then your data type would be 'String'.

### Data Type

In computers every data will occupy some memory space. So while building application we have to carefully use different data to minimize the storage space and optimize the program running speed. The main classification of data type is mainly differentiating between the Numeric Data and Non-Numeric Data.

**Numeric Data Type**: Numeric data types are used to perform mathematical operations and it is used to handle the numbers in various representations format.

| Data Types | Memory Size | Value Range |
|---|---|---|
| **Byte** | 1 byte | 0 to 255 |
| **Integer** | 2 bytes | -32,768 to 32,767 |
| **Long** | 4 bytes | (-)2,147,483,648 to (+)2,147,483,648 |
| **Single** | 4 bytes | (-)3.402823E+38 to (+)3.402823E+38 |
| **Double** | 8 bytes | (-)1.79769313486232e+308 to (+)1.79769313486232e+308) |
| **Currency** | 8 bytes | (-)922,337,203,685,477.5808 to (+)922,337,203,685,477.5807 |
| **Decimal** | 12 bytes | 79,228,162,514,264,337,593,543,950,335) & Up to 28 Decimal Places |

**Non-Numeric Data Type**: Non-Numeric data types are not manipulated by the arithmetic operators. These are comprised of texts, date, etc.

| Data Types | Memory Size | Value Range |
|---|---|---|
| **String(fixed size/length)** | Equivalent to String's length(in bytes) | 1 to 65,400 characters |

| | | |
|---|---|---|
| **String(variable length)** | String's length + 10 bytes | 0 to 2 billion characters |
| **Boolean** | 2 bytes | True/False |
| **Object** | 4 bytes | Embedded object |
| **Data** | 8 bytes | January 1, 100 to December 31, 9999 |
| **Variant(numeric)** | 16 bytes | Any value |
| **Variant (text)** | Text's length + 22 bytes | 0 to 2 billion characters |

Whenever we use variable in program code, it reserves some space in memory. So if we tell the correct data type to variable while declaring, we can effectively use the memory space.

## Variables

Variable is a named memory location used to hold a value that can be used for data manipulation and same can be changed during the script execution. we can implicitly declare variables using the assignment (=) operator and the VBA consider that variables as "Variant" data type. The variant type variables required more memory space than usual variables.

EName =" Knish"

Another way by Explicitly, we can declare variables using "**Dim**" keyword which is short name of Dimension. Explicit variable reduces the naming conflicts and spelling mistakes. Since we are indicating the data type while declaring the variable, it occupies less memory space. It is recommended always declare the variables before using them. The syntax of variable declaration "Dim variable name As Data type"

**Dim** EName as String

Ename = "Krish"

If we do not declare any data type, then VBA consider that variable to variant type.

Rules for Declaring Variable
1. Variable can have short names (like **x** and **y**) or more descriptive names (age, sum, total_Volume).
2. Variable names can contain letters, digits and underscores (_).
3. Variable names should not be start with number and it should be a letter.
4. space and period (.) is not allowed in between characters.

5. Variable names are **Not** case sensitive and it automatically correct the variable name to match the name while declaring.
6. Reserved words (like for, String) cannot be used as variable names
7. String value should be written with quotes and for numeric value without quote to be written.
8. We can also declare many variables with same data type by a separation of comma. Dim A, B, C As integer

**Constants Variable**

Constant is a named memory location like any variable used to hold a value that CANNOT be changed during the script execution. All rules for constant variable is same like other variable, but while declaration we have to use "**Const**" key word instead of "Dim" and we have to assign the value while declaration.

Const myDOB as Date = #12/10/2020#

**Method to Declare Variable**

We have to follow certain rules for different data type while declaring in variable.

**String Variable**

The String data type is one of the most common data types in VBA and string is traditionally a sequence of characters set correspond to the letters and Symbols and form text either a word or sentence. There are two types of string variables: fixed length and variable length. A variable-length string can contain up to 2 billion characters and a fixed-length string can contain 1 to 64 K characters.

Dim Ename as String        '--- Variable type no limitation
Dim Ename as String * 20    '---Fixed type store only 20 charecter
Ename = "Krish"        '--Always use double quote for string

**Date Variable**

Date variables are stored as floating-point numbers. Date literals must be enclosed within number signs (#), for example, #January 1, 1993# or #1-12-2023#. The format of date and time will be displayed according to computer system settings.

Dim DOB as Date

DOB = #25-12-2023#

## Numbers

In VBA the numbers are classified in to Integer, Long, Double and Currency. The value range and required memeroy space is explained in data type section.

Dim X1 as Integer      '-Store whole number
Dim Y1 as Double       '-Store Decimal number
X1 = 12                '- Write as it is without quote
Y1 = 10.23

## Variable Scope

The scope of variables is determined by where we declared that variable. We may declare the variable within Procedure or in Module

**Procedure Level**: Here the variables are declared inside procedure either Sub or Function.

Sub sub1()
    Dim A, B, C As integer
    A=12 : B=2 : C=0
    C=A*B
End Sub

Here all variable A, B,C are declared inside the procedure, so we can't use this value to another procedure.

**Module Level**: Here the variables are declared outside of all the procedures, at the top of the module in General Section.

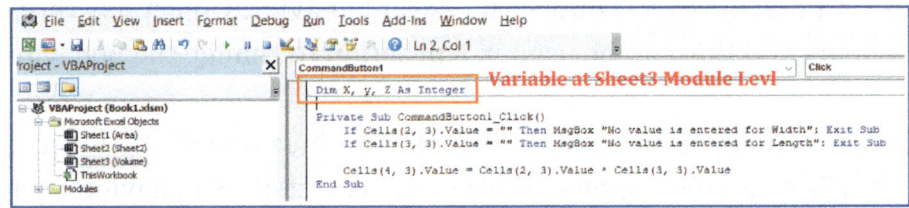

We can use this variable value for all procedures written in that module. If we declare our variable in Module with prefix of Public keywords, then that can be used in all procedure of all modules in same work book.

Public x, y, z As integer

## 5. VBA Excel Object Model

In object oriented programing model the entire application is built with several objects and each object also has several child objects. Excel is also made up of several Objects and few important objects are Application object, Workbook object, Worksheet object and Range Object. Each of the above object will has a collection of Objects like Excel Application has many workbooks and each workbook has many Worksheets, and each worksheet has many different Ranges, Shapes, Chart objects and controls.

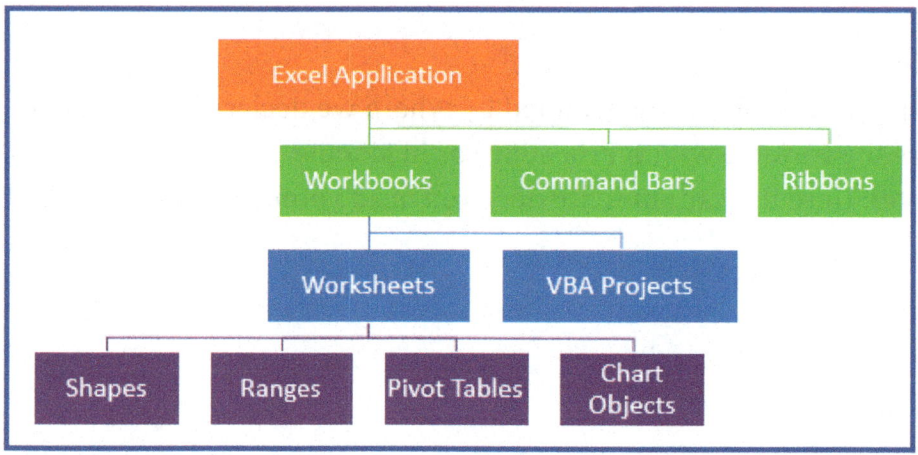

Every object has a related Properties and Methods stored as a part of that object and that can be controlled by VBA code. Although Visual Basic is not a complete object-oriented programming language, but it deals some part. Objects are used in Sub and Function Procedures to control the Excel behavior. Object has three important components and that can be used in a program to change the behavior of that object.

**Property**: - Property is an attribute of an object that defines one of the object's characteristics, such as size, color, screen location, an aspect of its behavior, such as whether it is enabled or visible. To change the characteristics of an object, you have to change the values of that properties. So, all Objects are accessed via Properties.

**Method**: - They are used to perfume some actions with that object data. The tasks are executed inside a method. For example, Add is a method of the Combo Box object, because it adds a new entry to a combo box.

CB1.Add "Mango"

**Event**: - Events occur whenever any VBA code is executed by triggering an object.

For understanding, A Car is an object made up of Engine, Wheel, Break, Steering, Doors, windows, etc. All the components of the car are its child objects. Next, each child has some of its properties (Colors, shape, Material), and it also has some Events (Door Open and close, Engine speed raise or Lower). Similarly, the Microsoft Excel worksheet is an object, and a Range of Cells present in that worksheet are its child objects

## Excel Objects

The important Excel objects are Application object, Workbook object, Worksheet object and Range Object.

### Application object

Excel application object is used in other applications like MS Access, AutoCAD, MS Word and so on. If you want to get data from excel from AutoCAD or MS Access, then we have to use Excel application object.

```
Dim app As Object
On Error Resume Next
    Set app = CreateObject("Excel.Application")
    Set app = GetObject( , "Excel.Application")
```

First we have to declare Variable to assign the application object. Next we have to use VBA in-build function create or Get object to evoke the Application from the system and assign to Variable **app**. The syntax of Create object is **CreateObject**("Applicationname.Object type"). Here we written Excel as application name and Application is as object type. So, if excel application is not active in the system, it creates an excel application object and assign to app variable. Some time we may get some data from Word document to Excel file, then the code will be

Set app = CreateObject("**Word**.Application"). After an object is created, we can refer it in code by using the object variable we defined(**app**). If some reason, the excel application is already opened then this GetObject will assign the excel application to the variable **app**. But before that the create Object throw error, since the application is already created, so to avoid that we have to use on Error Resume Next command. This will move the code to next line if error occurs. The syntax of GetObject is **Getobject**([File with pathname], [ Applicationname.Object type]). It has two optional value, just specify the file name with path, otherwise leave first option and put a comma and then write the Application name and Object type.

**Excel Workbook Object**

Excel workbook is child object of Excel application. We have to use different syntax while using in excel application or in other application.

While using in excel application

Dim wb As Workbook
If you want to assign the current working work book, then
    Set wb = Application.ActiveWorkbook
If you want to open another work book and assign, then
    Fpath ="D:\DMS\Comment-Log.xlsx"
    Set wb = Workbooks.Open(Fpath)
    OR
    Set wb = Workbooks.Open FileName:-Fpath, ReadOnly:=True

If you want to assign another opened work book, then
    Set wb = Workbooks("D:\DMS\Comment-Log.xlsx")

While using in other than excel application

If you want to open an excel work book from other Application, then
    Dim app As Application
    Dim wb As Workbook
    Dim ws As Worksheet
    Dim Fpath As string

    On Error Resume Next
    Fpath ="D:\DMS\Comment-Log.xlsx"
    Set app = CreateObject("Excel.Application")
    Set app = GetObject(, "Excel.Application")
    Set wb = app.Workbooks.Open(Fpath)

**To close the workbook**
    wb.close
    workbooks("D:\DMS\Comment-Log.xlsx").close SaveChanges:=True

while closing you can add the option Save Changes as True or False, otherwise if any data is manipulated, it popup the message for saving the document.

**To Activate the Workbook**

    wb.activate
    workbooks("D:\DMS\Comment-Log.xlsx").Activate
    Thisworkbook.Activate                       'Activate current workbook

Here wb is a mere variable name. So you can name it anything like wbook or workbook1, but it should communicate to developer a meaning. Connecting each object variable and getting property, we have to use dot(.) like app.wb

## Set Keyword

    We can assign any value to variable by just using equal (=) sign and that variable will store that value for future reference. Remember that the value is a single element either a string or an integer. Here the Sname variable will have only the value of "Krish" and only it repeats that value in all the function.

    Dim Sname as string
    Sname="Krish"

Unlike variables, objects cannot be assigned to variables using a mere "=" (equal to) sign. They are special since they hold several or large data's and values. The "**Set**" keyword must be used in order to assign object references to any variable. If you assign an object variable without Set key word, then it throws error message. Before set the object variable, we have to declare the variable by Dim either to a specific object or just object.

Dim wb as workbook         or     Dim wb as object

But in good practice always refer a specific object while declaring. The application is an object which can be assign to an object variable by **Set** and create or Get function

Set app = CreateObject("Excel.Application")        ' Assign the application object reference to app variable.

Set wb = app.workbook    ' Here it take a child object workbook from the application (app) object and assign to variable wb.

Set app = Nothing        'It will release the object and make it nothing

Set Rng = Sheets(1).Range("A1:C5")     ' It assign a range of cells to Rng variable

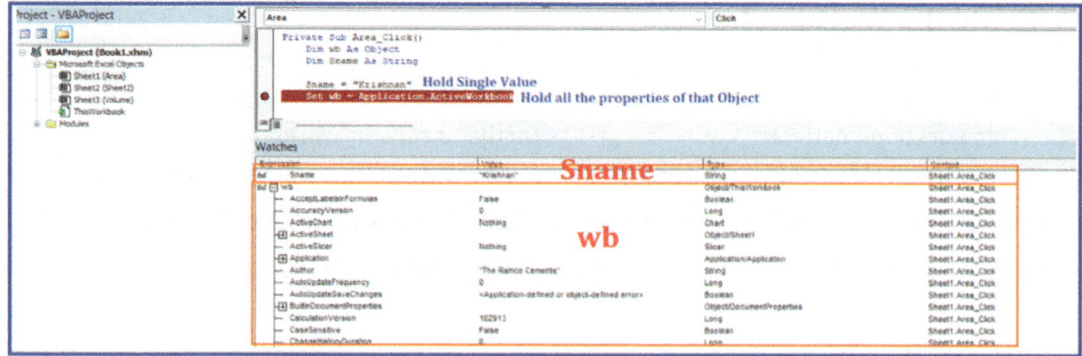

If you see the above image, Sname variable just hold one string value, but **wb** object variable has huge amount of properties and values. Always the object variable show a plus(+) sign in watch window and we can expand it to view all its properties and values.

**Worksheet**

In VBA we can refer the worksheet in two ways either sheets or worksheets, and both methods are almost equal.

Sheets("Sheet1").Activate   **or**   Worksheets("Sheet1").Activate

In excel some time we may use ChartSheet type worksheet that contains only a chart without cells and other controls. Sheets can handle both worksheet and chartSheet, but worksheets handles only worksheet. The excel workbook have many number of sheets as shown in Image, and we have to select or Activate the desired sheet to do data manipulation in that sheet.

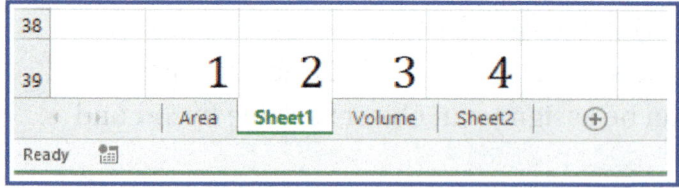

We can select or activate a particular sheet by its name or by its index number. In the above image there are four sheets and their index number starts from left as 1 and end at right by 4.

wb.sheets("Sheet2").activate      ' By sheet name
wb.sheets("Area").activate         ' By Sheet name
wb.sheets(2).activate              'By Index number

We can also use select instead of activate to make the sheet to current sheet like wb.sheets(2).Select

In general, we assign the worksheet object to an object variable by Set function.

Dim ws as worksheet
Set ws = wb.activeSheet

Active Sheet is the sheet that's currently active, that is sheet1 will be active and its property is assigned to object variable **ws**. To assign other sheets to variable

Set ws = wb.sheets("Sheet2")        ' By sheet name
Set ws1 = wb.sheets("Area")         ' By Sheet name
Set ws2 = wb.sheets(2)              'By Index number

Once we created a worksheet object variable, then we can activate that sheet just specifying the variable name and activate function

ws.activate

we can also combine all object in single line and activate the sheet. This command line activates other workbook sheet.

workbooks("D:\DMS\Comment-Log.xlsx").Sheets("Sheet1").Activate

## Ranges and Cells

Ranges and cells are very important object in excel and all our task will start and end from this objects.

## Cells

Excel spreadsheets store data in Cells and Cells are arranged into Rows and Columns. Each cell can be identified by the intersection point of its row and column like B3. For referring the cell object, we can use Cells function with two parameters and it can be written as Cells(row Index, Column Index). The column number is a simple count like A=1, B=2, C=3, D=4 and so on. We can write the column either the column index number or letters of specific column. For example referring the cell B3 we have to write Cells(3,2) or Cells(3,"B"). Here the number 3 is the row number, 2 is the column number and comma (,) is the separator of row and column. This is called cell address and by this, we can Read or Write the content of cell. Also we can change the cell format. To use the cell object in active work sheet

    Activesheet.Cells(4,2).select        OR
    Cells(4,2).select                    OR

If we already assign the worksheet object to variable **ws** then we can refer ws.Cells(4,2).select. The following code is frequently used in cells object.

Cells(4,2).select   ' It will move the cursor to B4 cell and make it active

X = Cells(4,2).Value   ' It will get value from B4 cell and assign to X
 Cells(4,2).Value = "Test"     ' It will write value 'Test" in cell B4
Cells(4,2).Interior.Color =vbRed ' It will fill red color in cell B4
Cells(4,2).Font.Bold = True ' It will change the font to Bold
Cells(4,2).Font.Name = "Arial"  ' It will change the font family
Cells(4,2).Font.Size =  14  ' It will change the font size

**Ranges**

Range is a property in VBA that helps to specify a single cell or Multiple cells.
1. Range("B3")                '-Refering Single Cell
2. Range("B3","C6","H4")      '-Refering a Group of cells
3. Range("3")                 '-Refering a Single Row
4. Range("A")                 '-Refering a Single Column
5. Range("B3:E10")            '-Three-dimensional range of cells

The argument parameter of range is a string value referring top left most cell address and bottom right most cell address with separation of Colon (:). We can also form range by cell reference like Range(Cells(1,3), Cells(4,2)) to refer the range A3:B4.

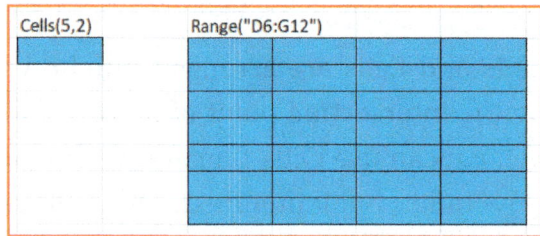

Some of frequent codes used to refer range
Range("D6:G12").select    '-Select a range of cells in active sheet as shown in the
                                above image.
ws.Range("B2:D7").select  '-Select a range of cells in Specified sheet(ws)  as shown in
                                the above image
X = Range("B2").Value     '- Get value from B2 cell and assign to X variable
Range("B2:C4").Value = "Test"    'write value 'Test" in all cells of
                                (B2, B3, B4, C2, C3, C4)
Range("B2:C4").Interior.Color =vbRed   ' It will fill red color to all cells
Range("B2:C4").Font.Bold = "Arial"     ' It will change the font family
Range("B2:C4").Font.Name = True        ' It will change the font to Bold
Range("B2:C4").Font.Size =  14         ' It will change the font size to all cells
Range("2:2").select       'It will select the entire row number two

Range("C:C").select        'It will select the entire column "C"
Range("B2:C4").merge       'it will merge all the cells in that range
Range("B2:C4").ClearFormats  'it will clear all the format in specified range of cells

The parameter in the range may be a contiguous cells or non- contiguous cells. contiguous cells mean the range of cells in Excel is a group of adjacent cells that are selected together and non-contiguous is selection of multiple cells in different location.

Range("B2:D7").select       'contiguous cells
Range("B15:C20, G15:G18").select 'Non-contiguous cells
Range("B1:C5 C5:G18").select    'Here we avoided the separating Coma(,). So it will select the intersection of cells. (C15, C16, C17, C18).

We can make the range as an object variable by set command
Set Rng = Range("B1:H50")

## Testing Application: -1

In this Testing, we are going to build a simple application to workout area and volume for different shapes. Open a blank excel sheet and create two sheet in the name of Area and Data. Write and format the respective sheet with respective data as shown in the image.

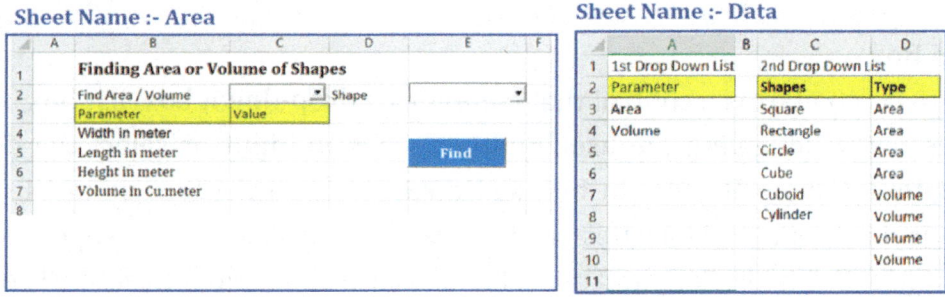

In this example we are going to use three controls, so enable the Developer Tab, if it is hided. To insert a Controls, you have to go Developer Insert controls (1) and select combo box in **ActiveX** Controls. Then move your mouse and click at one location, then Drag with left key pressed condition and leave it. While doing this action you may notice that the Design Mode controls (2) is selected. VBA use the name combo box for a simple drop down list.

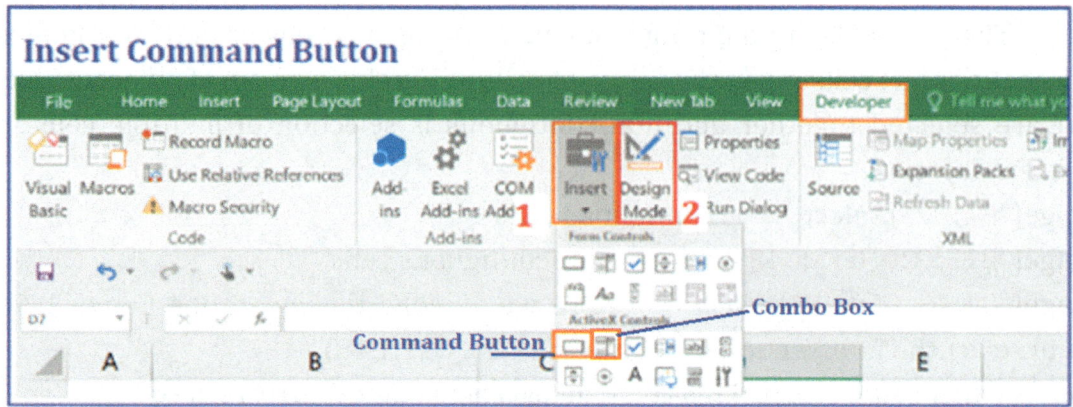

You can resize or change the position of combo box by click over the button and adjust the size by the handles appear around the button. Please remember that all editing on controls is only possible with **Design Mode** in selection condition. Same way you have to Insert the second combo box. Insert one command button and you can see a text "CommondButton1" is written over the command button. VBA assigns a name for each controls automatically by its type and a serial number like ComboBox1, ComboBox2 and CommondButton1.

We can change the name of controls and Display text on button as we like. Select 1st combo box, right click and open the property window. Change the name of control to **CB1** and same way name the 2$^{nd}$ combo box as **CM2**. Change the Name of command button to **Find** and change the caption property to "Find". You can also change properties of font, Back color, Fore Color, width and height as you like

**Combo Box**

A combo box is a control that combines a drop-down box, list box, and an editable text field, giving the user multiple ways to input or select the desired information. Combo Boxes can be used directly in excel sheet or in VBA User Form. It has many properties and in which most of the properties like Appearance, Behavior, Font and miscellaneous are almost identical to all controls and it is used to format the controls size and appearance. We can build the combo box with single column or multiple columns, but it considers only one column value after selection. For combo box the important properties are categorized under **Data** and some of item in **miscellaneous**. Data category has ten properties.

**Bound column**: When the user chooses a row in a multicolumn Combo Box, the Bound Column property identifies which column value from that row to be consider. For example, if each row contains 3 columns with different items and we set Bound Column as 2, then system stores the information in the second column of the currently-selected row as the value of the object.

**Column count**: Number column to be considered for each row. If you specify 3 then it form three column list.

**Column Heads**: Display the data column headings in first row if the setting value is "True".

**Column Widths**: Specifies the width of each column in a multicolumn combo box. Unless specified otherwise, column widths are measured in points (72 points = 1 inch). To specify another unit of measure, include the units as part of the values like 6 cm; 7 cm; 3 cm or 1.5 in; 2.5 in. If the value is blank all columns are divided in to equal length by its controls width. To separate column entries, use semicolons (;) as list separators.

**List Rows**: Number rows should be shown in first click. It is a mere number like 10 and default value is 8.

**List Style**: Specifies the visual appearance of the list. If value is "0" then it Looks like a regular list box, with the background of items highlighted. If value is "1", then it Shows option buttons, or check boxes for a multi-select list (default).

**List Width**: Specifies the width of the list in combo box. The value should be entered as explained in column width.

**Text**: It store the text selected in combo box.

**Text Column**: Values for the Text Column property range from -1 to the number of columns in the list. The Text Column value for the first column is 1, the value of the second column is 2, and so on. Setting Text Column to 0, it display and store the List Index value. Setting Text Column to -1 displays the first column that has a Column Widths value greater than zero.

**TopIndex**: Sets and returns the item that appears in the topmost position in the list. Returns the value -1 if the list is empty or not displayed.

Miscellaneous category has two main properties to source the data.

**ListFillRange:** This is used to fill the item list. For that we have to specify the range of data like A1:B10. This will add two column list to combo box control. Microsoft Excel reads the contents of every cell in the range and inserts the cell values into the list box. If the list in the list box was created with the AddItem method, this property returns an empty string ("").

**LinkedCell**: It output the selected value to a referred Cell. Alternatively, if you write a value in linked cell, it adds the value to combo box control.

We can add the list item to combo box by two methods. First method we can refer the data range in ListFillRange property and second method we can add VBA code in module. Both option has some merits and demerits. If we add the list item by a referred cell range, anybody can add new item to control, by just add the text in that range location. But by this method referring the range from other work book is not possible.

Using VBA code filling item list is very flexible and effective to add a filtered item based on some user input. We test both option for first combo box item list which require only two item: Area and volume. This list is constant for this application and it will not change based on some action or query. So this list should be loaded while opening the workbook. Double click the "ThisworkBook" module it will open the code window for this module. Select Workbook in controls (left drop down list) and Open in event list drop down list. It automatically creates a procedure start and end declaration as shown below. Add the code in-between the declaration.

```vba
Private Sub workbook_Open()
'------------Populate the list to first drop down list
    Sheets("Area").CB1.Clear
    Sheets("Area").CB1.AddItem "Area"
    Sheets("Area").CB1.AddItem "Volume"
End sub
```

Alternatively, we can assign a range from worksheet within same work book or from other opened work book to combo box list

```vba
Private Sub workbook_Open()
    Dim wb as workbook
    Dim ws , ws1 as worksheet
    Set wb = Workbooks("Home Budget-BE.xlsx")
    Set ws = wb.Sheets("Main Category")
```

```
    Set ws1 = Activeworkbook.Sheets("Area")
    ws1.CB1 = ws.Range("A3:C100").Value
End sub
```

After completion of code, save and close the excel file. Again open the excel file and click the first combo box, you notice it shows the value list Area and Volume. Please remember, all Sub procedure written in workbook_open event will be executed while opening the excel file.

**Code Explanation**
1. We declared the sub as private, since it going to work only in this module.
2. The procedure name is a combination of object and event: **workbook_open**.
3. first statement is comment line, so it starts with apostrophe (').
4. Since we are working in excel application, so no need to create an Application object variable.
5. we are going to play all our working in same work book, so no need to create Workbook object variable.
6. CB1 is the control name of 1st drop down, which is located in sheet "Area". So always we have to specify the sheets where the controls is located Sheets("Area").CB1
7. AddItem is in-build method which will add the string next to this ("Area") to that control.
8. The next line is adding another item "Volume" to controls. Like that we have to add any number of items as a separate line.

In second method we have to add the Cell range in **ListFillRange** properties. If the data is in same sheet, then just enter the range like A3:A4. If the data is in another sheet, we have to refer the sheet name and range. In our case the data is available in "Data" sheet so we have to fill the value like Data!A3:A4

We are going to use more Drop down list while building our application, so at that time you may famirize to create the Drop down list. Now you can test it the combo box1 and see the result. Both the method will give same results. Please remember you should use any one method otherwise it generates Error.

We can get the selected value by the control name value (CB1.Value) and use it for other process in VBA code. Sometime if you want to show the selected value in one cell and it automate other process, then you have to use LinkedCell properties and enter the cell reference value like C2. This will change the C2 cell value whenever we selsect an item from combo box. The combo box control is used as input field to do some calculation. We can assign the value to combo box control either by a selected value from the list or through the linked cell. If we write a value in linked cell by event, it automatically assigns that value to Combo box control, even though that value is not in the list item.

Now we have to add the item list to 2nd combo box. This item list should be filtered list based on the selection of 1st combo box. So the event code should be added in 1st combo box events which will trigger while selection. Don't fill the LinkedCell and ListFillRange property and leave it as blank. Activate the Area sheet and double click the 1st combo box, it opens the VBA editor and add a Sub procedure as shown below in Area Sheet module. In this code we added conditional statement and Loop statement, which will be explained in detail in coming chapter.

```
---------------------------------Code start----------------------------------
Private Sub CB1_Change()
    Dim ws As worksheet
    Dim opt As String
    Dim LR As  Integer
    '---------------Fill item list to 2nd combo box
    Set ws = Sheets("Data")              '---Create Sheet object variable
    '—find the Last row of sheet that column "C" has value
```

```
    LR = ws.Cells(ws.Rows.Count, "C").End(xlUp).Row
    '---------Looping all record
    opt = CB1.Value
    Sheets("Area").CB2.Clear
    For k = 3 To LR
       If ws.Cells(k, "D").Value = opt Then
          Sheets("Area").CB2.AddItem ws.Cells(k, "C").Value
       End If
    Next
         CB2.Value = ""
         Msgbox "Combo Box-2 Item filled"
End Sub
```
-----------------------------------Code end----------------------------------

Save the code and open the excel Area sheet. Select any one value in combo box-1, it popup a message "Combo Box-2 Item filled" and click ok button. Click the second combo box, now you can see a filtered value of shapes based on 1st combo box selection. If you not get the result, you have to debug the program which is explained in next chapter.

**Code explanation**

1. The event name is CB1_Change, means for every change in value of combo box, it triggers the event.
2. We declaring one object variable "ws", one string variable "opt" to store the 1st combo box value and one integer variable "LR".
3. We assign the sheet("Data") object to variable "ws". This means the "ws" variable have the total properties and value of Data sheet.
4. Next line will get last used cell in specified column from that sheet. A detail description is given next to this section.
5. Assigning the selected value of combo box-1(CB1) to variable opt
6. CB2.clear will clear the old item list and kept empty, before assigning a new filter item list. Always we have to use clear method before filling the item list.
7. Next statement is the loop statement build with **for**...**Next** loop and we will learn in detail in next chapter. Here it navigates the row from row number "3" where our data is start and loop up to the last row (LR). In data sheet the "D" column has the option value for each record either "Area" or "Volume". So we are comparing the "D" column value of each row with the CB1 selected value which is stored in opt variable by **IF** condition. If the value is matched, then it adds the "C" column value to

CB2 item list. Like that it adds all the "C" column value if the "D" column value matched to CB1 selection.

8. Next statement assigns set an empty value to CB2 controls.

Note: - whenever you refer a cells, you have to specify the sheet reference(ws.cells()). Cell object has many property, so you should always specify the value (cells(). value) property to get or assign the value.

**Finding Last Row**

The excel sheet has rows up to 1048576 in every sheets. In general, we will not use all rows for entering our data, so we have to find the last row which has a data. This will help while searching a data form the sheet. We can find the last row by different method like SpecialCells, Row.Count, Used.Range and Range.Find.

**Special Cells method**

Special Cells is an in-built function of VBA and it accept many excel cell Type parameter.

LR = Range("C:C").SpecialCells(xlCellTypeLastCell).row

Some of excel cell type parameter are

| Name | Description |
| --- | --- |
| xlCellTypeAllFormatConditions | Cells of any format. |
| xlCellTypeAllValidation | Cells having validation criteria. |
| xlCellTypeBlanks | Empty cells. |
| xlCellTypeComments | Cells containing notes. |
| xlCellTypeConstants | Cells containing constants. |
| xlCellTypeFormulas | Cells containing formulas. |
| xlCellTypeLastCell | The last cell in the used range. |
| xlCellTypeSameFormatConditions | Cells having the same format. |
| xlCellTypeSameValidation | Cells having the same validation criteria. |
| xlCellTypeVisible | All visible cells. |

In which xlCellTypeLastCell is one of parameter will get last cell which has data in a specified selection. Here we used range("C:C") which will select the entire "C" column. If you want to search from different sheet, then we have to specify the Sheet object variable reference like ws.range("C:C"). The specialCell function locates the last cell reference by the parameter. Row method will find the row number of located cell.

## Row Count method
It was built by two in-build function.
      LR = ws.Cells(ws.Rows.Count, "C").End(xlUp).Row    OR
      LR = ws.Cells(ws.Rows.Count, 3).End(xlUp).Row

Cells(ws.Rows.Count, "C") will count how many rows are there in the third column ("C"). We can also specify the column reference by its index number (3). The Range.End(Direction) is a function will move to a specific cell within the selected range. The direction parameter has four option: xlDown, xlUP, xlToRight and xlToLeft. Here End(xlUp).Row will find the last used cell in that specified range that is in "C" column. Then the Row method find the row number.

## Used.Range method
Used range means the cells are used by some data on a specified sheet.
      LR = ws.UsedRange.Row(ws.usedRange.rows.count).Row

The used range of worksheet ws method will get the number of used rows as a parameter and row command get the row count. Here we are not specified any column, so it consider a last cell from any one of column has the value as lost row. So if you very specific in one column, then this concept is not useful.

**Range.Find Method**: It is very length process and the code will be

LR = Cells.Find(What:="*", After:=Range("C1"), LookAt:=xlPart, _
    LookIn:=xlFormulas, SearchOrder:=xlByRows, _
    SearchDirection:=xlPrevious, MatchCase:=False).Row

The variable using the Cells.Find method. Here, we declared seven parameters. In What parameter we used ("*") which will find the first non-empty cell. SearchOrder:=xlByRows parameter will move right-to-left and also loops up through each row until it finds a non-empty cell.

## Finding Last Column
We can also find the last column which has data by the same method.

**Special Cells method:**
LC= Ws.Cells.SpecialCells(xlCellTypeLastCell).Column

**Column Count method:**
LC = ws.Cells(6, ws.Columns.Count).End(xlToLeft).Column

Cells(**6**, ws.Columns.Count) will count how many columns are there in Row 6.

**Used range Method:**

```
LC=Ws.UsedRange.Columns(Ws.UsedRange.Columns.Count).Column
```

# 6. Debugging

When we write code in any programming language, we may encounter errors that need to be analyzed, checked, and fixed. To overcome this problem most IDEs support debugging. Debugging is the process of executing our programming codes step by step and checking which steps currently compiler is executing, what are their values, and what is their output.

Many factors can lead to errors, including syntax problems, runtime issues, and logic flaws. Debugging the code allows you to find these flaws and correct them before they have an impact. The primary categories of issues that arise while executing in code are Syntax Errors, Logic Errors and Run-time Errors.

**Syntax error:** syntax errors are writing wrong statement format or using wrong keyword. Same way missing closing declaration like without end if in if statement or without next in for loop statement. This error is identified by VBA editor while writing the code and show red alert and popup message.

**Logic Error**: Using wrong operator which will give wrong result and this will not generate any error. For example, using Multiplication sign instead of divide sign, using Greater than operator instead of less than operator. This is very complicated error and no debug tool locate this error. So the developer has to keenly look at each line of code and locate the error.

**Run time Error**: Runtime errors cannot be detected by simply looking at the code; they are a result of your code interacting with the specific inputs or data at that time. For example, if we do a divide function with two variables, unfortunately the divisor number become Zero like 3/0, then it can't do the calculation and through error. Same way if you write a code to get property of non-object variable, then it throws error. Also some time you written a loop with wrong condition, then the loop will not terminate. So this error will be resolved only by more testing of the code and sometime this may be occurring after a long period based on user input.

In VBA there are some Techniques such as breakpoints, stepping through code, and monitoring variable values are much helpful to debug the code. Excel VBA editor has in-built debugging tool and it is very easy to use. Also it provides watch window, local window and immediate window to observe the code value or change in action while debugging. We can access the debugging tool from top menu bar or we can activate a floating debugging tool box by clicking the menu command View->Toolsbars->Debug

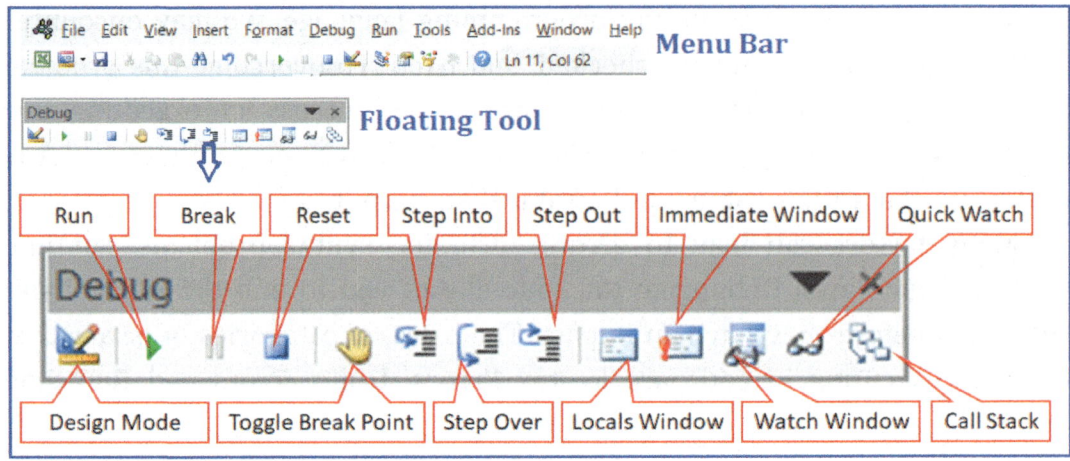

**Debugging the code**

Now we will test our CB1 change event sub procedure by VBA debugging tool. Change over to Area sheet and select any one option in CB1 combo box, the events is trigged and work in back ground. If no error in the code, it popup a message "Combo Box-2 Item filled", just click ok button and it fill the shapes name in combo box-2. Now change to VBA editor section and place the cursor point at any line of CB1 change event procedure. If the event is not shown, double click the Sheet1(Area) object in project explorer window. Click **run** button in debugging tool, again the code run in back ground and popup the message "Combo Box-2 Item filled".

**Break point**

The first step in debugging process is placing break point in the procedure code. This enable you to halt the execution of the code at that break point and we can run our code step by step of each line. To add the break point, click on the left gray bar at the location of desired code line. A Brown dot will appear on the gray bar and the code line is also highlighted with brown back ground color. To remove break point, we have to click again on the dot. Alternatively select the code line and click the Toggle Break Point button in Debugging tool or Just click "F9" key. This break point can be placed anywhere of the code except the Variable declaration line(Dim).

Placing break point at starting of the code, will consume more time to complete the process in big sub procedure. So we have to predetermine the location where we want to analyze the code and place the break point. If any

51

logical error in the code, VBA itself throw an alert message show the error and give an option to end the program or to Debug the code.

Our procedure is small event, so place the break point at first statement as shown in the above image. Change over to Area sheet and select any one option in CB1 combo box, it triggers the above event and focus the VBA editor window and high light the break point line and stop running the code. Now the program execution is in debugging mode. Alternatively, if already one option is selected in CB1, you can click the **Run** button in Debugging tool.

**Local windows**

In debug mode, Click the local window button in debug tool or from menu **View->Locals Window**. It opens the local window at bottom and list out all variable of our testing procedure and show empty value. Click **Step Into** button or press F8 key, it move the code to next line and that line will be highlighted. So we can know which line is now executing. Continuously click the step into key, it goes to next line and you can notice the variable in local window get a value from the execution and we can check whether it is representing correct value as per our requirement.

So local window will automatically display all the declared variables in the current procedure and their values. When the Locals window is visible, it is automatically updated every time there is a change in value during run time. Some variable name has a **+** symbol on left side, then that variable is object variable and it has more properties related to that object. Just click the plus sign, it expands and show all properties list.

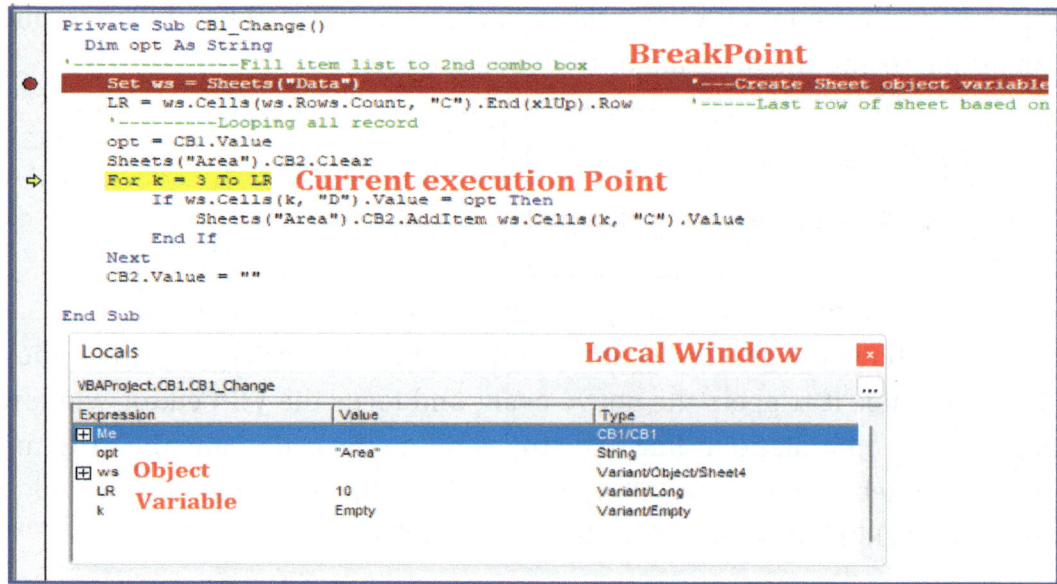

We can resize the column headers by dragging the border to the right or the left and also we can resize over all window size and position it at any location. Whenever you want close that window just click Close button located at top right corner. To stop the code debugging just click the **Reset** button in debugging tool which will terminate the code running and empty out the local window.

## Debug Mode

VBA debugging mode can be classified in to three types: Run mode, Break Mode and Design Mode.

**Run Mode**: Run mode or Runtime is simply the duration during which code runs or executes. Runtime duration and speed can be controlled in debugging process using the Run(F5), Step into(F8), Step Over(Shift+F8) and Step Out(Ctrl+Shift+F8) buttons or the key combination mentioned in brackets. Run button will just run the selected procedure and stop the execution at break point. Step into button will move the execution one step or go to next line.

Step Over button is useful to skip debugging process on calling procedure.

Sub shape()

W=2

L=3

H=4

Call Volume(W,L,H)   '—Second procedure call

Msgbox "Volume:-" & cells(2,2)

End sub

Sub Volume(W,L,H as integer)
    '----converting in to meter
    x = W/1000
    y= L/1000
    z =H/1000
    Cells(2,2) = x * y * z
End sub

In the above code if we set break point at W=2, then by step Into or Step Over process, it go line by line up to the second procedure call line. After that step into process go to first line of second procedure and again continue line by line in second procedure. Where as in Step Over process, it run the second procedure in back ground and complete the execution and return back to first procedure and continues to the next line.

    Step out executes all remaining code in that procedure and terminate the debugging process. If you use step out during execution of second call procedure, it executes all reaming code in second procedure and return back to 1st call procedure and stopped at second procedure call code.

**Break mode**: Break mode is entered when a running procedure stops because of either an error in the code or a deliberate act by the programmer. It may be placing break point or inserting stop statement in the procedure code. Stop statement work like break point and it stop the execution at that point. We can make break mode by clicking the Break button in debugging tool or key Ctrl+Break.

```
opt = CB1.Value
Sheets("Area").CB2.Clear
Stop
For k = 3 To LR
    If ws.Cells(k, "D").Value = opt Then
        Sheets("Area").CB2.AddItem ws.Cells(k, "C").Value
    End If
Next
```

**Design Mode**: The Design mode specifies that, the code does not run anymore until the Design mode is turned off. Design mode is the time during which no code from the project is running. Also, the events from the host or project will not execute. This mode is most often used when a sheet has an ActiveX control in it or while editing User Forms.

### Immediate window

The VBA Immediate Window is a tool that allows you to get immediate answers about your Excel files, and quickly execute some testing code. We can open Immediate window by clicking the button in debug tool or from menu View->Immediate Window or Just click Ctrl+G keys. For this window also we can resize the window and position it at any location.

```
Immediate
?Activeworkbook.Worksheets.Count
 2
?sheets(1).name
Area

?sheets(2).Cells(sheets(2).Rows.Count, "C").End(xlUp).Row
 10
```

In the above example we tested three code with print (?) command and this window give the result immediately below the code. Like that we can test any statement before writing the code.

### Watch Window

Watch window is identical to the Locals window, except that, It lists only developer-selected variables or expressions, not the entire scope-local variables. Another thing we can watch any expression in watch window and we can't do in local window. We can open watch window by clicking the button in debug tool or from menu View->watch Window. For this window also we can resize the column and window size and position it at any location. Watch window has additional column of Context than local window. The Context refers to the module or procedure where the variable values are evaluated.

The Watch window automatically pops-up when you add Watches. For adding a new watch, we have to highlight the variable name or expression in the code window and right click the mouse, then click add watch command. Another way, highlight the variable and click the Quick watch button in the Debugging tool. It will open the Add watch dialogue box with various option, click ok button. It adds the highlighted variable or expression to watch window.

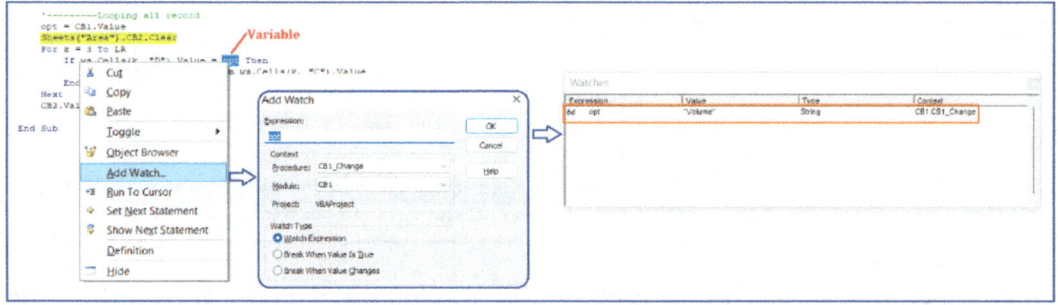

Alternatively, drag and drop the highlighted variable or expression into the Watch window. To edit a Watch, select it in the Watch window and select Edit Watch from the Debug menu. Another way is to right-click on the Watch in the Watch window and pick Edit Watch from the pop-up context menu. To delete a Watch, first select it in the Watch window. Next, hit the Delete (Del) key. Alternatively, right-click the Watch and select Delete Watch from the context menu. The variable or expression listed in watch window show the result value while it code is executed.

## Call Stack

The Call Stack is a queue of all procedures scheduled for execution in the current scope. Often, you'll link your procedures using Call statements. So, completing a task will require running a series of procedures (think of them as sub-tasks). The Call Stack lets you can see this queue of procedures.

This option is available during execution by debugging, click the call stack button in debugging tool box and it popup a dialogue box and show the list of procedures in que. Select any one procedure and click Show button, it navigates to that particular procedure for edit or look.

## Debug in Test Application-1

Add the following variable and expression to watch window

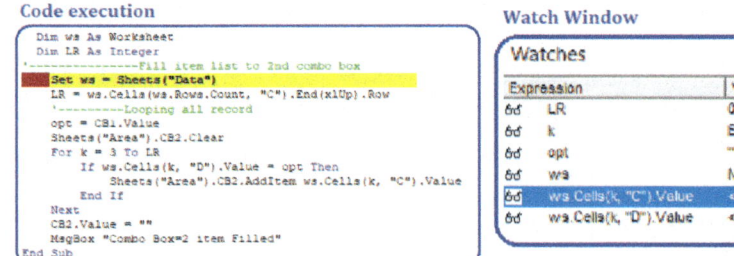

You may notice the Set ws line is highlighted, means the execution is in that line. Also the variable in watch window shows like: LR has zero value, k has empty value, opt has null string and ws is nothing. Click the Step Into button in debugging tool, the code execution will move to next line.

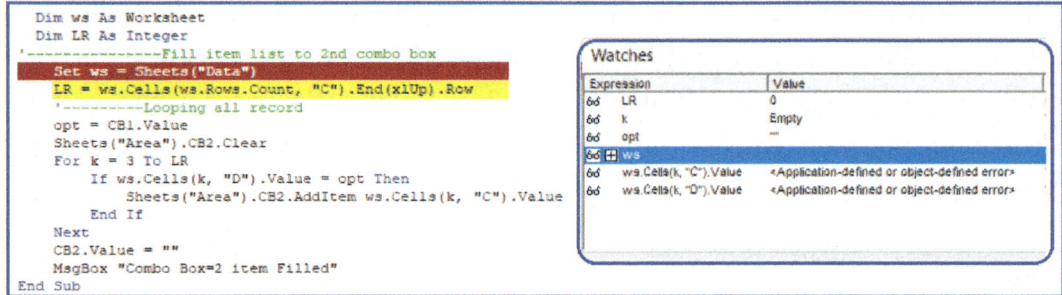

Now the Set ws code is executed, so the ws variable has changed and it showing a + sign at left side. Since ws is object variable, so it holds many properties of sheet object. Click the Plus sign to expand, it shows all the properties as shown in the image. Some property list is also having + sign and if expand it, it shows another list. Like object variable will hold more data and same can be extracted by code and use it.

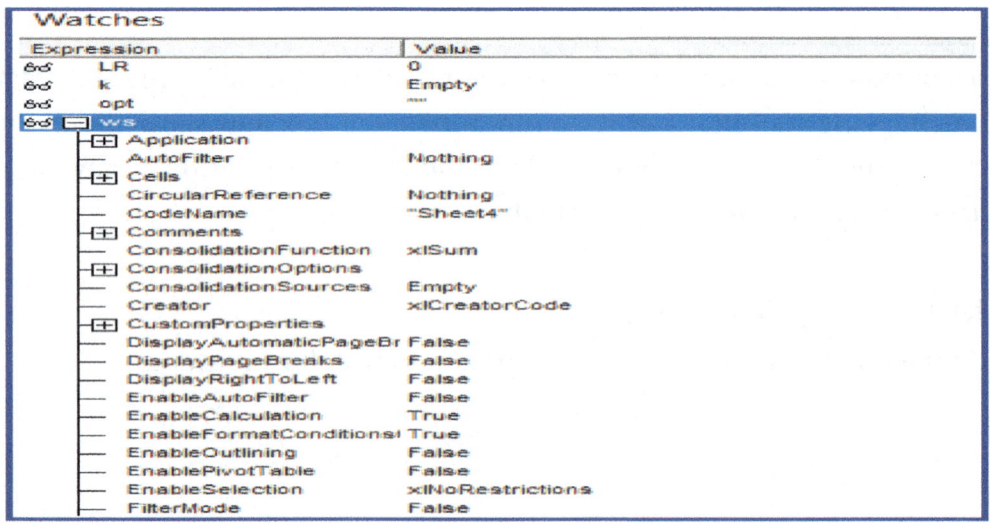

Click Step into button two times, the code execution will move another two lines.

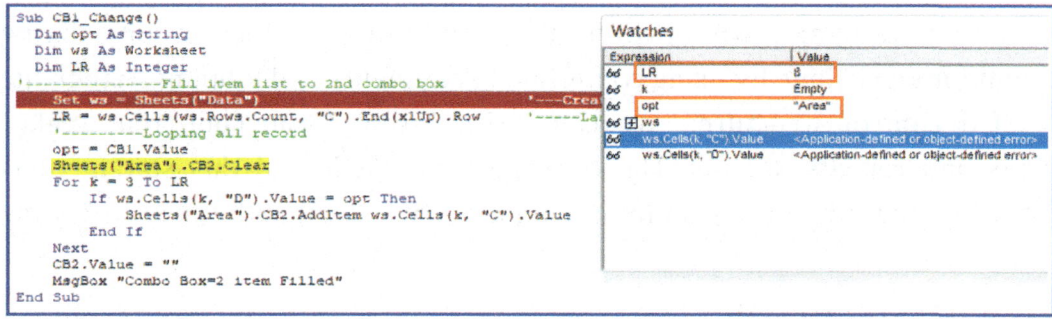

Now It executed the last row function and assign the value of 8 in LR variable. Same way it gets the Combo box-1 value and assign to opt variable(Area). Again click Step into two times it clears the Combo box-2 list and start for loop. Here the starting value of for loop is 3, so it assigns the value 3 to k variable. This loops will run up the value 8 (LR value). Click the Step into button, it will check the Data sheet D3 cell (ws.Cells(k, "D").Value) and compare it with opt variable. If the value is same it go to next line and get the Data sheet C3 cell value (ws.Cells(k, "C").Value) and add it to Combo box-2 item list. Like the loop continue for last record (8) and fill the item list. We will see in detail about for loop and if conditional statement in next chapter.

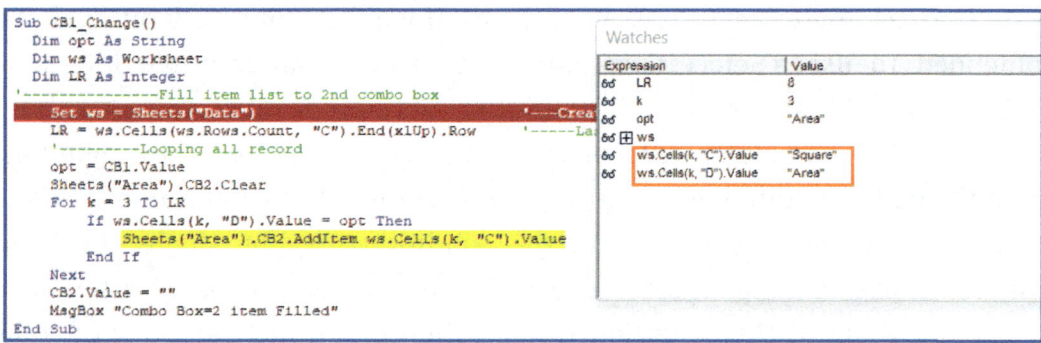

# 7. Conditional check and Loops

In any program, we have to use conditional statement or looping statement for work flow. By using conditional statements and looping statements also called control structures, we can write Visual Basic code that makes decisions and repeats actions. The concept and function of this statement is almost same like other programming language, but slight difference in coding pattern.

## Conditional statement

Conditional statements evaluate whether a condition is True or False, and then specify one or more statements to run, depending on the result. Usually, a condition is an expression that uses a comparison operator to compare one value or variable with another. In VBA there are two conditional statement: If...Then...Else which Branching flow of code when a condition is True or False and another one is Select Case statement which divert the flow of code by a group of case steps.

### If else Statement

Use the If...Then...Else statement to run a specific statement or a block of statements, depending on the value of a condition. If...Then...Else statements can be nested to as many levels as you need. However, for readability, it is recommended to use a Select Case statement rather than multiple levels of nested If... Then... Else statements.

To run only one statement when a condition is True, use the single-line syntax of the If...Then statement omitting else keyword. The condition is written in-between if and then keyword and the condition may be single check or combination of check. if the result is true, it executes a block of code written next to then keyword and if the condition is false, then it execute the block of code written next to else statement.

```
'------Simple statement
    If opt = "Area" then
        A=20 * 30
    End if
'------Normal statement
    If opt = "Area" then
        A=20 * 30
    Else
        A= 10*40
    End if
```

```
'--------Nested statement
        If opt = "Area" then
            A=20 * 30
        else
            If opt = "Volume"
                A= 10*40
            Else
                Msgbox" No Option is selected"
            End if
End if
```

We can also write the If statement in single line like
If opt = "Area" then A=20 * 30 Else A= 10*40

### Select Case statement

The Select Case statement is an alternative way to write nested If...else statements. It Executes several groups of statements, based on the value given to Select case function.

```
Mon=5
Select Case Mon
    Case 5
        CMonth = "May"
    Case 6
        CMonth = "June"
    Case 7
        CMonth = "July"
End Select
```

In the above example, we assigning a month number to a variable Mon. This variable is assigned as expression in select case statement. If we assign any value from 5 to 7 for Mon variable the select statement compares the value in $1^{st}$ case, if the value matched to it value, then it executes the statement next to $1^{st}$ case and exit from the select statement. If it not matched, then it goes to $2^{nd}$ Case and compare. Suppose if we assign a value of "7" to Mon variable, this statement skip two case and execute the $3^{rd}$ case and assign a value of "July" to CMonth variable.

## Loop Statement

Looping allows you to run a group of statements repeatedly. Some loops repeat statements until a condition is False; others repeat statements until a condition is True. There are some loops that repeat statements to a specific number of times or for each object in a collection. There are three loop statement in VBA: Do...Loop, For...Next and For Each...Next. we can use nested loop with the combination of Do... Loop and For...Next loop. Also we can build a nested loop with more do loop or with more For loop

## Do Loop

Do loop repeat the looping while or Until a condition is true. The Do While Or Until loop repeats a block of statements while Or Until a given condition is true. In other words, the loop runs as long as the condition is true. Once the condition becomes false, looping stops and VBA exits the loop.

| While | Until |
|---|---|
| Dim k As Integer<br>    k = 1<br>    Do While k < 11<br>        Cells(k, 1).Value = k<br>        k = k + 1<br>    Loop | Dim k As Integer<br>    k = 1<br>    Do Until k = 11<br>        Cells(i, 1).Value = k<br>                k = k + 1<br>    Loop |

In the above example, we writing the incremental number from 1 to 11 in "A" column of excel sheet. Both loop statement will do the same task. The first while loop run the code whenever the k value is less than number 11 and the second Until loop run the code whenever the k value is equal to the number 11. The do loop statement repeats all the statement up to loop key ward and again return back to Do while line. We can also exit the loop by apply some conditional statement and if the statement is true, by exit loop key word, we can exit from the loop intermittently.

## For Next Loop

In for Next loop, the block of code is executed for a specific number of times. Hence, this loop must be used when the number of iterations (repetitions) to be performed is known in advance. The syntax of for loop is we have to create a variable (k) and assign a range with start (3) and end number (LR). It should be an integer value either we can put a number or we can put an integer type variable.

| | |
|---|---|
| For k = 3 To LR<br>    If ws.Cells(k, "D").Value = opt Then<br>        Ws1.Cells(2, "A").Value = ws.Cells(k, "A").Value<br>        Exit for<br>    End If<br>Next | For k = 3 To LR<br>    For J = 1 to 5<br>        Ws1.Cells(k, J).Value = ws.Cells(k, J+2).Value<br>    Next J<br>Next k<br><br>**Nested Loop** |

Suppose the last row (LR) is 22, then Here the for loop repeat the loop for 22-3=19 times. So we can put any number as start number but it should be less than end number. While running the loop it assigns the run cycle number from start number to k variable. So we can use this k variable value in the statement to refer row or column of cells. In the first statement, opt is a variable has some value like "Area". The **if** condition get the D3 cell value from worksheet1 (ws.cells(k,"D") and compare with opt variable. You know that ws is object variable of worksheet1. In cell reference cells(k, "D") means cells(3,"D"). Here the k is for loop variable and at first start it assigns value 3, so the cell reference is referring row 3 and column "D". if the value is not matched to opt variable value, it skips the conditional statement and go to **next** key word. Then the execution is return back to **for** statement and add one increment to k variable and it become 4. Now the if condition checks the D4 cell value and compare. Like the loop run up to the last row. If the condition is true then it execute the code in **if** statement that is, Get the value of A4 from worksheet1 and write the value in A2 cell of worksheet2. Also the task is completed, so it terminates the **for** loop by **exit for** statement. We can exit from loop any time with some conditional statement. In default incremental value in for loop is one, but we can make different incremental value by Step key word.

        For k = 3 To LR   step 2    '—It increment the value 2 for each looping
        For k = LR To 3   step -1    '—It reduce the value 1 for each looping

The second statement is a nested **for** loop statement build with two **for** loop. The first loop moves the excel record from 3rd row to last row and second loop moves in to columns. In the first action, the value of k = 3 and J = 1. In first iteration of second for loop, it get the value from cell C3 (ws.cells(k, J+2)) of worksheet1 and write it in A3 (ws1.cells(k, J)) cell of work sheet2. Like it run the second loop five times and fill the value at row number 3 from column "A" to "E" of work sheet2. Then again it run first loop and change the k value to 4 and run the second loop. Placing the variable name after Next key word is optional and it will help to identify the loop position in multiple nested loop statement while debugging.

## For Each Loop

        For Each loop helps in looping through a collection of objects. These objects include cell ranges, worksheets, workbooks, shapes or other objects on a worksheet. With this loop, we can go through every object of a collection and perform a task on it like hide or unhide the sheets based on condition. The for

Each loop is used when the number of objects (or elements) in a collection is Unknown. Hence, the number of repetitions to be performed is also not known in advance.

```
Dim Ws As Worksheet
    For Each Ws In ActiveWorkbook.Worksheets
        If Ws.Name <> "Main" Then
            Ws.Visible = xlSheetVeryHidden
        End If
    Next Ws
```

Here we are assigning all work sheets to Ws variable and by for each loop, we check each sheet name by a condition. If the sheet name is not "Main", then we hiding that sheet and continue the loop up to all the collection of sheets. Putting the for loop variable name (either Ws or K) after next key word is optional and it will help while writing a nested loop statement.

**GoTo Statement**

To exit from the procedure or from Loop, we use Exit keyword like Exit for, Exit Do, Exit Sub and Exit Function. Some time we may skip or jump to a specific code based on the condition within the procedure. For that VBA GoTo statement is used to jump in to a specified line. The Syntax

```
GoTo SpecifiedName
----Statement1-----
SpecifiedName :
----Statement2-----
```

First we have to write the GoTo keyword with a Name in any one of conditional statement to branch out the code execution. The name should not have a space or any special character. Then write the name with Colon(:), can be placed anywhere in the same procedure whether before or after the GoTo statement.

```
        If cell(2, 4).Value = "Fruit" Then
                GoTo SecA
        Else
                GoTo SecB
        End If
        -----Some Statement--------
SecA:
        MsgBox "Fruit Selected - Section-A"
SecB:
        MsgBox "Vegetable Selected - Section-B"
```

In the above code user enter one option either Fruit or Vegetable in D2 cell. Then the If Condition is the value, if the value is "Fruit" then it execute the first GoTo Statement and Jump to Label SecA and display the Message "Fruit Selected - Section-A" other wise it execute the second GoTo statement and Jump to Label SecB and display the message"Vegetable Selected - Section-B".

## 8. VBA Operators

Like all program language VBA support all operators and it has four type of operators as listed below

1. Arithmetic Operators
2. Comparison Operators
3. Logical operators
4. Assignment operators

### Arithmetic Operators

| Operator | Description | Example A=10; B=20 |
|---|---|---|
| + | Adds two values | A+B result 30 |
| - | Subtracts $2^{nd}$ value from $1^{st}$ value | A-B result 10 |
| * | Multiply two value | A*B result 200 |
| / | Divide $1^{st}$ value by $2^{nd}$ value | B/A result 2 |
| ^ | Exponentiation | B^2 result 400 |

We can write all arithmetic operation in a single line, remember that the BODMAS order of operators will be followed. The full form of BODMAS is Brackets, Orders, Division, Multiplication, Addition and Subtraction.

Example: - Result = (A+B/C*D^2) – (B*C)     '—Here All letters are variables

### Comparison Operators

| Operator | Description | Example A=10; B=20 |
|---|---|---|
| = | Checks two values if equal take as true statement | (A=B) False (vsk=ksv) False |
| <> | Checks two values if not equal take as true statement | (A <> B) True |
| > | Check left value is Greater than right value | A > B False |
| < | Check left value is Less than right value | A < B True |
| >= | Check left value is Greater than or Equal to right value | A >= B False |
| <= | Check left value is Less than or equal to right value | A <= B True |

## Logical Operators

| Operator | Description | Example<br>A=10; B=20 |
|---|---|---|
| AND | In this all condition should be satisfied. if satisfy the result is true or it is false. | A > 7 **AND** B < 25 is true. |
| OR | In this any one of the condition should be satisfied or true | A >7 **OR** B=12 is true. |
| NOT | Use to reverses the logical state of its operator. If a condition is true then Logical NOT operator will make false. | A > 7 **AND NOT** B < 25 is false. |
| XOR | This operator is a combination of **Not** and **OR**. It will return true if one of the condition is true | A>B **XOR** B>0 |

## Concatenation Operator

| Operator | Description | Example |
|---|---|---|
| + | Is same as the addition operator and will add two values or two strings of text | C = "Hi" + " Krish" then C = "Hi Krish" |
| & | It will join together two string of text. | C = "Hi" + " Krish" then C = "Hi Krish" |

**Example:** txt1= "What a very" ; txt2 = "nice day"

    Txt3 = txt1 + " " + txt2    results    What a very nice day

    Txt3 = txt1 + txt2    results    What a verynice day

    X = 5 + 5    results    10

    X = "5" + 5    results    55

    X = "hellow"+ 5    results    hellow5

## Testing Application 1 - Continue

Again open the Area sheet and double click the CB2 combo box in deign mode. It will open change event procedure in sheet module, add the following code.

```vb
Private Sub CB2_Change()
    Cells(4, 2) = ""
    Cells(5, 2) = ""
    Cells(6, 2) = ""
    Select Case CB2.Value
    Case "Square"
        Cells(4, 2) = "Face length in meter"
        Cells(7, 2) = "Area of Square in Sq.meter"
    Case "Rectangle"
        Cells(4, 2) = "Width in meter"
        Cells(5, 2) = "Length in meter"
        Cells(7, 2) = "Area of rectangle in Sq.meter"
    Case "Circle"
        Cells(4, 2) = "Diameter in meter"
        Cells(7, 2) = "Area of Circle in Sq.meter"
    Case "Cube"
        Cells(4, 2) = "Face Width in meter"
        Cells(5, 2) = "Height in meter"
        Cells(7, 2) = "Volume of Cube in Cu.meter"
    Case "Cuboid"
        Cells(4, 2) = "Width in meter"
        Cells(5, 2) = "Length in meter"
        Cells(6, 2) = "Height in meter"
        Cells(7, 2) = "Volume of Cuboid in Cu.meter"
    Case "Cylinder"
        Cells(4, 2) = "Diameter in meter"
        Cells(5, 2) = "Height in meter"
        Cells(7, 2) = "Volume of Cylinder in Cu.meter"
    End Select
End Sub
```

Deselect the Design mode and select one option in Combo box-1, it populates a filter list in combo box-2. Then select any one value from combo box-2, it changes the Question label in "B" column from row number 4 to 7. In this we used a simple select case conditional statement which is explained in detail in earlier chapter.

# 9. VBA Procedure

We learned the basic of Sub and Function in previous chapter. Sub or function are procedure to execute some task or some calculation.

## Subroutine(Sub)

A Subroutine is a piece of code that performs a specific task described in the code but does not return a result or a value. Subroutines are used to break down large pieces of code into small manageable parts. Subroutines can be recalled multiple times from anywhere in the program. Any application has thousands and thousands of source code lines and create a complexity. Subroutine is help by breaking down the program into small manageable chunks of code. Also each subroutine is a block of code to do some particular task, which may be used in other program or other subroutines by calling. So reusability of subroutines is major advantage to reduce developer working time. Subroutines and functions are self-documenting which clearly indicate it purpose to developer.

The most common way to define a subroutine in VBA is by using the **Sub** keyword, followed by a unique procedure name and it may or may not carry a list of parameters and with lot of statement with **End Sub** keyword. It has more optional prefix in syntax which will declare the scope of that procedure. We should follow certain rule to write the procedure name and it is almost same rule as explained for variable name.

**Syntax**:

Sub name ( arglist as type)
    statements
End Sub
    Or
[ Private | Public | Friend ][ Static ] Sub name [( arglist )]
    statements
End Sub

**Private / Public / Friend**: - This is optional parameter, here if we specify private sub procedure, then it can only be used by other procedure in the same module. If the option is public, then it allows to use this procedure from other procedure located all modules in that workbook. Friend option is Used only in a class module. Indicates that the Sub procedure is visible throughout the project, but not visible to a controller of an instance of an object.

**Static:**- Indicates that the Sub procedure's local variables are preserved between calls. The Static attribute doesn't affect variables that are declared outside the Sub, even if they are used in the procedure.

In sub procedure we can call any other sub procedure and they will do some task, but it will not return any result to calling procedure.

# Function

VBA has lot of in-build function to do some manipulation in string or integer value. Apart from in-built functions, VBA allows to write user-defined functions as well. We can also use this function in work sheet like other VBA in-build function. A function procedure is almost same like subroutine, but it returns the result to calling procedure. In general sub procedure will be used to execute some task and it change the excel behavior, but function will be used to do some calculation and return the result to sub procedure for further process. A function can return multiple values separated by a comma as an array.

The most common way to define a function in VBA is by using the **Function** keyword, followed by a unique function name and it may or may not carry a list of Arguments and also it defines the return data type and end with **End Function** keyword. Function name will be follow the rules as explained in subroutines.

**Syntax:**

                                  **Argument  Data Type**        **Return Data type**

        Function name [( arglist  as type ) as Type]
            statements
        End Function

                                      Or

        [ Private | Public | Friend ][ Static ] Sub name [( arglist ) as Type]
            Statements
        End Sub

The optional keyword private, public, Static is same like sub procedure.

## Parameter / Argument

The parameter is referred to as the variables that are defined during a Sub or function declaration or definition. These variables are used to receive the values (arguments) that are passed during a Sub or function call. So parameter is a variable defined in procedure on declaration and Argument is the value receive while calling by another procedure. These parameters are used during the execution of the procedure and do some action in worksheet or do some calculation and return results. We have to specify the parameter list in parentheses immediately following the procedure name. For each parameter, you have to specify a name, a data type, and a passing mechanism (ByVal or ByRef).

```
Sub Drg(ByVal width As Integer, ByVal length As Integer) As Integer
    Cells(4,3) = width
    Cells(5,3) = Length
End sub
```

We can also write without passing mechanism and VBA consider ByRef as a default passing mechanism. We can also write the parameter without its data type and VBA consider it as Variant type. But some time it throws error like data mismatch or wrong results. So It is recommended always use data type while declaration. If the parameter is same data type, then you can write all variable name with comma separation and at last specify the data type

```
Function Area(ByVal X As String, ByVal Y, Z As Integer) As Integer
```

We can also write a function without parameter, which will do some action or return a constant value. However, we have to use empty parentheses after function name.

| Function GetValue() as Integer<br>    GetValue=50<br>End function | Function GetValue()<br>    GetValue= "Welcome"<br>End function | Function GetRange() as Range<br>    Set GetRange = Range("A1:G4")<br>End Function |
|---|---|---|

The first function returns a constant value 50 to call procedure. The second function returns the value of "Welcome" to call procedure. The third function returns the value of range A1:G4 to call procedure. Here specifying the return type will give correct result.

**ByRef / ByVal parameter**

When an argument is passed as **ByRef** argument to a different sub or function, the reference of the actual variable is sent. Any changes made in to the copy of variable, will reflect in original argument. We can say that, instead of value, the location of value is sent to function using ByRef to a function. This is the default argument in VBA. We don't need to write ByRef before argument.

Sub x(A as Variant)        Or    Sub x(ByRef A as Variant)

When an argument is passed as **ByVal** argument to a different sub or function, only the value of the argument is sent. The original argument is left intact. Any changes made in foreign function or sub will not reflect in the original argument. To declare an argument as ByVal you need to use the ByVal keyword before the argument.

Sub x(ByVal A as Variant)

We can test it the effects of ByRef and ByVal by two subroutines as shown in image. First Sub is X that takes a variant argument as ByRef. Next, it is setting the value of A = 20 then prints the value of A. Sub Y is the main subroutine that calls subroutine X. It sets the value of A=10 then calls subroutine X and passes A as an argument. Then it prints value of A in Y. When you run Sub Y we get the result in immediate window as shown in the image. Both X and Y print the value of 20.

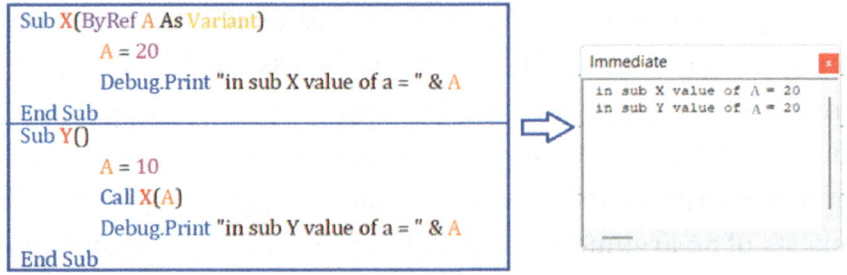

Now just change the ByRef to ByVal in first Sub X parameter and run the code.

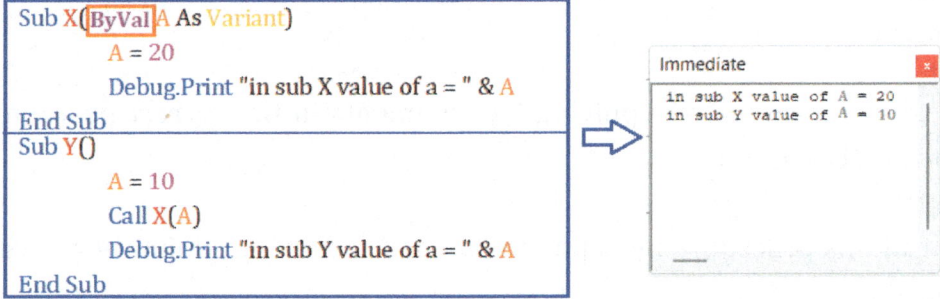

Both examples are same with the only difference of argument passing. Here in X, arguments are declared as **ByVal**. When you run Y subroutine this

72

time the output is as shown above print. The value of original a is NOT changed by sub X. It is 20 for X and 10 For Y. When Y Call X with A parameter, it only sends the value of A not the address of A. Hence any change made in A is not reflected in the original variable.

**Call sub procedure**

We can call any sub procedure to current sub procedure, just type the name of procedure and include required argument values with coma separator. We can also use **call** statement for calling another procedure, but you have to specify the parameter in parentheses.

DrawLine W, L          Or          Call DrawLine(W, L)

In general, we get return value from Function procedure, so while calling the function procedure, we have to assign the function to a variable and enclose the arguments in parentheses

Area = RectArea (W, L )

If you are not interested in the return value of a function, you can call a function the same way you call a Sub procedure. Omit the parentheses, list the arguments, and don't assign the function to a variable.

When you call sub or function procedure the parameter order is followed in argument list. Each argument in called function should match in counts and data type to call procedure parameter. The value will be assigned based on its position like $1^{st}$ parameter is assigned to $1^{st}$ Argument and $2^{nd}$ parameter is assigned to $2^{nd}$ argument and so on. So if the order is misplaced, it give wrong result. You can supply the arguments by name without regard to position. A named argument consists of an argument name followed by a colon and an equal sign (:=), followed by the argument value.

```
Sub Emp(EName As String, Age As Integer, DOB As Date)
    Debug.Print EName, Age, DOB
End Sub
```

You can call this procedure by supplying its arguments in the correct position, delimiting each with a comma

Emp "Mary", 29, #2-21-69#

You can also call this procedure by supplying named arguments, delimiting each with a comma.

Emp Age:=29, DOB:=#2/21/69#, EName:="Mary"

Named arguments are especially useful when you are calling a procedure that has optional arguments. If you use named arguments, you don't have to include commas to denote missing positional arguments. Using named arguments makes it easier to keep track of which arguments you passed and which you omitted.

We can pass the parameter value straight away by a value or through variables. Since the parameter value will change time to time based on input, so always the parameters should be specified by variables.

| Sal = GetSalory("Krish") | EName ="Krish"<br>Sal = GetSalaory(EName) |

## Function Return

Custom build function is also work like in-build Function directly in work sheet and write the function result in cell. Some time we use function to do task directly without return the result like Beep 2 times while calling function. For returning the result the function name will work as variable and we have to assign the result to function name (FunctionName = Result). This will return the result to calling procedure.

## Return Data type

We can control or specify the return data type while function declaration. This data type should be specified after the parameter closing bracket. This is optional and we can write the function without that. If we not specified the return data type, then it pass the value as variant type.

Function Area(ByVal X As String, ByVal Y, Z As Integer) **As Integer**

To do some testing, Open the excel work book and select the "Data" sheet. Write the VBA in-built function =Left(C4,2) in cell C12. After entered the formula it shows "**Re**" in cell C12. This is a function to extract the specified number of character from given string start from left. The cell C4 has a string value of "Rectangle" and the left function extracted two letter from left and shown the result as "Re". Now we can build our own function in Module1 as shown below

```
Public Function InputMonth(X As Date)
    Dim Mnumber As Integer
    Dim Mname As string
    Mnumber = Month(X)
    Mname = MonthName(Mnumber)
    InputMonth = Mname
```

End Function

Again change over to Data Sheet and select cell C12. Write equal sign (=) and type Input, Excel shows the InputMonth in the available function list while start typing. So excel will consider all custom build function to use it in work sheet. Select the function or Type fully and type open bracket and type a date like "23-12-2023" and close the bracket and press enter key. Now the function result text "December" is written in cell C12. In this function it receives the input as date type and check the month number by Month(X) function and assign to Mnumber variable. Next line use MonthName(Mnumber) function and get the month name and assign to Mname variable. Then the result Mname is assigned to function name and it returns the result to cell C12. Month() and MonthName() are VBA in-build functions.

Another testing, we write one sub procedure and one function procedure as shown below.

| Sub AreaCal() <br>     Dim Width, Length, X as integer <br>     Width=10 :    Length=20 <br>     X = RectArea(Width, Length) <br> Msgbox "Area of rectangle" & X <br> End sub | Function RectArea(X, Y As Double) <br>     RectArea = X * Y <br> End Function |
|---|---|

In the above example, a sub procedure is written to workout Area of shape. In this we are assigning the width and length of rectangle to variable W and L. Then calling a function RectArea passing the above variable as a parameter and Assigning the function return result to Variable X and popup it by message box. The function receives the input of width and length of rectangle as a function parameter X and Y. The value is multiplied (Formula of Area) and returned to calling function by its name. Please note that, the variable name in calling procedure is Width and Length, whereas the parameter variable name in function is X and Y. So please remember, there is no link between call procedure variable and called procedure variable. It just passes the value to argument list.

## Exit Procedure

Some time we execute the procedure based on some conditional check. If the condition parameter matched, then we should terminate the procedure, without running the code up to last line of procedure. For that we have to use Exit Sub for sub procedure and Exit function for function procedure.

    Sub check(X as integer)

If X < 10 then Y = 10 *2 : Exit sub
If X > 10 And X < 20 then Y = 10 *3 : Exit sub
If X > 20 then Y = 10 *3 : Exit sub
End sub

## 10. Message and Input Box

A Message Box is nothing but a dialog box that you can use to inform your users by showing a custom message or get some basic inputs. While the Message box is displayed, VBA code running is temperedly stopped and wait for user input. User has to click any one of the buttons to continue the code running.

### Message Box

Message Box is one of the most frequently used functions in VBA application. The message box is a dialogue box that appears on the screen as an extra window and show some message to user. The syntax of Message box is

MsgBox( prompt [, buttons ] [, title ] [, helpfile, context ] )

### Prompt

Prompt is mandatory value for MsgBox function and all others are optional. Prompt specifies the message information to user or take some decision from user. You can also display tables, dates, and numbers in the prompt. You can also add multiple lines in the prompt area. To display a text string, you have to write it within quote and for variable value, write the variable name without quote.

Msgbox "Record Updated"          '-----Only Text String
Msgbox Area                      '----Only variable
Msgbox "Area of rectangle" & Area   '----Text string and variable

We can write the prompt in multiline by adding Carriage return character (13) or Line Feed character (10).

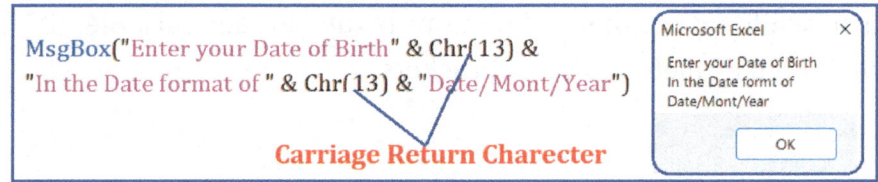

### Buttons

If we not specify the button option, VBA display a default button "Ok" in the message box. While typing the code, after prompt is typed we have to add comma to add next option. After typing the comma, VBA displays a list of buttons that can be added to the MsgBox function. You can select and add the button according to your requirement.

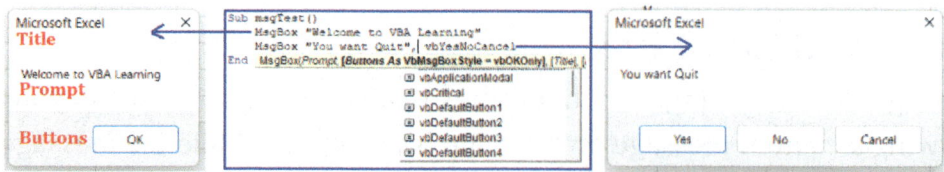

The image showing two type of message box and the first message box code is without button option and second message box code has vbYesNoCancel button option.

When the user clicks a button it returns some value as shown in the table. We can use this value in our code and write the decision taking statement and divert the flow of code based on button click.

| Constant | Value | Description |
|---|---|---|
| vbOK | 1 | OK |
| vbCancel | 2 | Cancel |
| vbAbort | 3 | Abort |
| vbRetry | 4 | Retry |
| vbIgnore | 5 | Ignore |
| vbYes | 6 | Yes |
| vbNo | 7 | No |

Sub buttonTest()
    Ans = Msgbox ("Click any Button", vbYesNoCancel)
    If Ans = 6 Then MsgBox "Yes Button Clicked"
    If Ans = 7 Then MsgBox "No Button Clicked"
    If Ans = 2 Then MsgBox "Cancel Button Clicked"
End sub

The above test code popup different message based on button click. You have already learn while assigning a function result to an variable, it is mandatory to enclose all parameter value in brackets.

**Title**

In the MsgBox, function the third argument is for writing your custom title. The title of a message box specifies what is the purpose of the displayed information or what action it will do by clicking the button. The title will be shown at top left side corner of dialogue box in single line. Title is not mandatory while writing the message box code and if we omitted title option then, VBA display a default title "Microsoft Excel".

MsgBox "Wecom Mr.Krish", vbOK, "VBA Learning Class"

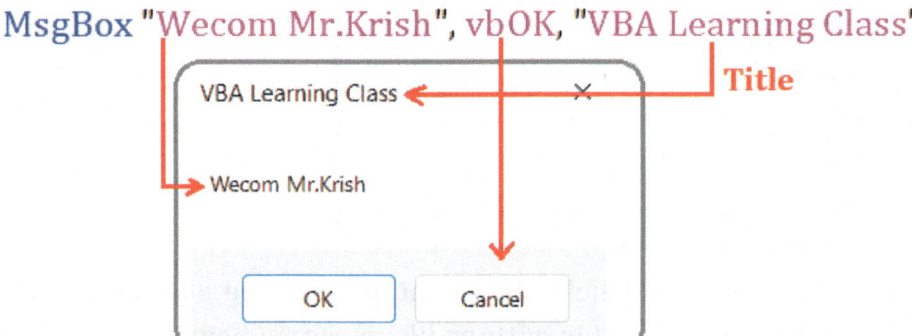

## HelpFile and Context

This the String expression that identifies the Help file to use to provide context-sensitive Help for the dialog box. If helpfile is provided, context must also be provided. Context is a Numeric expression that is the Help context number assigned to the appropriate Help topic by the Help author. Both option work in combination, so we can't assign one option for this.

## Input Message Box

Input Box is a dialogue box that helps users to take value, and do later computations according to the entered value. The input box is similar to the message box, but the message box is used to display the data while the input box is used to enter the data. By default, a message box shows only the OK button in its dialogue box but the input box shows both the OK and Cancel buttons in its dialogue box. The Syntax of input box is

InputBox(prompt[,title][,default][,xpos][,ypos][,helpfile, context])

Like message box prompt is mandatory argument and all others are optional argument. Since this input box returns a value, so always we have to assign this to a variable and all arguments are enclosed in brackets.

Ans = InputBox("Enter your Date of Birth" & Chr(13) & "In the Date formt of " & Chr(13) & "Date/Mont/Year")

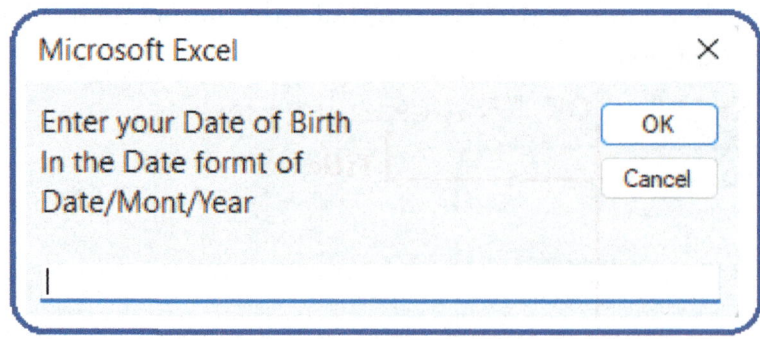

The Input Dialogue Box has a Text field at bottom to enter the user input data. Input Box is not having any options for buttons like message box, it has only Ok and cancel buttons. The Argument Prompt, Title, HelpFile and Context are same like message box and follow the instruction as explained.

**Default**

    Default argument provide a default text that will be pre filled in the text box of the dialog box. Users have the option to accept or modify this default text. If you omit default, the text box is displayed empty.

**XPOS**

    This numeric parameter represents the X -axis position of the dialog box. It specifies the value in twips, the horizontal distance of the left edge of the dialog box from the left edge of the screen. If xpos is omitted, the dialog box is horizontally centered.

**YPOS**

    Similar to XPOs, YPOs determine the Y-axis position of the dialog box. It specifies the distance of the dialog box from the top of the screen vertically. If left blank, the input box will be centered vertically.

**Skip Argument**

    We can skip the argument with just place comma separator and place the decided optional argument. For example, you want to skip the title argument and want to place the default argument then

InputBox("Your Name", ,"Krish")

Another method to skip the argument is specifying the argument name

InputBox(Prompt := "Your name", Default := "Krish"). This is applicable for message box also.

## Testing Application 1 - Continue

Till now we completed the list filling in two combo box and change the Question label based the second combo box selection. Now we have to write the code for **Find** command button, which will collect the input data and calculate the area or volume of selected shape. In this process first we have to validate the input data before doing any calculation. Open the excel file and select "Area" sheet and Double click the **Find** button. It opens the VBA editor and focus the Area sheet module and add the sub procedure for the button. You may notice it automatically created the **click** event. VBA will create the frequent use events for any control while double clicking the control. For combo box it create **change** event and for button it creates **click** event. Add the code as shown below.

```
Private Sub Find_Click()
    Dim W, L, H As Double
    Dim Shp As String
    Dim Res As Double

    '----Validate the value is in number
    If IsNumeric(Cells(4, 3)) = False Then MsgBox "Enter Number in C4 cell": Exit Sub
    If IsNumeric(Cells(5, 3)) = False Then MsgBox "Enter Number in C5 cell": Exit Sub
    If IsNumeric(Cells(6, 3)) = False Then MsgBox "Enter Number in C6 cell": Exit Sub
    W = Cells(4, 3).Value
    L = Cells(5, 3).Value
    H = Cells(6, 3).Value
End sub
```

After completing the code, deselect Design mode and select one option in two combo box. The second combo box change event will fill Zero in Cells C4 to C7 as a default value. Click the find button, it will execute at back ground and will not do any task. Change the C4 value to any of text string like "Ten" and click the Find button. Now it pop up the message like "Enter Number in C4 cell".

**Code explanation**
1. First line is declaring three variable of Integer type.
2. Second line is comment line and 3$^{rd}$ line will check the C4 value, whether it is a number. If it is number, then it goes to next line otherwise it popup validation message and exit from the procedure. Same way other line will validate cell C5,C6 .
3. After validation check it assign the cell value to variable W, L and H.

The second validation check is whether the input value is greater than Zero. The input data will vary from one to three based on the shape selected. So we have to validate the corresponding question value based on shape selected. Modify the code as shown below

```vb
Private Sub Find_Click()
    Dim W, L, H As Double
    Dim Shp As String
    Dim Res As Double
    '----Validate the value is in number
    If IsNumeric(Cells(4, 3)) = False Then MsgBox "Enter Number in C4 cell": Exit Sub
    If IsNumeric(Cells(5, 3)) = False Then MsgBox "Enter Number in C5 cell": Exit Sub
    If IsNumeric(Cells(6, 3)) = False Then MsgBox "Enter Number in C6 cell": Exit Sub
    W = Cells(4, 3).Value
    L = Cells(5, 3).Value
    H = Cells(6, 3).Value
    '-------Validate the input value is greater than zero
    Select Case CB2.Value
    Case "Square"
        If W = 0 Then MsgBox "Value for Face length is required": Exit Sub
    Case "Rectangle"
        If W = 0 Then MsgBox "Value for Width is required": Exit Sub
        If L = 0 Then MsgBox "Value for length is required": Exit Sub
    Case "Circle"
        If W = 0 Then MsgBox "Value for Circle Diameter is required": Exit Sub
    Case "Cube"
        If W = 0 Then MsgBox "Value for Face length is required": Exit Sub
        If H = 0 Then MsgBox "Value for Height is required": Exit Sub
    Case "Cuboid"
        If W = 0 Then MsgBox "Value for Width is required": Exit Sub
        If L = 0 Then MsgBox "Value for length is required": Exit Sub
        If H = 0 Then MsgBox "Value for Height is required": Exit Sub
    Case "Cylinder"
        If W = 0 Then MsgBox "Value for Circle Diameter is required": Exit Sub
        If H = 0 Then MsgBox "Value for Height is required": Exit Sub
    End Select
End Sub
```

After completion of the code run application and check whether all validation statement is working correctly.

**Code Explanation**
1. To check the shape selection, here we used select Case conditional statement. The select statement takes the check value from CB2.value
2. Next it checks the case and execute the statement in the matched case.

3. It will check the value of W, L and H is greater than zero. Also it checks only for the required data value based on the selection of shape.

Now we have to add the formula for each calculation and populate the result. This is a very simple application, so we can add the formula in the above select statement. But to learn some function, we are going to create function procedure for each calculation in Module1. Open the Module1 code window and type the following function code.

---

```
Function Area(X, Y, Z) As Double
'--Calculating Area of different shape
  If X = "Square" Then Area = Y * Y        '--Calculating Area for square
  If X = "Rectangle" Then Area = Y * Z     '--Calculating Area for rectangle
  If X = "Circle" Then Area = (3.1416 * Y ^ 2) / 4  '--Calculating Area for Circle
End Function
```

---

2nd Function to workout Volume

```
Function Volume(ByVal P As String, ByVal Q, R, S As Double) As Double
'--Calculating Volume of different shape
  If P = "Cube" Then Volume = Q * Q * S       '-----Caluculating Volume for Cube
  If P = "Cuboid" Then Volume = Q * R * S     '-----Caluculating Volume for Cuboid
  If P = "Cylinder" Then Volume = ((3.1416 * Q ^ 2) / 4) * S  '--- for Cylinder
End Function
```

---

Modify the Find click event and add the code after select statement as shown below

```
Private Sub Find_Click()
  Dim W, L, H As Double
  ................
  ................
  Case "Cylinder"
    If W = 0 Then MsgBox "Value for Circle Diameter is required": Exit Sub
    If H = 0 Then MsgBox "Value for Height is required": Exit Sub
  End Select
  '-----------Calling function
  Shp = CB2.Value
```

82

```
    If CB1.Value = "Area" Then Res = Area(Shp, W, L)
    If CB1.Value = "Volume" Then Res = Volume(Shp, W, L, H)
    Cells(7, 3).Value = Res
End Sub
```
---

We have to test this application in debugging mode, so that you can understand the entire flow of code in each procedure. So mark a break point at first line of Find event procedure. Save the procedure and select the Area Sheet. Change the range C4:C7 format to number with two decimals. Select option Area in first Combo Box and select "Rectangle" in second Combo Box. It fill the relevant question in B4 and B5 cells. Fill some number in C4 and C5 cells and Click the Find button, the execution pause at first line and by Step into button you have to navigate. I am not going to explain all steps in debugging mode. As a first validation. If all your code written correctly, it flows in all steps and write a result in C7 cells.

**Output**

|   | A | B | C | D | E | F |
|---|---|---|---|---|---|---|
| 1 |   | **Finding Area or Volume of Shapes** |   |   |   |   |
| 2 |   | Find Area / Volume | Area | Shape | Rectangle |   |
| 3 |   | Parameter | Value |   |   |   |
| 4 |   | Width in meter | 21.50 |   |   |   |
| 5 |   | Length in meter | 32.20 |   | Find |   |
| 6 |   |   | 0.00 |   |   |   |
| 7 |   | Area of rectangle in Sq.meter | 692.30 |   |   |   |
| 8 |   |   |   |   |   |   |

**Code Explanation**
1. After input data validation it goes to function calling code. The first step is assigning the CB2 value to a variable Shp to know which shape is selected.
2. We created two function to calculate Area and volume for different shapes. So we have to call the relevant function based on CB1 selection whether Area or Volume. For that, if conditional statement is used to select the calling function. If the CB1 value is area then it execute the statement Res=Area(Shp,W,L).
3. The Area is a function name and it has three parameter Shp,W,L. So it passes the parameter value to function Area for calculation. The variable value as per the above Image Shp = Rectangle, W =21.5 and L=32.2.

4. In Area function, we declare three parameter X, Y, Z and we are not specified the data type to explain different concept. Here X receives the value from Shp, Y receives from W and Z receive from L
5. Next we checking which shape is selected by If conditional statement. In this example, we selected Rectangle in CB2, so it assigns to Shp variable and it passes to X variable. So it execute the code If X = "Rectangle" Then Area = Y * Z
6. Area formula for rectangle is Width x Length, So we are multiplying the Y and Z value and assign to function name for returning the result.
7. The return result is stored in Res variable in find Event and write it in Cell **C7**.

Test all option and check the result and it is the End of Testing Application-1.

# 11. Arrays

In VBA, an Array is a single variable that can hold multiple values. It can store different data type by variant data type, however, it is also possible to declare an array of a particular data type if needed. The syntax of array is Dim Name(Size) as Data type.

Arrays declaration is similar to declaring a variable, by using Dim, Static, Private and public Statements. But in Array declaration, we have to specify the size of variable in parenthesis or empty parenthesis. Array can be classified as Single Dimensional Array and Multi-Dimensional Array and further it classified in to Static array and Dynamic array.

## Static Array

Static Arrays that cannot change size and store the value only up to the size specified. Imagine, Array is just like a range of cells and each cell store a different value. Array values can be accessed by their position (index number) within the array. For example, if we have an array of 5 size, the first number will be present at index 0 and the last element will be present index 4.

Dim Ename(5) as String

| Data | Jhon | Krish | Peter | Mohan | Imbrahim |
|------|------|-------|-------|-------|----------|
| Index | 0 | 1 | 2 | 3 | 4 |

In order to access an element of an array using its index, we need to make use of the access operator ( ). If we want to access its 3rd element, we have to use index 2

Employee = Ename(2)

The above code extract the 2nd index value "Peter" from Ename array and assign to Employee variable.

If we unable to predict the array size, then static array is not suitable. For example, if we assign a cell value to Array variable by a loop statement, if the cycle exceeds the specified size, then it throws an error "Subscript Out of Range".

```
Dim Cnt(3) as Integer      '--size as 3 with Integer data type
   For k = 1 To 5
      Cnt(k) = k+10
   Next        '--it throws error subscript out of range while the k value change to 4.
```

We can declare the size in various methods like

Dim Cnt(1 To 4) As Integer    '--Creates array with positions 1,2,3,4

Dim Cnt (4 To 7) As Long       '--Creates array with positions 4,5,6,7
Dim Cnt(0 To 3) As Integer '--Creates array with positions 0,1,2,3
This almost equal to Dim Cnt (3) as Integer. The size can be 0 to any number, but should not be a negative number.

**Array Index Base**

Whether an array is indexed from 0 or 1 depends on the setting of the Option Base statement. Use the **Option Base 1** statement at the top of a module, that is first line of module which will change the default index of the first element from 0 to 1.

Option Base 1                    '—In General Section
Dim Ename(5) As String
Employee = Ename(2)

Since index base is changed to 1 by Option Base 1 statement, now the Value "Krish" is extracted from Ename array and assign to Employee variable.

**LBound and UBound**

Lower Bound and Upper bound is in-build function used to determine the Subscript number of an array. Lower Bound is the starting of array index number and Upper Bound is the ending of array index number. The syntax for LBound and UBound is

X = LBound(Array, [Dimension])   And   X = UBound(Array, [Dimension])

The Bound function takes in two arguments: array and dimension, where array is a mandatory argument and dimension is an optional argument. The array argument is an array name for which you want to determine the lower bound. The dimension is an integer value specifying the dimension for which you want to return the lower bound. If omitted, the function will return the lower bound of the first dimension. The default LBound for any dimension is either 0 or 1, depending on the setting of the Option Base statement. The UBound of the fixed array is the size specified, but you have to subtract 1 to find the last index, if the index base is Zero. The length of Array is the difference between UBound and LBound. We can also declare the fixed array size by specifying the LBound and UBound number like Ename(3 to 5).

# Examples

```
Dim Emp(8) As String           '—Lbound=0 and UBound = 8
Option Base 1                  '—In General Section
Dim Ename(5) As String         '—Lbound=1 and UBound = 5
Dim Esal(3 to 15) As Indeger   '—Lbound=3 and UBound = 15
X = LBound(Esal)               ' --Give X Value as 3
Y = UBound(Esal)               '-- Give Y Value as 15
Length of Array = Ubound – LBound = 15 - 3  = 12
```

## Initialize Arrays

We can assign the values to array by its position or by Array function. For example, assigning the value to Ename Array

Ename(0) ="Jhon"
Ename(1) ="Krish"
Ename(2) ="Peter"
Ename(3) ="Mohan"
Ename(4) ="Ibrahim"

Here we specifying the Array variable name and the position of variable by its Index number in the bracket.

We can also assign the value to array by VBA in-build array function.

Ename = Array("Jhon", "Krish", "Peter", "Mohan", "Ibrahim")

Here all the value is placed inside bracket of Array function. Each value should be separated by a comma. You have to follow the discipline like write the string value within quote and Number value in plain without quote. We can also do it by For…Next loop or For each statement to fill the Array value by its position.

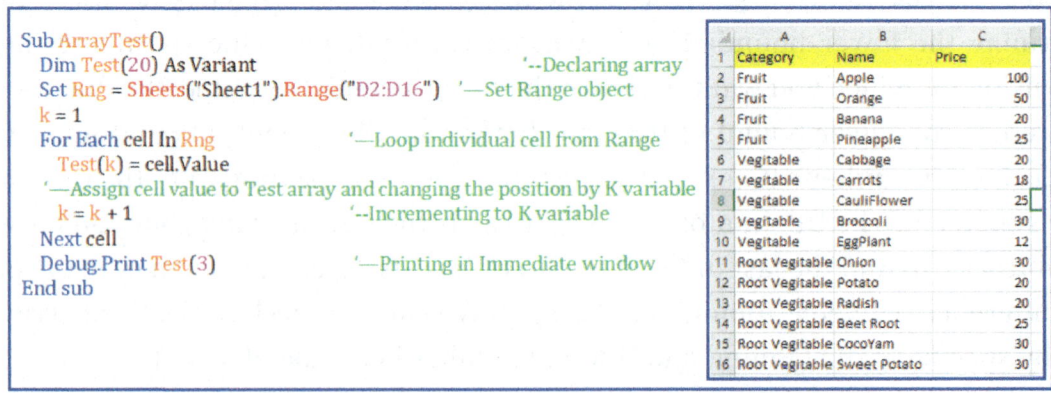

```
Sub ArrayTest()
    Dim Test(20) As Variant                            '--Declaring array Test
    Set Rng = Sheets("Sheet1").Range("D2:D16")    '—Set Range object
```

87

```
    k = 1
    For Each cell In Rng              '—Loop individual cell from Range
        Test(k) = cell.Value
     '—Assign cell value to Test array and changing the position by K variable
        k = k + 1                     '--Incrementing to K variable
    Next cell
    Debug.Print Test(3)               '—Printing in Immediate window
End sub
```

In the above example we are setting a range D2:D16 from excel file and using a for each loop with that range. This loop move the cell selection one by one and that cell value is assigned to Test() array variable. The index number is dynamically changed by the loop by incrementing one to K variable. Then it prints the result as "Banana"

## Multi-Dimensional Array

All the above example we dealt single dimension arrays. In Visual Basic, you can declare arrays with up to 60 dimensions. In which most of the application uses two dimensional or Three dimensional arrays. To create multidimensional array with more than one dimension, use comma separator to define each separate dimension.

Dim Emp(3,10) as variant    '—Two Dimensional array

Dim Emp(3, 4,10) as variant    '—Three Dimensional array

Dim Emp(1 to 3, 4 to 10) as variant

'—Two dimensional with Lower bound and Upper Bound size.

If you think of the array as a matrix, the first argument represents the rows and the second argument represents the columns. Think of a 1D array is like a single row or single column of Excel cells, a 2D array like an entire Excel worksheet with multiple rows and columns, and a 3D array is like an entire workbook, containing multiple sheets each containing multiple rows and columns.

## Initialize Arrays

Same way, we can assign the values to array by its position or by Array function.

```
Esal(0,0) ="Jhon"
Esal(0,1) = "EID-1001"
Esal(0,2) = 3000
ESal(1,0) ="Mohan"
ESal(1,1) =" EID-1002"
Esal(1,2) = 4000
ESal(2,0) ="Krish"
ESal(2,1) =" EID-1003"
Esal(2,2) = 2500
```

|  | | Index 2nd Number | | |
|---|---|---|---|---|
| Index 1st Number | | 0 | 1 | 2 |
| | 0 | Jhon | EID-1001 | 3000 |
| | 1 | Mohan | EID-1002 | 4000 |
| | 2 | Krish | EID-1003 | 2500 |

In this we have to specify the multi dimension size with comma separator. By array function

```vba
Dim Esal() As Variant
    Esal = Array(Array("Jhon", "EID-1001", 3000), Array("Mohan", "EID-1002", 4000),
        Array("krish", "EID-1003", 2500),)
```

We can also do it by For…Next loop or For each statement to fill the Array value by its position.

```vba
Sub Test()
   Dim ws1, ws2 As Worksheet
   Dim wsData(16, 3) As Variant    '---Declare the array
   Dim rw, col  As Integer
'---get the information from the source sheet and populate the array
   Set ws1 = Worksheets("Sheet1")
   For rw = LBound(wsData, 1) To UBound(wsData, 1)
      For col = LBound(wsData, 2) To UBound(wsData, 2)
          wsData(rw, col) = ws1.Range("A2").Offset(rw, col).Value
      Next col
   Next rw
'---Check the third position value from array
   Debug.Print wsData(3, 0)
   Debug.Print wsData(3, 1)
   Debug.Print wsData(3, 2)
'-------Write the Array value to Sheet2
  Set ws2 = Worksheets("Sheet2")
   For rw = LBound(wsData, 1) To UBound(wsData, 1)
      For col = LBound(wsData, 2) To UBound(wsData, 2)
         Ws2.Range("A1").Offset(rw, col).Value = wsData(rw, col)
      Next col
   Next rw
End Sub
```

## Output

**Source (Sheet1)**

| | A | B | C |
|---|---|---|---|
| 1 | Category | Name | Price |
| 2 | Fruit | Apple | 100 |
| 3 | Fruit | Orange | 50 |
| 4 | Fruit | Banana | 20 |
| 5 | Fruit | Pineapple | 25 |
| 6 | Vegitable | Cabbage | 20 |
| 7 | Vegitable | Carrots | 18 |
| 8 | Vegitable | CauliFlower | 25 |
| 9 | Vegitable | Broccoli | 30 |
| 10 | Vegitable | EggPlant | 12 |
| 11 | Root Vegitable | Onion | 30 |
| 12 | Root Vegitable | Potato | 20 |
| 13 | Root Vegitable | Radish | 20 |
| 14 | Root Vegitable | Beet Root | 25 |
| 15 | Root Vegitable | CocoYam | 30 |
| 16 | Root Vegitable | Sweet Potato | 30 |
| 17 | | | |

**Destination (Sheet2)**

| | A | B | C |
|---|---|---|---|
| 1 | Fruit | Apple | 100 |
| 2 | Fruit | Orange | 50 |
| 3 | Fruit | Banana | 20 |
| 4 | Fruit | Pineapple | 25 |
| 5 | Vegitable | Cabbage | 20 |
| 6 | Vegitable | Carrots | 18 |
| 7 | Vegitable | CauliFlowe | 25 |
| 8 | Vegitable | Broccoli | 30 |
| 9 | Vegitable | EggPlant | 12 |
| 10 | Root Vegit | Onion | 30 |
| 11 | Root Vegit | Potato | 20 |
| 12 | Root Vegit | Radish | 20 |
| 13 | Root Vegit | Beet Root | 25 |
| 14 | Root Vegit | CocoYam | 30 |
| 15 | Root Vegit | Sweet Pot. | 30 |
| 16 | | | |

## Code Explanation

1. First line is declaring an object variable Ws1 and Ws2
2. Second line declaring the 2D array WsData with size of 16,3
3. Declaring local variable rw(Row) and Col(Column)
4. Set the worksheet1 object variable Ws1 which is the source sheet to extract data.
5. Next step, we are using two for loop to get data by row and column. In first loop rw is for loop count variable and starting number is worked out by Lbound function. Here the Array name is WsData and Dimension is 1 means it take the minimum subscript from first position of dimension that is 16. The loop end number is worked out by UBound function. Here the Array name is WsData and Dimension is 1 means it take the maximum subscript from 16. So the lBound function give a value 0 and UBound function give a value of 16. So for loop start number is 0 and end number is 16.
6. In Second loop col is for loop count variable and starting number is worked out by Lbound function. Here the dimension is 2 means it take the minimum subscript from second position of dimension that is 3. Same way UBound function workout the maximum subscript. So the LBound function give a value 0 and UBound function give a value of 3. So for loop start number is 0 and end number is 3.
7. Next line extract data from cell and assigning to Array. In first running, the Variable value of rw and col is set to zero, because the start number of for loop is zero. We used offset VBA in-built function which will move the

cell selection based on argument value given in bracket from the reference cell. For detail of offset function, refer in In-built function chapter. Here the reference cell is A1 and the value of rw and Col is zero(0), so it maintain the same cell and get the value from A1 and assign to array variable WsData(0,0). Then the second loop increment one to col variable and again start. Now the value of rw is zero(0) and Col is one(1). The offset function shift the cell selection from A1 to one column and get the value from B1 and assign to array variable WsData(0,1). Like that the second for loop move the cell selection up to three columns and assign the column value to Array variable. Then the first for loop increment one to rw variable and repeat the cycle. So the first loop move cell by row and second loop move by columns and get all cell value.
8. Next code is show the 3rd element of Array WsData. It prints the result in Immediate window like Fruit, Pineapple and 25.
9. Next code is extracting data from WsData array and populate in Sheet2. The process is reverse as explained above.

## Dynamic Array

In Dynamic Array, the size is always change based on the program requirement. For example, if we assign one column value from row number 1 to Last row to Array variable. The last row is dynamic and it change time to time based on data addition or deletion, so we should assign it in to a Dynamic Array. We can resize the array and add more value to it while running the code. For declaring Dynamic array, we have to specify the array variable name with empty parenthesis.

Dim Cnt()

Dim Cnt() as variant

Once the array variable is declared, we have to Re-dimension the array size by ReDim function.

### Redim

ReDim is used in sub procedure to reallocate the storage space for Dynamic array variables. The ReDim statement is used to set or change the size of Array that has already been declared.   The syntax is

ReDim [ Preserve ] varname ( subscripts )[ As type ]

Preserve is optional Keyword used to preserve the data in an existing array when you change the size of the last dimension. Varname is the array variable name which is already declared. Subscripts is the dimension of an array which can be either a number or a variable name. As Type is an optional to specify the data type.

We can use the ReDim statement as many times in code to resize the array variable size. If you have a large array and you no longer need some of its elements, ReDim can free up memory by reducing the array size. On the other hand, if your array needs more elements, ReDim can add them. The ReDim statement cannot change the data type of an array variable or its elements. ReDim releases the existing array value and creates a new array with the same rank and with Preserve Modifier it preserves (Retain) the data in the existing array when you change the size of only the last dimension.

**Example**

```
Dim Esal(10) As Integer
ReDim Preserve Esal(20)
ReDim Preserve Esal(15)
ReDim Esal(10)
```

The Dim statement creates a new array with single dimensions and declared with a bound of 10. The first ReDim creates a new array which replaces the existing array in variable Esal and Preserve keyword copies all the elements from the existing array into the new array and add 10 more position with empty value. The 2$^{nd}$ ReDim creates another new array in the name of Esal and copies all the elements that fit. However, five positions are lost along with data. Reducing the size of a large array can free up memory that you no longer need. The third ReDim creates another new array in the name of Esal and removes another five position. This time it does not copy any existing elements, because the statement doesn't include the Preserve modifier, it sets all array elements to their original default values.

**Example**

```
Sub Test()
    Dim ws As Worksheet
    Dim wsData() As Variant    '---Declare the array
    Dim rw, col, LR, LC  As Integer
    '---get the information from the source sheet and populate the array
    Set ws = Worksheets("Sheet1")
    LR = ws.Cells(ws.Rows.Count, "A").End(xlUp).Row  '—Find last data row
```

```vb
    LC = ws.Cells(1, Columns.Count).End(xlToLeft).Column   '—Find last data column
    ReDim wsData(LR, LC)            '---Set dimension to Array variable
    For rw = 0 To LR-1
       For col = 0 To LC-1
            wsData(rw, col) = ws1.Range("A2").Offset(rw, col).Value
       Next col
    Next rw
'---Check the third position value from array
    Debug.Print wsData(2, 0)
    Debug.Print wsData(2, 1)
    Debug.Print wsData(2, 2)
End sub
```

**Code Explanation**

1. First line is declaring an object variable Ws for work sheet
2. Second line declaring the 2D array WsData without size.
3. Declaring local variable rw, Col, LR and LC
4. Set the worksheet1 object variable Ws which is the source sheet to extract data.
5. Next finding the last row and column of sheet which has data and assign to LR and LC variable.
6. Next we are re sizing the WsData by specifying the dimension. Here the first position is number of row which is assigned by the variable LR. And second dimension is number of column which is assigned by variable LC. This variable value is always change based on record addition or deletion.
7. Next step, we are using two for loop to get data by row and column. In first loop rw is for loop count variable and starting number is zero(0) and end number is last record of sheet(LR). Since we are using zero base array, we have to subtract one from last row count, so we used end number as LR-1.
8. In second loop col is For loop count variable and starting number is zero(0) and end number is last column of sheet(LC). Since we are using zero base array, we have to subtract one from last column count, so we used end number as LC-1.
9. Next line extract data from cell and assigning to Array. Which is as explained in previews example.
10. Next code is show the 2$^{rd}$ element of Array WsData. It prints the result in Immediate window like Fruit, Banana and 20.

# 12. Data Manipulation by In-build function

VBA provides a large number of built-in functions that can be used in our code. The list is bigger and you can see the list in Annexure-A attached in last pages of this book. In which some of function is called work sheet function marked as (WS) at end of each function. We can't use this work sheet function directly in VBA code. For example max() function will work directly in sheet cells, but it will not work in VBA code. We have to write such function like
Application.WorksheetFunction.Max().

In this section, the most popular built-in functions are explained in detail and for all other functions, you have to browse in web based on your requirement. There is no necessity to memory all the function in mind, which will make us tired. So no need to read this section in detail, you can refer this section whenever you are using in any application development.

## String

String is an array of characters which will form word or Sustenance with combination of Alphabetic, Numbers, Space and special characters. VBA provide various in-built function to manipulate the string in the program. Some of important functions are explained in this section.

**Left(), Right() and Mid() function**

To extract some portion of string, we can use three type of function in VBA. This function counts the space also as one character.

St = "Welcome to VBA Learning Class"
X = Left(St , 2)

Left function extracts a specified number of character (2) from left side. The above statement assigns the value "**We**" to X Variable.

X = Right(St , 4)

Right function extracts a specified number of character (4) from Right side. The above statement assigns the value "**lass**" to X Variable.

X = Mid(St , 4 , 2)

Mid function extracts a specified number of character (2) from the 4$^{th}$ character from left side. The above statement assigns the value "**co**" to X Variable.

### Len() function
This function counts the number characters including space and returns an integer value.
X = Len(St)    It assign a value of 29 to X variable

### LTrim(), RTrim() and Trim() function
Trim function is used to trim (remove) the empty space in a string at starting or ending point.
X = LTrim("    Check    ") Assign the value "Check    " to X
X = RTrim("    Check    ") Assign the value "    Check" to X
X = Trim("    Check    ") Assign the value "Check" to X

### Lower(), Upper() and Proper() function
This function is used to convert the character case either to Lower case or Upper case.
X = Lower("WElCOmE")   Returns "welcome" to X
X = Upper("WElCOmE")   Returns "WELCOME" to X
X = Proper("WElCOmE")
The proper function changes all first letter of word in to Upper case and change balance character of that word in to lower case, so it Returns "Welcome" to X.

### InStr() and InStrRev() function
InStr function return the position the first occurrence of one sub string within a search string, starting from **left** side of search string.
InStr([Start Position], Search String, Search Char, [Compare Method])
It has four arguments and in which the Search string and Search char is mandatory and other two arguments are optional. We have to specify the string argument in double quote.
St = "Welcome to VBA Welcoming Class"
X = Instr(St,"co") '--It gives a result 4 and assign to X variable.
X = Instr(7, St,"co")
X = Instr(7, St,"co", vbTextCompare)

It gives a result 19, Since the start position 7 is after the first occurrence, so it finds the next occurrence.  Compare method has two option "Text" and

"Binary". Binary comparison compares the numeric Unicode value of each character in each string, and is case sensitive. Whereas text comparison compares each Unicode character based on its lexical meaning in the current culture, and is not case sensitive.

A=a    '--by binary comparison is false
A=a    '--by text comparison is True

InStrRev function return the position the first occurrence of one sub string within search string, starting from **right** side of search string.
InStrRev(Search String, Search Char, [Start Position], [Compare Method])
The function is reverse of InStr. If we place Negative value in start position of InStr or InStrRev function, it acts in reverse order.

## Chr() and Asc() function

Chr function returns the character associated with the specified character code(ASCII).
X = Chr(65)    '—Returns Character "A" to variable X
Msgbox "First Line" & chr(13) & "Second Line"
This message box function write two lines in dialogue, because Chr(13) is Line feed character, so it create next line and write the second string.

Asc function returns the character code(ASCII) associated with the specified character.
X = Chr("A")    '—Returns Character 65 to variable X

## Split() and Join() function

The Split function is used to split strings into multiple substrings based on a delimiter provided to the function and a comparison method.
Split(String to be split, [Delimiter], [Limit], [Compare])
Split function has four arguments, in which String to be Split is mandatory and all others are optional.
Delimiter: Delimiter is a separating character like , ; - and if we omit this delimiter it split the string with space.
Limit: Limit is How many substrings do you want from the supplier string.
Compare: Compare is method to compare the text by binary or Text.
For this function we have to assign the result to Array variable

```
Sub Test()
Dim X() As String
St = "Welcome to VBA Welcoming Class"
X = Split(St)
    Debug.Print X(0)
    Debug.Print X(4)
End Sub
```

Immediate
Welcome
Class

Join function Returns a string created by joining a number of substrings contained in an array.

Join(Source Array, Delimiter) as String

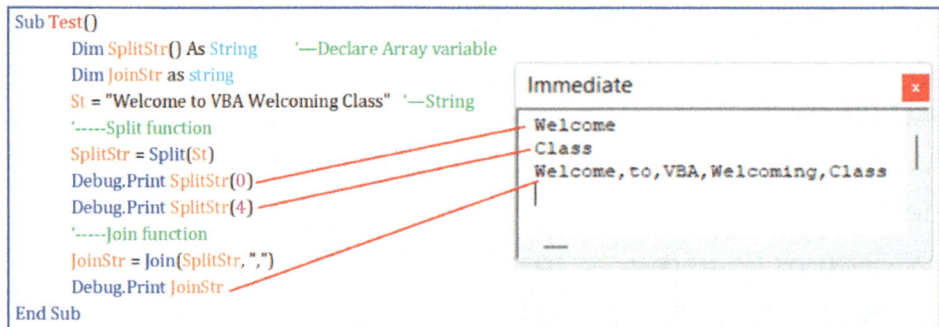

The above test example splitting the St string by split function and assign to SplitStr array. Then it printing the 0 and 1st element of SplitStr array. Again by Join function we are Joining the Array in to a single string with comma delimiter and assign to JointStr variable. Then printing the JoinStr. The results are shown in Immediate window. If you omit the delimiter character, then it leaves space between words.

**Replace() function**

This function replaces a specified substring to a given string as specified number of times.

Replace(Original String, Find String, Replace String, [Start], [Count], [Compare])
Replace function has six arguments and first three value is mandatory.
In which Original String, Find String and Replace String is mandatory and others are optional.
Start: The position in the Expression from where the search should begin. By default, it starts from the first character.
Count: The number of occurrences to replace. If omitted, all occurrences will be replaced.

Compare: Specifies the type of string comparison.

```vba
Sub Test()
  Dim JX, Y As String
  St = "Welcome to VBA Learning Class. VBA is Microsoft Programing
     language"
  X = Replace(St, "VBA", "Visual Basic")
  Debug.Print X
  Y = Replace(St, "VBA", "Visual Basic", 2, 1)
  Debug.Print Y
End Sub
```

The 1st Debug print show the output like "Welcome to **Visual Basic** Learning Class. **Visual Basic** is Microsoft Programing language". Here the replace function replaced the all "VBA" word with "Visual Basic". Here we are not specified the count, so it replace all the "VBA" character with "Visual Basic".

The second Debug print show the output like "Welcome to **Visual Basic** Learning Class. **VBA** is Microsoft Programing language". Here it replaces the first occurrence, since we given 1 as count argument.

## Date and Time

Excel normally stores dates in form of numbers referred to as date-serial numbers to help during calculations. A date is usually given a numerical value starting from January 1, 1900 and this date is equal to the number 1 that is the first date in Excel's date system. And November 10, 2023 is equal to the number 45,240. That is, this date is 45,240 days after January 1, 1900.

Now let's look at time. One day is equal to the number 1, one hour is equal to 1 divided by 24 (1/24) and the minutes and seconds are converted in to hour. The equal number value for 11:30:40 is 0.4796. If we combined the date and time, then the value is 45240.4796. There is many in-build function to deal the date type.

### Date(), Time() and Now() function

The Date function returns the current system date in a format specified in your computer date/time/time zone settings. Since it has no arguments, so in some versions of Excel, the date() function can automatically change to Date without Parentheses. We can store date in a variable of type Date, Variant or String.

X = Date()      '--- result of X = 11/8/2023

Time function returns the current system time. For this also we can write without Parentheses in some Excel Version

X = Time()      '--- Result X = 12:31:27 PM

Now function returns the current system date and current system time to variable. For this also we can write without Parentheses in some Excel Version

X = Now()      '---result of X =11/8/2023  12:31:27 PM


## DateAdd() Function

DateAdd Function is used to add a specified date or time interval to a date or time. This function will return the resulting date/time to a variable. The syntax of the DateAdd Function is:

DateAdd(Interval, Number, Date)

**Interval**: Interval is a string that specifies the type of interval as listed below.

| Day | Week | Week Day | Month | Quarter | Year | Day of the Year | Hour | Minute | Second |
|---|---|---|---|---|---|---|---|---|---|
| "d" | "WW" | "W" | "m" | "q" | "yyyy" | "y" | "h" | "n" | "S" |

**Number**: The number of intervals that you want to add to the original date/time.
**Date**: The original date/time.

X = DateAdd("m", 10, "11/12/2023")     '--Result  9/12/2024

Here the Number type is month(m), so it adds 10 months to given date and give the result.

## DateDiff() Function

DateDiff Function is used to get the difference between two dates, based on a specified time interval. The syntax of the DateDiff Function is:

DateDiff(Interval, Date1, Date2, [Firstdayofweek], [Firstweekofyear])

**Interval**: It is same like as explained in DateAdd function
**Date1**: A date value representing the earlier date.

**Date2**: A date value representing the later date.

**Firstdayofweek** (Optional): A constant that specifies the weekday that the function should use as the first day of the week. If blank Sunday is used as the first day of the week. Firstdayofweek can be vbSunday, vbMonday, vbTuesday, vbWednesday, vbThursday, vbFriday and vbSaturday. If we specify vbUseSystemDayOfTheWeek, it uses the first day of the week that is specified by your system's settings.

**Firstweekofyear** (Optional): A constant that specifies the first week of the year. If blank, then the Jan 1st week is used as the first week of the year. It can be

vbFirstJan1:- uses the week containing Jan 1st.

vbFirstFourDays:- uses the first week that contains at least four days in the new year.

vbFirstFullWeek:- uses the first full week of the year.

vbSystem:- uses the first week of the year as specified by your system settings.

X = DateDiff("m", "11/11/2021", "10/12/2023")   '--Result 23

Here the Number type of interval is month(m), so it find the difference of two dates in month and give a result as 23.

## Day(), Month(), Year(), Weekday() Function

This is short form of DatePart function, give the part of date.

X = Day("12/5/2023")         '---Result 5
X = Month("12/5/2023")       '---Result 12
X = Year("12/5/2023")        '---Result 2023
X = WeekDay("12/5/2023")     '---Result 3

## Hour(), Minute(), Second() Function

X = Hour("2:14:22 AM")       '---Result 2
X = Minute("2:14:22 AM")     '---Result 14
X = Second("2:14:22 AM")     '---Result 22

## MonthName(), Function

MonthName Function is return the name of a month from an input supplied month number. The syntax is

MonthName(month as Integer, [Abbreviate as Boolean])

**Month**: Month is an integer value between 1 and 12.

**Abbreviate** (Optional): - Specifies whether the month name should be abbreviated. If you specify false it give full month name. If blank the default value of False is used.

X = MonthName(11, False)   '--Result November
X = MonthName(11, True)   '--Result Nov
X = MonthName(11)         '--Result November

## WeekDay() function

Weekday Function is return an integer from 1 – 7 representing a day of the week from an input date. The syntax is

Weekday(Date, [Firstdayofweek])

**Firstdayofweek** (Optional): A constant that specifies the weekday that the function should use as the first day of the week. For detail Refer DayDif function

Weekday("11-8-2023")   '--Result 4
Weekday("11-8-2023", VbMonday)   '--Result 3

## WeekDayName() function

WeekdayName Function is return the name of a weekday from an input supplied weekday number. The syntax is

WeekdayName(Weekday, [Abbreviate], [Firstdayoftheweek])

X = WeekdayName(5)   '--Result "Thursday"
X = WeekdayName(5, True)   '--Result "Thu"
X = WeekdayName(5, True, vbMonday)   '--Result "Fri"


## DateSerial() , TimeSerial() function

DateSerial Function is take an input year, month and day in integer value and returns a date. The syntax is:

DateSerial(Year, Month, Day)

X = DateSerial(2023, 5, 20) '--Result 5/20/2023

TimeSerial function is take an input hour, minute and second in integer value and returns a Time. The syntax is:

TimeSerial(Hour, Minute, Second)

X = TimeSerial(1, 10, 15)   '--Result 1 : 10 :15 AM
X = TimeSerial(13, 10, 15)   '--Result 1 : 10 :15 PM

## DateValue(), TimeValue() function

The DateValue Function returns a Date when given a string representation of a date.

DateValue("November, 12, 2023")   '-- Result 11/12/2023
DateValue("10-12-2023")           '-- Result 10/12/2023

The TimeValue function returns a Time when given a string representation of a date or time.

TimeValue("November, 12, 2023")   '-- Result 12 : 00: 00 AM
TimeValue("10:12:20")             '-- Result 10 : 12 : 20 AM

## Comparing date

We can compare a date with comparative operators of Greater than(>), Less than(<) and equal(=)

## Activity Function

### Find function

The VBA Find function uses the Range object to search for a specified value in a Range of cells provided. The syntax is

Range("A1:A10").Find(what, [After], [LookIn], [LookAt], [SerchOrder], [SerchDirection], [MatchCase], [SerchFormat] )

Here the only required parameter is What and all other parameters are optional.

| Parameter | Type | Description | Values |
|---|---|---|---|
| What | Required | The value you are searching for | Any data |
| After | Optional | A single cell range that you start your search from | for example: Range("A5") |
| LookIn | Optional | What to search in eg: Formulas, Values or Comments | xlValues, xlFormulas, xlCommentsThreaded, xlNotes |
| LookAt | Optional | Look at a part or the whole of the cell | xlWhole, xlPart |
| SearchOrder | Optional | The order to search | xlByRows or xlByColumns. |
| SearchDirection | Optional | The direction to search | xlNext, xlPrevious |
| MatchCase | Optional | If search is case sensitive | True or False |
| MatchByte | Optional | Used for double byte languages | True or False |
| SearchFormat | Optional | Allow searching by format. The format is set using Application.FindFormat | True or False |

By this function we can locate the row and column number which has the first match value

x = ws.Range("C:C").Cells.Find("Stop").Row
x = ws.Range("C:C").Cells.Find("Stop").Column

### Offset function

VBA Offset function is use to move or refer a cell in worksheet by skipping a particular number of rows and columns from the reference range. In Excel, the range is nothing but a cell or range of the cell. The syntax is

Range("A1").offset(row offset, Column Offset)

range is the reference position and here the reference position is A1 cell. Offset is in-build function has two arguments row offset and column offset. Row offset is how many rows do you want shift(offset) from the current cell(Reference Cell-A1) and column offset is how many columns do you want shift from the current cell. If you specify the row number with positive number, then it move to Right side and if it is in negative number it moves Left. Same way If you specify the column number with positive number it move to Downward and if it is in negative number then it moves Upward.

Example

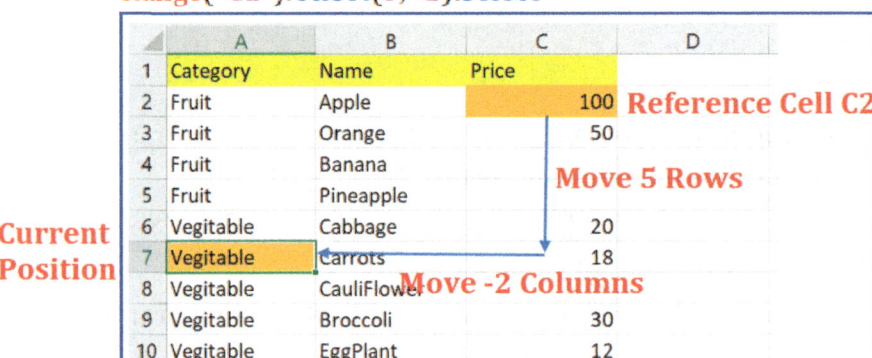

## Sorting Method

Sorting refers to ordering of data in an increasing or decreasing fashion according to some linear relationship among the data items. They may be by alphabetic order or Number order. Sorting reduces the time to search any particular data. We can sort the excel sheet data by VBA and it has lot of options and syntax is

Expression.Sort (Key1, Order1, Key2, Type, Order2, Key3, Order3, Header, OrderCustom, MatchCase, Orientation, SortMethod, DataOption1, DataOption2, DataOption3)

The Expression is the Range object or the range object variable.

Sheets("Sub Category").Range("A1:B100").AutoFilter()

Or

```
Set Rng = Sheets("Division").Range("A1:D100")
Rng.Sort()
```

The key1,2,3 are Specifies the sort field, either as a range name (String) or Range object. The key numbers are used for first sort, second sort and third sort of various columns. The Order1,2,3 are sorting order like xlAscending and xlDescending corresponding to key numbers. Type is used for PvotTable sorting.

```
Set ws =Worksheets("Sheet1")
Set Rng =ws. Range("A1:E6")
Rng.Sort.SortFields.Clear
Rng.Sort Key1:=Range("A1"), order1:=xlDescending, Header:=xlYes
```

The 'Clear' method is used initially to ensure that every sort parameter for that worksheet is set back to the default values. A user may have previously set the parameters to different values, or an earlier sort in VBA may have changed them. It is important to start from a default position when sorting, otherwise it give incorrect results.

For sorting, We need to provide three main parameters.

**Key**:-The range of cells from single or multiple columns we need to sort.
**Order**:-Specify the sorting order either ascending or descending.
**Header**:-Declare whether the columns to be sorted have a header or not.

In the above code we specifying the total range "A1:E6" which is to be sorted and the key range is "A1" which means it consider only A1 column data for sorting. The order is Descending and if we omit this parameter it consider the default value of Ascending.

We can also sort multilevel fields and the syndax is

```
Rng.Sort Key1:=Range("E1"), Key2:=Range("C1"), Header:=xlYes,
Order1:=xlAscending, Order2:=xlDescending
```

In the above code, there are two keys in the sort statement (Key1 and Key2). Key1 (Col-E) is sorted first with all columns and then Key2 (Col-C) is sorted based on the first sort. Also there are two order parameters. Order1 associates with Key1 and Order2 associates with Key2. It is important to ensure that keys and orders are kept in step with each other.

The above parameters are key parameter which will fulfil our requirement and all other parameters are additional options.

**Match Case**:- Set to True to perform a case-sensitive sort, False to perform a non-case-sensitive sort;

**Orientation**: - Specifies if the sort should be by row (default) or column. Set xlSortColumns (xlLeftToRight) value to 1 to sort by column. Set xlSortRows (xlTopToBottom) value to 2 to sort by row.

**Sort Method**: - It Specifies the type of sort. Set xlPinYin value to 1 to sort by Phonetic Chinese sort order for characters. This is the default value. Set xlStroke value to 2 to Sort by the quantity of strokes in each character.

**Data Option**: - DataOption1 specifies how to sort text in the range specified in Key1. Same way other option2 and 3 sort text in the range specified in Key2 and 3. Set xlSortNormal value to 0 Sorts numeric and text data separately. This is the default value. Set xlSortTextAsNumbers value to 1 Treat text as numeric data for the sort.

You learn more while building the sample project at end of this book.

### Filter Method

Filtering data in excel sheet is to display records that meet certain criteria. Take any data sheet with column headers. To switch on the filter mode, select all column headings and click Data in menu and click the Filter. You notice a Drop down Arrow is added to all Column header. Click any one of Drop down arrow, it expands and show options like Sorting by Ascending, Descending and by color. Also it shows all the unique Data of the selected column. Deselect all Check box and select any one Check box, here I am selected a value 12. After selection click the Ok button, then it shows only the records has the value matching to checked value in that column and hide all other records.

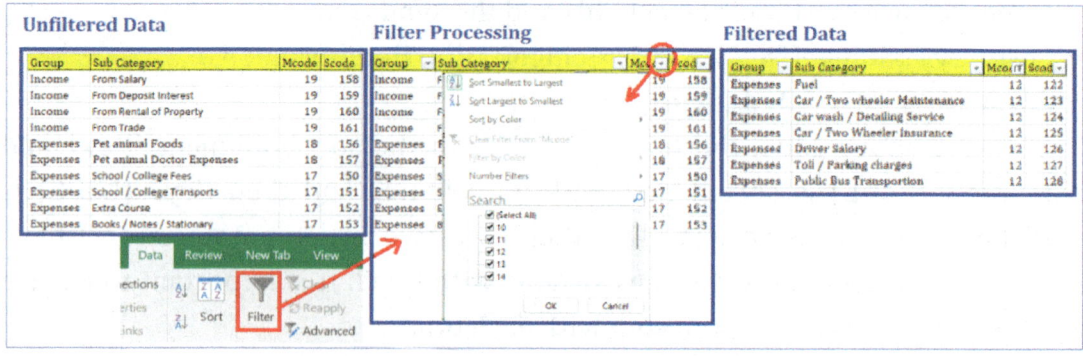

Same filter action, we can do in VBA by Auto filter and Advanced Filter function.

105

## Auto Filter

Excel VBA auto Filter Method is very useful for filtering the records to suit our requirement. You can retrieve specific limited records from the large number of records based on some criteria. The syntax is

Expression.AutoFilter (Field, Criteria1, Operator, Criteria2, SubField, VisibleDropDown)

The Expression is the Range object or the range object variable.

Sheets("Sub Category").Range("A1:B100").AutoFilter()

Or

Set Rng = Sheets("Division").Range("A1:D100")

Rng.AutoFilter()

In this function apart from the Expression all other parameters are optional. For simple filter we have to use parameters field and creterial. In the field parameter, you have to set the column number. The leftmost column ("A") is field one and it increase by one increment for next column. Criteria is the value you want search and filter. We can use a string value or any variable which supply a string value.

'-----Filter column "C" (3) and show the record has "BSC" text in column "C".

Rng.AutoFilter Field:=3, Criteria1:="Bsc"

We can make our filter criteria for different value in same column with operator. Here we have to give two criteria value for Creteria1 and Creteria2 and add any one Operator.

'-----Filter column "C" (3) and show the record has "BSC" Or "Bcom".

Rng.AutoFilter Field:=3, Criteria1:="Bsc", Operator:=xlOr, Criteria2:="Bcom"

We can also make our filter criteria with two columns.

Rng.AutoFilter Field:=3, Criteria1:="Bsc"

Rng.AutoFilter Field:=4, Criteria1:="Maths"

In the above example the first statement filters the entire sheet data by column "C" with criteria value of "Bsc". Then the second statement again apply filter to previous filtered data for column "D" with criteria value of "Maths".

The VissibleDropDown parameter is used to show or hide the Arrow symbol. If it is True, then it displays the AutoFilter drop-down arrow for the field header. If it is False, then it hides the AutoFilter drop-down arrow. If we not use this parameter, then it considers the default value of True and show the Drop-Down arrow. Always you have to reset the filter before run another filter. Resting of filter will remove the filter condition and show all data.

Rng.ShowAllData

You learn more while building the sample project at end of this book.

## Advance Filter

Auto filter allows filtering data with a maximum of two criteria for a specified column. But advanced filter allows to apply several filter criteria simultaneously to the entire data, which auto filter does not do. The syntax is

Expression.AdvancedFilter (Action, CriteriaRange, CopyToRange, Unique)

The Expression is the Range object or the range object variable.

The Action parameter is mandatory and it has two option xlFilterInPlace or xlFilterCopy. The action xlFilterInPlace will filter the source data and show it in same place of source data range which is specified in Expression. The action xlFilterCopy will filter the data and make a copy of that and past it to a specified range.

CriteriaRange is optional parameter which will be assigned by a Range with criteria value in same sheet or in different sheet. The column and column header should be identical to Main data sheet. We have to specify our criteria in next row of headers corresponding to decided columns.

| C | D | E | F | G | H | I | J | K | L | M |
|---|---|---|---|---|---|---|---|---|---|---|
| **Main Data** | | | | | | **Creteria Range** | | | | |
| ID | Name | Division | Group | Total Mark | | ID | Name | Division | Group | Total Mark |
| 120 | William | Bsc | Maths | 79 | | | | Bsc | | |
| 121 | Peter | Bsc | Science | 84 | | | | | | |
| 123 | Ganesh | Bcom | Commerce | 63 | | | | | | |
| 124 | Seetha | Bcom | Commerce | 79 | | | | | | |
| 120 | William | Bsc | Maths | 83 | | | | Sheet-2 | | |
| 121 | Peter | Bsc | Science | 84 | | | | | | |
| 123 | Ganesh | Bcom | Commerce | 67 | | | | | | |
| 124 | Seetha | Bcom | Commerce | 79 | | | | | | |

In the above example we specified the criteria for Total mark column as <80. If you apply these criteria it shows only the mark has less than 80 in the total mark column. Create a test sub procedure in module1 and type all the code given below. Run the code by debugging tool.

---

```
Sub test()
    Dim RngMain As Range
    Dim RngCriteria As Range
'----define the ranges
    Set RngMain = Sheets("Sheet2").Range("C2:G10")
    Set RngCriteria = Sheets("Sheet2").Range("I2:M3")
'---filter the Main data using the criteria
    RngMain.AdvancedFilter xlFilterInPlace, RngCriteria
```

End Sub

---

| Main Data | | | | |
|---|---|---|---|---|
| ID | Name | Division | Group | Total Mark |
| 120 | William | Bsc | Maths | 79 |
| 123 | Ganesh | Bcom | Commerce | 63 |
| 124 | Seetha | Bcom | Commerce | 79 |
| 123 | Ganesh | Bcom | Commerce | 67 |
| 124 | Seetha | Bcom | Commerce | 79 |

| Creteria Range | | | | |
|---|---|---|---|---|
| ID | Name | Division | Group | Total Mark |
| | | | | < 80 |

**Result**

In the above code we are assigning two range object variable **RngMain** and **RngCriteria** with different columns and rows of same sheet. Then Applying advance filter for **RngMain** data which is primary data. The **Action** is **xlFilterInPlace** and the **Cretieria range** is **RngCreteria**. It takes criteria value from RngCreteria and hide all the record which is not matching to criteria in Main data. Add another criterion to Division as "Bsc" and again run the code.

| Main Data | | | | |
|---|---|---|---|---|
| ID | Name | Division | Group | Total Mark |
| 120 | William | Bsc | Maths | 79 |

| Creteria Range | | | | |
|---|---|---|---|---|
| ID | Name | Division | Group | Total Mark |
| | | Bsc | | < 80 |

Now you can notice it applied both criteria and shown only one record. Like you can add any number of criteria for any column.

**Filtering Unique Value**

The main data source has many duplicate value, to filter that we have to use Unique parameter. The value for this parameter is True or False. Correct the Advance filter statement of test procedure like

**RngMain.AdvancedFilter** xlFilterInPlace, RngCriteria, ,True

Here we are skipping the **copytorange** parameter, so we are using an empty space between **Creteriarange** and **Unique** parameter. To avoid confussion, we can use named argument in the statement like

**RngMain.AdvancedFilter** Action:=xlFilterInPlace, CreteriaRange:=RngCriteria, Unique:=True

| Main Data | | | | |
|---|---|---|---|---|
| ID | Name | Division | Group | Total Mark |
| 120 | William | Bsc | Maths | 79 |
| 121 | Peter | Bsc | Science | 84 |
| 120 | William | Bsc | Maths | 83 |

| Creteria Range | | | | |
|---|---|---|---|---|
| ID | Name | Division | Group | Total Mark |
| | | Bsc | | |

The result is show only the unique record in main data sheet. If anyone column has different value it will be treated as unique record. For example, take William record, the total mark is different, so it is showing. Whereas the Peter record has same value for all columns, so it hided one of the record.

**Copy a unique record**

If you want to copy the filtered data and past in in a specified range, then you have to add CopytoRange parameter. Also you have to change the Action parameter to xlFilterCopy. Modify the test procedure code as shown below.

```
Sub test()
   Dim RngMain, RngCriteria, RngCopy As Range
'----define the ranges
   Set RngMain = Sheets("Sheet2").Range("C2:G10")
   Set RngCriteria = Sheets("Sheet2").Range("I2:M3")
   Set RngCopy = Sheets("Sheet3").Range("B2:F15")

'---filter the Main data using the criteria and copy to next sheet
   RngMain.AdvancedFilter xlFilterInPlace, RngCriteria,RngCopy,True
End Sub
```

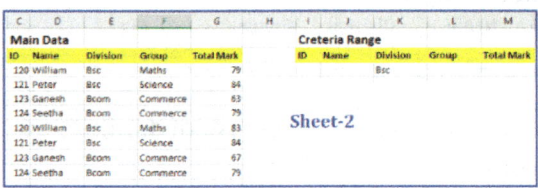
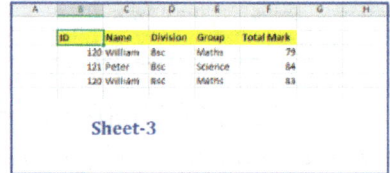

The above filter statement will not change the Main data, since we used Action as xlFilterCopy. It filters the data as per CriteriaRange and past it in sheet-3 as specified in CopyToRange parameter.

**Removing Duplicate Data**

We can use advanced filter to remove the duplicate data and past it in new sheet. For that we have to remove CreteriaRange parameter.

RngMain.AdvancedFilter Action:=xlFilterCopy, CopyToRange:=RngCopy, Unique:=True

# 13. Error Handling

VBA Error Handling refers to the process of anticipating, detecting, and resolving VBA Runtime Errors. These errors are normally caused by something outside your control like a missing file, database being unavailable, data being invalid, attempting to divide by zero etc. If we think an error is likely to occur at some point, it is good practice to write specific code to handle the error if it occurs and deal with it. There are three types of errors in VBA: Syntax, Compilation and Runtime. This was explained in detail in Debugging section.

Most VBA errors are handed by On Error Statement, which tells VBA what to do if it encounters an error. There are three On Error Statements: On Error GoTo 0, On Error Resume Next and On Error GoTo Line.

**On Error GOTO 0** :- It is a default setting, when error occurs with on Error GOTO 0, VBA will stop executing code and display its standard error message box. If we are not add any error statement, then also it show same type error message.

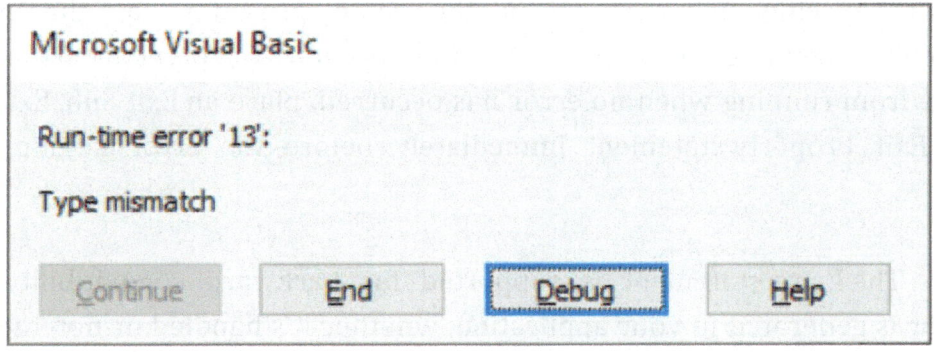

**On Error Resume Next**: - It simply tells VBA to skip to next line as if the line of code containing the error. It is good practice to write this statement at well-known code line which through Error. For example, if you assign a Excel application object to variable by Create method, it through an error if already the Excel file is opened.

    On Error Resume Next
        Set app = CreateObject("Excel.Application")
        Set app = GetObject(, "Excel.Application")

In the above code it tries to create Excel application object, if that Excel application is already opened, then it throws error. If we specify On Error Resume Next statement before this statement, then it skip that line if error is encountered or execute that line.

**On Error GOTO Line**:- On Error GoTo Line tells VBA to Jump to a specific line label or line number, when an error is encountered.

```
Private Sub Command1_Click()
    On Error GoTo Errhandler
    -----Code---------------
    Exit sub          '---If no error is encoundered it exit from sub
    Errhandler:
    MsgBox Err.Description
End Sub
```

In the above example if any error is encountered after On error GOTO statement it divert the code where the label (Errhandler) is written in this code and execute the code after this label. We can write any lable at on error GoTo statement, but we should not use space in that label. We can use underscore instead of space. The error handler line label should be same as declared in GoTo statement and end with colon(:). Like we can write any number of diversion statement. The specified line must be in the same procedure as the On Error statement; otherwise, a compile-time error occurs. To prevent error-handling code from running when no error has occurred, place an Exit Sub, Exit Function, or Exit Property statement immediately before the error-handling routine.

**Error Trap**:- The Error statement is supported for backward compatibility. When an error is generated in your application, whether it's handled or not, the properties of the Err object are assigned values with information about the error that just occurred. You can access this information, or generate your own errors explicitly using the Err.Raise method.

Err.Raise Number, [Source], [Description], [HelpFile], [HelpContext]

| Property | Value |
|---|---|
| Number | MSDN has listed various types of errors in DLL library which has a error number and description. We have to specify as argument to Error statement. Can be any valid error number. |
| Source | Returns or sets a string expression specifying the name of the object or application that originally generated the error |
| Description | Returns String value of containing a short Description of the Error |
| HelpFile | The fully qualified drive, path, and file name of the appropriate Visual Basic Help file. |
| HelpContext | The appropriate Visual Basic Help file context ID for the error corresponding to the **Number** property. |
| LastDLLError | Zero. |

On Error Resume Next
    Err.Raise(11)        '- This error number show "Division by Zero" error
    Err.Raise(7)        '—This error number show "Out of member" error
    If Err.Number <> 0 Then
        Msgbox Err.Number & "/" & Err.Source & "/" & Err.Description
        Err.Clear
    End If

Here the message box displays the Error Number, Source and Description. The Err.Clear method clear all the errors generated and reset it to null.

## 14. Project

In this excise we are going to build a Home Expenses Monitoring application. Please remember, this book is meant for learning and practice, so the application is not full-fledged application. It teaches how to use various elements to build the application, after learning you can further develop and add other features like monthly budget. The application is designed only for one computer, then the entire application is built with single excel file. If you want to work with many users in same company network, then we have to split the application in two parts like the **Front end** and **Back end**.

The front end is one part of application, that the user interacts directly and it is usually referred as "client side". The front end consists of everything that all users can interact with that application to view, Add and edit the data. It is built with lot of controls, Forms, Graphics, Photos with attractive colors and patterns. The back end is also known as the server side application. It organizes and stores data and it does not interact with users directly, it plays an indispensable role behind the scenes by adding key functionality to application. Without a clean and proper backend, the front end won't work properly. This application is simple and used by a single user, so there is no need to build front end and Back end. But for practicing, I am building this application with front end and Back end concept.

For Any standalone project, we have to create a separate Folder in any one of drive and we have to store all our project related file in that folder. I am created a project folder in D drive like D:\Budget Project. In this folder create three sub folder in the name of Application File, Report and Images. Then create another two sub folders in Images Folder like General and Bills. After that we have to create two excel work book in the name of "Home Budget-BE" and "Home Budget-FE" and store it in Application file folder. The Home Budget-BE is normal excel file used as Back end file and will not have any macro, so you can save this file as Excel work book format with an extension of "xlsx". But the Home Budget-FE is front end file have lot of VBA code, so you have to save this file as Excel macro enabled work book format with an extension of "xlsm". In general, the Back end file should be stored in local server of your company. But we are building home budget project, so we can save the back end file also in the same Application File folder.

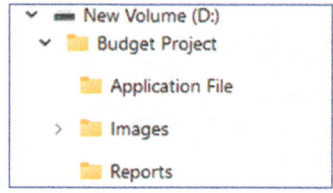

Always the Front end should be kept in developer computer for developing and debugging the code. Once the developer completed the application, they share that to other user and they have to copy that file and keep it in their local system. This file has to be replaced for every time, when any code modification is done in original. Here we are the developer and user, so we will keep all files in same folder.

## Project Concept

We very well know about the home budget and its expenses and most of us, maintain this in their personal diary. Home budget is recording the income and making monthly budget plan. Then recording the actual expenses for each item and compare with Graph or Report. In this project we are only doing the recording of Income and Actual expenses and Budget planning is not covered. After learning all concept, you can develop the monthly budget plan for this application.

This application has a Dashboard which is the first page, from that we can navigate to other page. In the dash board we can view some table statement and graphical view to show the summary of expenditure. The Dashboard form has three parts, Top part has the Application heading, Panel Image and all command control buttons. The second part is a table show the selected month expenditure for each category and also show the Annual expenditure for the same category. The third part is Graphical representation of all Expenditure.

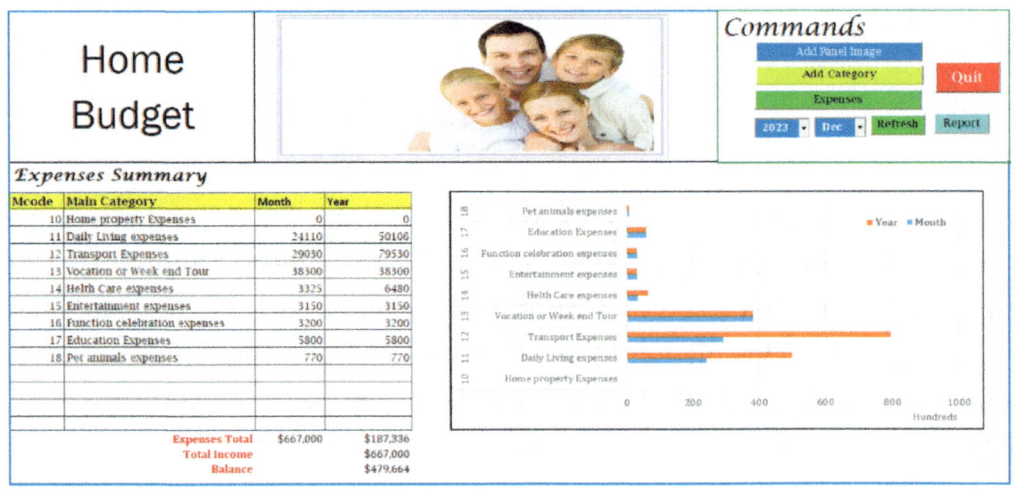

In this form, there are two drop down list shows the Year and month. While open the application, it automatically assigns the current year and month to this drop down controls. We can change any year and month and click the Refresh button, it modifies the bottom data table and chart based the selection. Same way the Report button will generate a PDF report for the selected Year and Month.

The form has a panel image at center to improve the look. we can change the panel image by using Add Panel Image command button. By clicking this button, it shows file Explorer window to select the Image file, and after selection, it uploads the file to Image General folder and then assign it to this page.

We can add all relevant category by clicking the Add category button which will pop up category Adding Form.

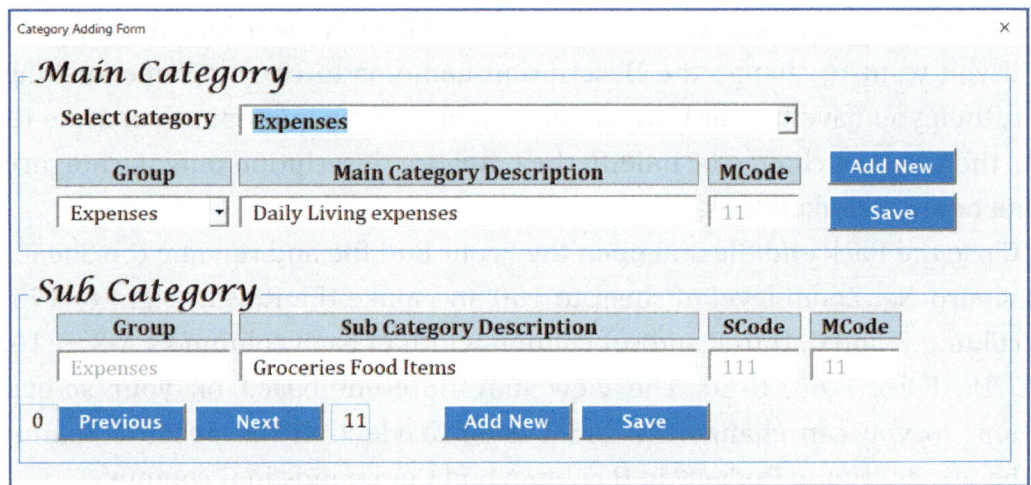

Same way we can add all our expenses by clicking Expenses button which will open Monthly expenditure form to add the actual expenses for different category.

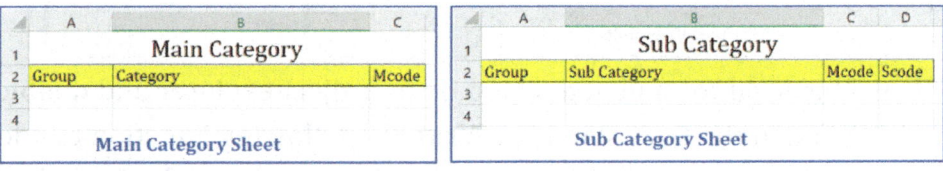

We will see in detail all the form function in project building section.

# Project Building
## Dashboard

    Open "Home Budget-BE" file and rename the sheet-1 as "Main Category". Create or rename the Sheet2 as Sub Category. This two sheets are used to classify our expenses in various groups.

Write the table Heading and column heading at top of the sheet as shown above. Here Mcode and SCode is the Main and sub category codes used as ID of record. Always you have to maintain a ID for each record and it should be a unique and should not be edited or Deleted. This ID is used to link all transaction of different data table. We can also use the Description of category as a link filed, but in future if you want to change the Description name or to correct some spelling mistake, then you have to edit it in all linked tables. If we maintain a separate ID column, then we can change or modify the Category description only in category table and not in all linked table.

Close the Back end file and open the Front End file and rename the Sheet1 as Dashboard. Set Zoom level of sheet to 100 and make the Row1 height to 175. Merge column B and C, D to F and set column width of each column as A-3, B-10, C-35, D-15, E-15, F-60, G-60. The view may different based on your screen resolution, so you can change the zoom level to view all the above columns. Write the text as "Home Budget" in **B** column and Commands in **G** column.

The first excise in dashboard is adding a panel image by VBA code, so that we can change the panel image by just a click of button. For that we have to add an Image ActiveX control and one ActiveX Button. Go to Developer tap and select Insert command and select Image ActiveX Control, click at first row of "D" column and drag it up to bottom of first row up to "F" column. Same way insert ActiveX command button below the Commands word in first row. Format and rename the controls name like PanelImg to Image control and AddPImage to command button. For Image control we have to set the following properties for show proper view

1. Name              = PanelImg
2. AutoLoad          = False
3. PictureAlinment   = 2-frmPictureAlignmentCenter
4. PictureSize Mode  = 1-frmPictureSizeModeStretch

We should ensure the panel Image Picture ratio to 16:9 for proper alignment.

Go to Visual basic editor and add a Module in project explorer and double click the module1 to open the Code window. Write the following Function to add image file to folder. This procedure is common to add any type of file by calling from any sheet module procedure. So we have to write this procedure in module1 with public statement.

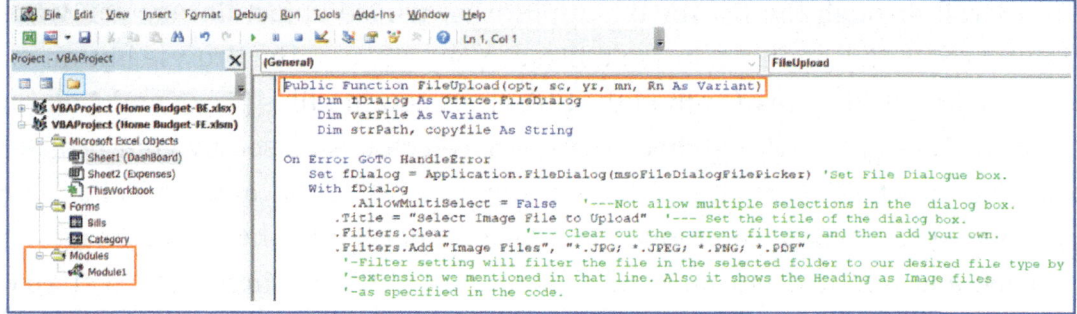

## Reference Library

Reference libraries are pre-written, reusable chunks of code that developers can use to create applications quickly and easily. You know all application has more in-built function to execute a particular task which are pre-written by the application developer. Also the application has many object model and it vary between application. If you use the objects of other applications as part of your Visual Basic application, then you have to establish a reference to that object libraries of those applications.

To add the references to your project, Go to Tools menu in Visual Basic editor, choose References which display the references dialog box. The References dialog box shows all object libraries registered with the operating system.

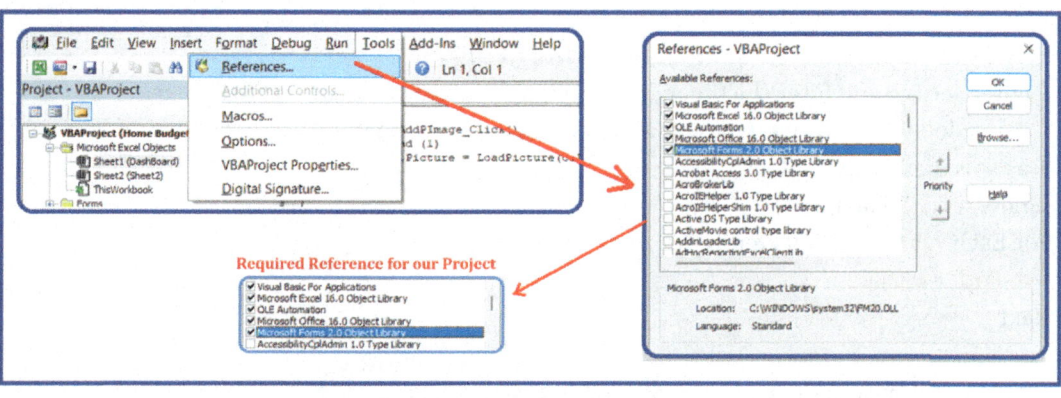

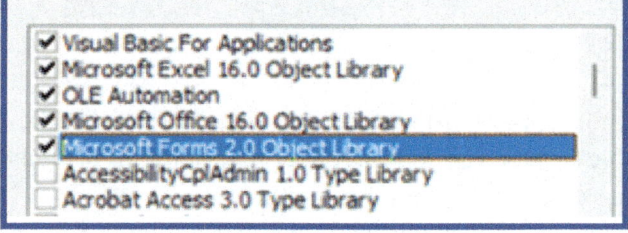

Scroll through the list for the application whose object library you want to reference. If the application isn't listed, you can use the Browse button to search for object libraries (*.olb and *.tlb) or executable files (*.exe and *.dll on Windows). References whose check boxes are selected are used by your project; those that aren't selected are not used, but can be added any time. For our project we needed some reference file which is marked in the above image, so you check and add it if not checked. For example, if the "Microsoft Excel 16.0 object Library" is not included, then it pops up error message for all VBA in-built function.

**File Upload Script**

```
---------------------------------------Code Start--------------------------------------
Public Function FileUpload(opt, sc, yr, mn, Rn As Variant)
    Dim fDialog As Office.FileDialog
    Dim varFile As Variant
    Dim strPath, copyfile As String

On Error GoTo HandleError
    Set fDialog = Application.FileDialog(msoFileDialogFilePicker) 'Set File Dialogue box.
    With fDialog
        .AllowMultiSelect = False   '---Not allow multiple selections in the dialog box.
       .Title = "Select Image File to Upload"   '--- Set the title of the dialog box.
       .Filters.Clear       '--- Clear out the current filters, and then add your own.
       .Filters.Add "Image Files", "*.JPG; *.JPEG; *.PNG; *.PDF"
        '—Filter setting will filter the file in the selected folder to our desired file type by
             extension we mentioned in that line. Also it shows the Heading as Image files
             as specified in the code.
       If .Show = True Then
          For Each varFile In .SelectedItems
            strPath = varFile
          Next
       Else
          MsgBox "You Have not selected any File Process Canceled."
          Exit Sub
       End If
    End With
    ext = Right(strPath, Len(strPath) - InStrRev(strPath, "."))   '---Get file extension
'-------Store the file based on option parameter passed to this procedure
    If opt = 1 Then         '-------for Panel Image file
      copyfile = "D:\Budget Project\Images\General\Panel-Img." & ext
```

   End If

~~If opt = 2 Then           '-------for Panel Image file~~
~~   Fname = "Bill-" & yr & mn & sc & Rn & "." & ext~~
~~   copyfile = "D:\Budget Project\Images\Bills\" & Fname~~
~~End If~~

'----------Copy file to folder
   FileCopy strPath, copyfile
   FileUpload = copyfile
Exit Function
HandleError:
  MsgBox Err.Description
End Function
-------------------------------End of Code------------------------------------

Add the following code in command button click event.
Private Sub AddPImage_Click()
  X = FileUpload(1, 0, 0, 0, 0)
  '----Calling FileUpload function and get return value and assign to X variable
  PanelImg.Picture = LoadPicture(X)
End Sub

Mark a break point at fourth line of FileUpload() procedure and click run button in browsing tool.

**Code Explanation**:
1. Click the Add Panel Image Command button, it executes it click event.
2. The first line of code is calling the sub procedure FileUpload() with a five parameters by variant type. The parameters are Option (opt), Sub catecory code(Sc), Year(yr), Month(Mn) and row number(Rn). For panel image upload only option function is used, so we can write the parameter (1,0,0,0,0). Now the execution is diverted to fileUpload() function located in module1.
3. The first step is declaring all variables.
4. Then writing the Error handler before starting the code execution.
5. In next line we are creating an object variable Fdialog and assigning the application dialogue box object.
6. Then setting the properties of file dialogue box object to our decided value by with function. For detail refer with statement in next section. You

can understand each property settings of dialogue box by the comment line added in the code. It will open the dialogue box as shown below

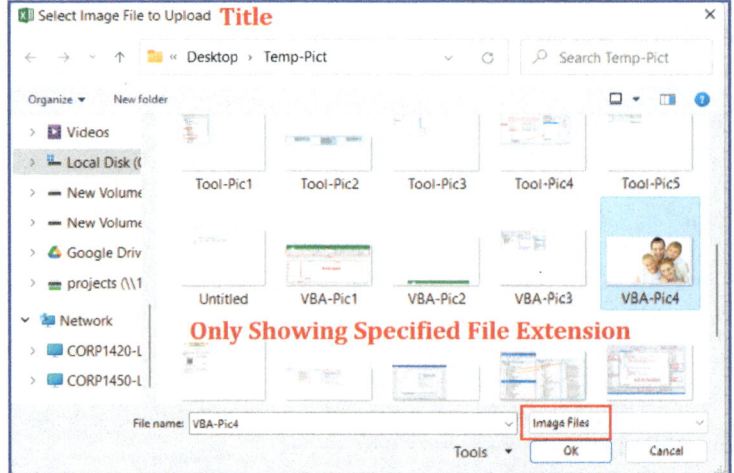

7. Select any one image and click Ok button.
8. If any file is selected, it assigns the selected file path to strPath variable. If no file is selected or Clicked cancel button, it popup a message "You Have not selected any File Process Canceled." And quit the procedure running.
9. Next line gets the file extension from the file path by string manipulation function like Right, Len, InStr and InstrRev.
10. Next line check the argument value passed to opt variable and if the value is 1, then it assigns the file path along with extension and store it in copyfile variable. This path is constant, which is located in our project folder.
11. Next line Filecopy function copy the file as per the source path strPath to target folder path copyfile. This function has two arguments, one is source path and another one is target path.
12. Next line is to return the function result to calling procedure. For return any value, you have to write the function name and write a value after the equal sign. Here we returning the Target file path (CopyFile).
13. After completing the FileUpload() function, it returns back to command button event and execute the next line. Next line is assign the picture to Image control by LoadPicture function. LoadPicture function has one parameter specify the full image file path which is it get from the return value of X variable.

By this command button, you can change image any time, however it delete the old image file from the folder and replace with new image file with same name.

**With....End with**

      By with statement, we have to specify the object name at starting after with keyword and then we can access all the properties and methods of that object by writing a dot (.) along with property name. Once all properties values are changed, then we have to close the with statement by "End with" key word.

```
Set fDialog = Application.FileDialog(msoFileDialogFilePicker)
With fDialog
    .AllowMultiSelect = False
    .Title = "Select Image File to Upload"
    .Filters.Clear
    .Filters.Add "Image Files", "*.JPG; *.JPEG; *.PNG; *.PDF"
    .Show = True
End With         Refered Object by With
```

```
Set fDialog = Application.FileDialog(msoFileDialogFilePicker)
fDialog.AllowMultiSelect = False
fDialog.Title = "Select Image File to Upload"
fDialog.Filters.Clear
fDialog.Filters.Add "Image Files", "*.JPG; *.JPEG; *.PNG; *.PDF"
fDialog.Show = True
        Directly Refered the Object without with
```

This is very help full to refer a long object variable name or a nested object names. The above image shows an identical statement which is valid.

# Category Form

      The first step of the project is creating master data tables. In our project the main category and sub category is master table which is going to be create one time at the starting of project. However, we may add a some of category during long usage of this application. For that we are planning to develop a User form which will add and Edit the Main category and sub category records.

## VBA User Form

      The User form is a very important part of programming in VBA. It allows you to build a professional looking user interface to communicate with the users of your VBA application. It also allows you to totally control the user in what they are doing to your workbook. We can add all type of ActiveX controls, such as drop downs, Label, Text box, tick box and command buttons in the user form and each controls have a many methods, events and properties to enhance the user experience.

Open the Home budget-FE excel file and open VBA editor. Now we have to Create a new object module for user forms. For that right click the project name in the project folder and click insert command and then click the userform sub command. It will create a new module in the name of **Forms** and add a **UserForm1** under this module. Also it shows the form template at code window, if not shown then, Double click the UserForm1. To add ActivX controls, click the Toolbox at top menu or select the menu command view->ToolBox.

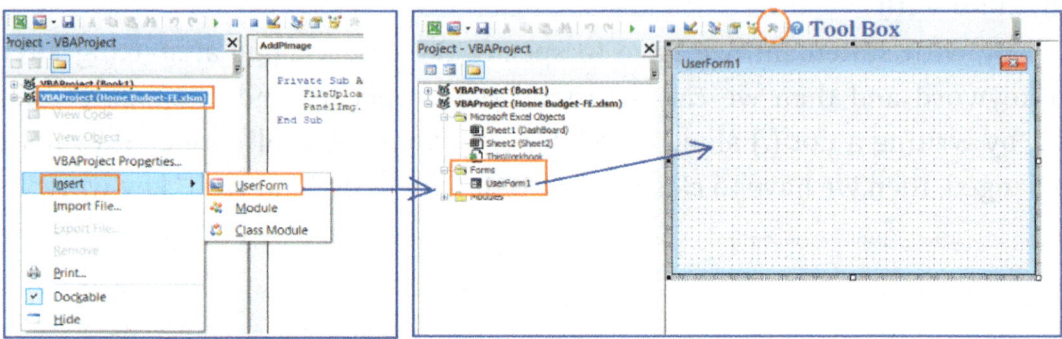

Select the form and right click over the form and select properties from context menu or Click the properties Icon on top menu tool bar. Change the following properties of that form

1. Name             : - Category
2. Caption          : - Category Adding Form
3. Width / Height   : - 675 / 300

After changing the above properties, you may notice the userform1 in project explorer is changed to Category, and the Title of form is changed to "Category Adding Form" and the width is increased. This form is going to use to add Main category and sub category by user, so it has to be divided in to two section. To make any section in the form, VBA frame is a good option.

---

### VBA Frame

The Frame control is used to hold a set of controls within its area as a group that work together, are related to each other or have some commonality. They also enhance the UserForm's layout by bunching and organizing a related set of items. Since it is a group control, user can move all the controls to anywhere of form by dragging the frame. It has a box Border and at top it shows the frame caption. The frame is also having number of properties like other controls.

**Appearance**: Appearance properties is almost same like other controls, by which we can change name, caption, back ground and fore ground color.
**Font**: We can change the font style and size of the font
**Picture**: We can use any background picture in frame which improve the look and separate out the entire group in different way in the form.
**Position**: We can resize the frame by position properties.
**Scrolling**: We can set any configuration for scrolling controls.

---

Add two frame to the form and change the properties as shown below and center the frame in form.

| SN | Properties | Frame-1 | Frame-2 |
|---|---|---|---|
| 1 | Caption | Main Category | Sub Category |
| 2 | Font | Lucida Calligraphy , Bold Italic, 20 Size | |
| 3 | Width | 650 | 650 |
| 4 | Height | 130 | 130 |
| 5 | Border Style | 1-frmBorderStyleSingle | |
| 6 | Border Color | &H80000012& | |

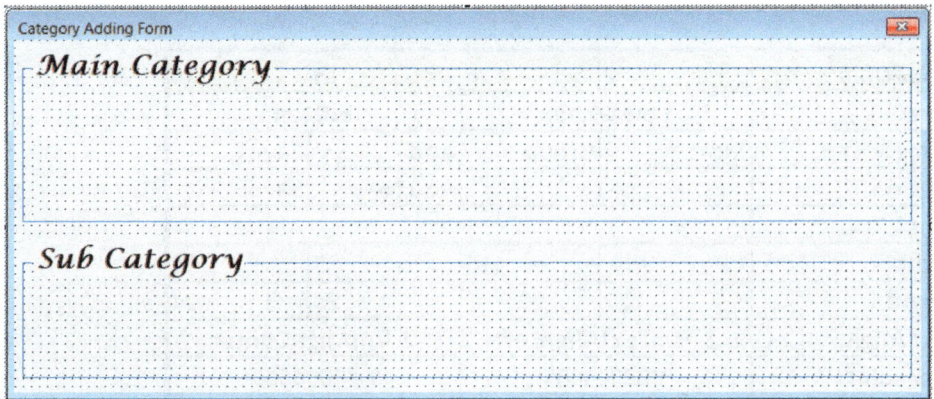

## Main Category

We have to add some label and text box controls to Frame-1 to get Main category inputs. **Labels** are simple text box displays the title or controls description. Like other controls, we can insert the label controls and edit all it properties. **Text Box** is used to show some data which can be viewed, typed or edited. Also Text box is used to input user data to application. The first control is a combo box (2) to show the main Category list which is already added to table. Then add three label(3,4,5) below combo box to show the title of Text fields. Add another combo box (6) as group field to classify the category in two group: Income and Expenses. Add two text box (7,8) to show the Category description and MCode. Add two command button(9,10) to add and save the record.

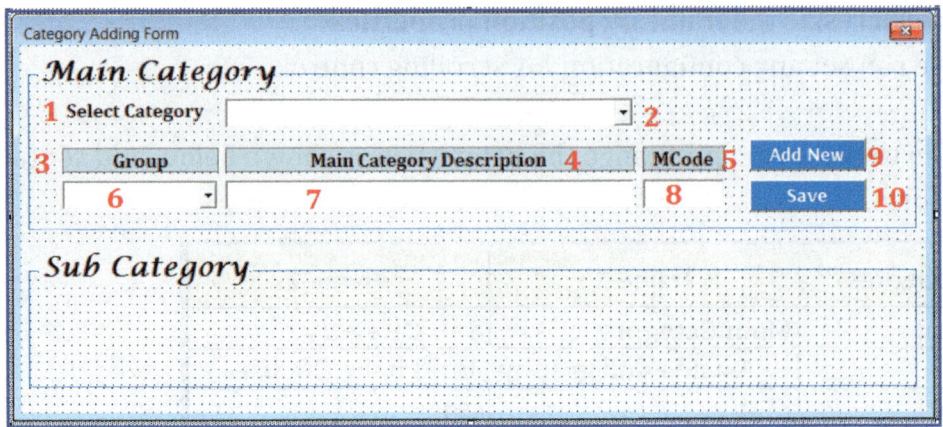

Format and set the following properties to each controls as shown in the picture. However, you can do it the properties settings as you like. The most common properties are Name, Caption, Width, Height, Text align, Back color and Fore color. The dedicate property of combo box is Column count, Bound column and Column widths.

| Sn | Properties | 2 | | 6 | | 9 | | 10 |
|----|-----------|---|---|---|---|---|---|----|
| 1 | Type | Combo box | | | | Button | | |
| 2 | Name | Mcat | | Group | | Add | | Save1 |
| 3 | Caption | | | | | Add New | | Save |
| 4 | Font | | | | | | | |
| 5 | Width | 366 | | 115 | | 85 | | 85 |
| 6 | Height | 22 | | 22 | | 24 | | 24 |
| 7 | Text Align | 1-frmTextAlignLeft | | | | 2-frmAlignCenter | | |
| 8 | Back color | H80000005 | | | | H8000000D | | |
| 9 | Fore Color | H80000008 | | | | H8000000E | | |
| 10 | Column count | 3 | | 1 | | | | |
| 11 | Bound Column | 3 | | 1 | | | | |
| 12 | Column widths | 80 pt;200 pt; 40 pt | | | | | | |

| Sn | Properties | 1 | | 3 | 4 | 5 | 7 | 8 |
|---|---|---|---|---|---|---|---|---|
| 1 | Type | Label | | | | | Text Box | |
| 2 | Name | Label1 | Label2 | Label3 | Label4 | TB1 | TB2 | |
| 3 | Caption | Select Categor | Group | Main Category | Mcode | | | |
| 4 | Font | Cambrial, Bold, 14 Size | | | | | | |
| 5 | Width | 120 | 115 | 300 | 60 | | 300 | 60 |
| 6 | Height | 18 | | 18 | | | 22 | |
| 7 | Text Align | 2-Center | 1-frmTextAlignLeft | | | | | |
| 8 | Back color | H8000000F | H80000003 | | | | H80000005 | |
| 9 | Fore Color | H80000012 | H80000012 | | | | H80000008 | |
| 10 | Enabled | TRUE | | | | | TRUE | FALSE |

Now we have to add a command button in Dash board to open the above user form and add the event procedure for that button. We can copy the Add image button and past it in the command row and edit the name and caption, this will save time and repeat the same look of each type of controls.

**Name** :- CatFrm
**Caption** :- Add Category

Private Sub CatFrm_Click()
   Category.Show          '-----This event show the category form.
End Sub

Deselect the design mode and Click the Add Category button, it will open the category form and show it at top of excel sheet. As a default the form is centered to screen, but we can change the properties of form to change the position of form. We can move the form to any direction by click and dragging. Once the form is shown, you can't access the sheet shown at back ground. But we can change this property by altering the **ShowModal** properties. If this property set to true, it will not allow to access the back ground window and if it is set to false, then it allow to access sheet as well as form. We can use the default close button located at top right corner of the form to close the form.

Now we have to add sub procedure to all controls to refer the back end file Main Category sheet to read and write the data. Since the Back end excel file is different workbook, we have to establish an object link which will be executed while opening the Front end excel file. For that open Project explorer, click **ThisWorkBook** object and write the following code

------Code to be write in ThisworkBook module------------------

```vb
Private Sub Workbook_Open()
    ActiveWorkbook.Sheets("Dashboard").Activate
'------------Open Database file
    Dim wb As Workbook
    Fpath = "D:\Budget Project\Application File\Home Budget-BE.xlsx"
    Set wb = Workbooks.Open(Fpath)
    ActiveWindow.WindowState = xlMinimized
End Sub
```
--------------------Code End----------------------------------------

We know that the work book open event is triggered while opening the work book and all code are executed before showing the work sheet.

**Code Explanation**

1. First step is making Dash Board work sheet as active sheet while opening
2. Declaring wb object variable to assign work book.
3. Fpath variable store the full path of back end file location, this may vary according to your Project folder created.
4. The workbooks.open function open the Back end excel file and assign as object to Wb object variable.
5. The next line will minimize the back end excel file after opening.

So now whomever open the Front end excel file it opens the Back end file and minimize it. Close the Front end excel file and re-open to test the above procedure.

Now we have to add sub procedure to user form controls. The main category table has three fields: Group, Description and MCode, so we provided three text box to get input data. In which the Mcode field is key ID for each record, which will be linked to other tables. So it should be a unique value and no duplicate is allowed. So we have to make arrangement to enter this ID automatically by procedure. So the Text Box-2 meant for Mcode, enable properties is set to false, which will not allow to enter any data by user manually. Before opening the form we have to initialize the list value to MCat and Group combo box. For that we have to double click the form and create a UserForm_Initialize() events and add the code as shown below.

-----------------Code Start--------------------------------------------
```vb
Private Sub UserForm_Initialize()
    Dim wb As Workbook
    Dim ws As Worksheet
    '----Fill Category Drop down list
    Set wb = Workbooks("Home Budget-BE.xlsx")
```

```vb
    Set ws = wb.Sheets("Main Category")
    LR = ws.Cells(ws.Rows.Count, "C").End(xlUp).Row
    ws.Range("A2:D" & LR).Sort key1:= ws.Range("B2:B" & LR), order1:=xlAscending,
    Header:=xlNo
    Mcat.Clear
    Mcat.List = ws.Range("A3:C100").Value

    '----Fill list to Group
    Group.AddItem "Income"
    Group.AddItem "Expenses"
End Sub
```
--------------------------Code End--------------------------------------

**Code explanation:**
1. User Form Initialize event will be executed every time when the form is open by show command.
2. First step is setting the Back end work book objects, which is already opened, to wb variable.
3. Then assign the Main category sheet to ws variable.
4. Next step is finding the last row of that sheet and assign to LR variable. Since always the last row record is vary based on record addition.
5. Next step is sorting the entire data in selected range from that sheet.
6. Next step clears the list from Mcat combo box
7. Next step assigns the range of data from worksheet to Mcat combo box list. This will create three column combo box and show the Group, Category and MCode value.
8. Next step filling the Group combo box list by add item method.

Select the category form and click the run command from debug tool box. You can notice there will be list in Group, but no list will be there in Mcat combo box. Since we not added any data to Main category table. Now we add code to Group combo box to generate the Mcode and fill the Text Box-2.

---------------Code start-------------------------------
```vb
Private Sub Group_Change()
If TB2.Value = "" Then
    '----Find last number of Code
    Set wb = Workbooks("Home Budget-BE.xlsx")
    Set ws = wb.Sheets("Main Category")
    x = Application.WorksheetFunction.Max(ws.Range("C:C"))
```

```
        If IsNull(x) = True Or x = 0    Then y = 10
        If x > 1 Then y = x + 1
        TB2.Value = y
    End If
End Sub
------------------------Code end---------------------------
```

**Code Explanation:**

1. Since the Mcode should be unique, it is decided to generate this code automatically while entering new data.
2. The first data for Main category is the group either Income or Expenses. While selecting the option, it triggers the above event.
3. First it checks whether the TB2 value is empty string. if it is empty string, then it executes the code inside the if condition. Otherwise it will not generate the Mcode.
4. If the TB2 value is empty, then it assigns the work book and work sheet object to wb and ws variable.
5. The Mcode column is "C" in main category sheet, so it finds the maximum value in that column by max function and assign to x variable.
6. It is decided that Mcode is formatted with two-digit number and start from 10 to 99. So the next If condition check the x value, if it is null (for first record) then it assign the value 10 to y variable. If we add second record, then the x value will be 10, so it adds one and assign 11 to y value.
7. Then it adds the y value to TB2 text box.

Mark a break point at first code and Test it by debugging mode. Select any one value from group and you notice that a value 10 is added to TB2 text box. Again change the Group option it will not change the TB2 text, since by TB2 empty condition, it will skip the code. Please remember, while checking this the Back end file is also in open condition. Now the data is available only in Form and same has to be written to Main category sheet. So add the following code to Save button.

```
------------------Code start------------------------------
Private Sub Save1_Click()
'--------Validation check
    If Group.Value = "" Then MsgBox "Enter Group field": Exit Sub
    If TB1.Value = "" Then MsgBox "Enter Data to Description field": Exit Sub
    If TB2.Value = "" Then MsgBox "Enter Data to MCode field": Exit Sub
```

```vb
    Set wb = Workbooks("Home Budget-BE.xlsx")
    Set ws = wb.Sheets("Main Category")
    LR = ws.Cells(ws.Rows.Count, "C").End(xlUp).Row
On Error Resume Next
    x = ws.Range("C:C").Cells.Find(TB2.Value).Row

    If x > 0 Then
        ws.Cells(x, 1) = Group.Value
        ws.Cells(x, 2) = TB1.Value
    Else
        ws.Cells(LR + 1, 1) = Group.Value
        ws.Cells(LR + 1, 2) = TB1.Value
        ws.Cells(LR + 1, 3) = TB2.Value
    End If
    Msgbox "Record Saved"
End Sub
```
---------------------------------Code end---------------------------------

**Code Explanation:**

1. The first step, before save any record, we have to check whether the mandatory data is available. So we have to validate the input before save the record. Validation may be to check whether it has empty string or string instead of date or number. Here the first three lines are used to check whether the three input filed is having a value otherwise it pops up a message and exit from the procedure.
2. Second and third line is assigning the work book and work sheet objects to object variable wb and ws
3. Next find the last row from the worksheet and assign to LR
4. Next line uses the find in-built function to find the match word equal to Text box TB2, in a range of C column. If it found then, it gets the cell address and by row method it gets the row number and assign to X variable.
5. The if condition checks the X value and decide whether it has to do edit of existing data or Add a new data. If X is greater than zero, then it selects the specified cell by row number (x) and replace the value. If X is not having any number, then it goes to one row after the last row (LR+1) and add the new data.
6. Then it popup a message "Record Saved"

To clear the data entry field, we have to add a procedure in Add New command button as shown below

--------------------------------Code start----------------------------
Private Sub Add_Click()
   Group.Value = ""
   TB1.Value = ""
   TB2.Value = ""
End Sub
---------------------------------Code End-----------------------------

This code just assigns an empty string to all three fields.

Test the above code and if it working properly, then add the following data to main category. Just fill the data in three fields and click the save button. To add second record, click the Add New button, it clears the field and enter the second record value and click the save button. Now close the form and again open by clicking the Add Category button. Select the category combo box and click the down arrow, now you notice the list value show the main category value whatever you entered. Since we written the list loading procedure in form initialize events, it load all category record while opening the form. Like add all main category records and check it in back end file.

| Group | Category | Mcode | |
|---|---|---|---|
| Expenses | Home property Expenses | 10 | Auto Generated Number |
| Expenses | Daily Living expenses | 11 | |
| Expenses | Transport Expenses | 12 | |
| Expenses | Vocation or Week end Tour | 13 | |
| Expenses | Helth Care expenses | 14 | |
| Expenses | Entertainment expenses | 15 | |
| Expenses | Function celebration expenses | 16 | |
| Expenses | Education Expenses | 17 | |
| Expenses | Pet animals expenses | 18 | |
| Income | Various Income | 19 | |

**Sub Category**

Now we have to add fields to sub category frame. Sub category has four fields like Group, Description, Scode and MCode. Here the MCode is linking field to main category. Go to VBA editor and double click the category form. Copy all the main category fields and past it in sub category frame and align it as shown in the image. Copy and pasting of controls will save time for formatting, since it has a similar format setting. Correct the second label description as Sub Category Description. Change all the Text field name to TB3, TB4, TB5 and TB6. Here except Description field all other fields are filled by program, so make all other field enable property to false. Copy any one of button in main category and past it in Sub category frame. Like make four buttons and rename the name property to PreRec, NextRec, AddNew and Save2.

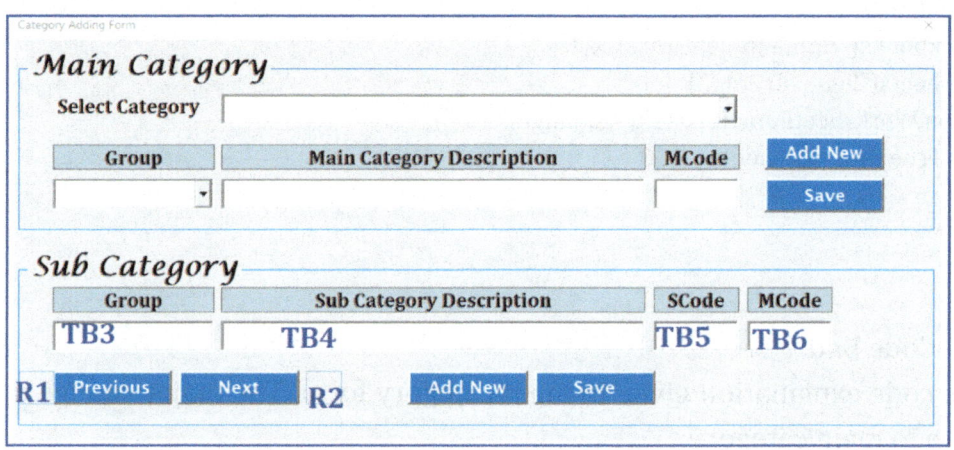

Add another two text box for navigation and name it R1 and R2. The concept is adding record in sub category linked with main category. So any addition or edit of sub category, we have to open the main category item from MCat combo box. Modify the MCat combo box event as shown below.

-------------------Code start-----------------------

```
Private Sub Mcat_Change()
If Mcat.Value <> "" Then
'----------Main category
   Group.Value = Mcat.Column(0)  '---Old code for main category frame
   TB1.Value = Mcat.Column(1)
   TB2.Value = Mcat.Column(2)
'---------Sub category
   TB3.Value = Mcat.Column(0)
   TB6.Value = Mcat.Column(2)
End If
End Sub
```

----------------------Code end-------------------------------

In the above code it Just fill the main and sub category fields. In which it will fill the Group value and Main code value to Text box TB3 and TB6. After completion of code, Test the procedure. Next step is generating the Sub Code (SCode) number automatically after entering the Description value. Create TB4 change events and enter the below code. It is almost same like the code we entered in main category Group change events.

-----------------Code Start--------------------------------

```vb
Private Sub TB4_Change()
    If TB5.Value = " " Then
    '----Find last number of Code
    Set wb = Workbooks("Home Budget-BE.xlsx")
    Set ws = wb.Sheets("Sub Category")
    x = Application.WorksheetFunction.Max(ws.Range("D:D"))
    If IsNull(x) = True Or x = 0 Then y = 100
    If x > 1 Then y = x + 1
    TB5.Value = y
End If
End Sub
```

-----------------Code End--------------------------------

You read the code explanation given in main category form. The major change in code compare to main category.

1. It compares TB5 text box value
2. Work sheet ws is assigned with Sub category sheet
3. The sub code will be three-digit number, so it starts from 100.

Next write the events to Add New button and save button as shown below. This is almost same like main category controls events.

-----------------------Code start---------------------------------

```vb
Private Sub AddNew_Click()
    TB3.Value = Group.value    '----Replace with main category Group field
    TB4.Value = ""
    TB5.Value = ""
    TB6.Value = TB2.Value      '----Replace with main category Mcode field
End Sub
```
-------------------------------------------------------------------------

```vb
Private Sub Save2_Click()
'--------Validation check
    If TB3.Value = "" Then MsgBox "First select the Main category": Exit Sub
    If TB4.Value = "" Then MsgBox "Enter Data to Description field": Exit Sub
```

133

```vba
    Set wb = Workbooks("Home Budget-BE.xlsx")
    Set ws = wb.Sheets("Sub Category")
    LR = ws.Cells(ws.Rows.Count, "C").End(xlUp).Row
    x = 0
    On Error Resume Next
    x = ws.Range("D:D").Cells.Find(TB5.Value).Row
    If x > 0 Then
        ws.Cells(x, 2) = TB4.Value
    Else
        ws.Cells(LR + 1, 1) = TB3.Value
        ws.Cells(LR + 1, 2) = TB4.Value
        ws.Cells(LR + 1, 3) = TB6.Value
        ws.Cells(LR + 1, 4) = TB5.Value
    End If
    MsgBox "Record Saved"
End Sub
```
------------------------Code End----------------------------------

**Code Explanation:**

1. The Add new button will replace TB3 with Group and Tb6 with TB2 text box located in main category frame.
2. TB4 and TB5 text box will be filled with empty string.
3. The first step in save2 button code is validation check
4. Second and third line is assigning the work book and work sheet objects to object variable wb and ws
5. Next find the last row from the worksheet and assign to LR
6. Next line uses the find in-built function to find the match word equal to Text box TB5, in a range of D column. If it found then, it gets the cell address and by row method it gets the row number and assign to X variable.
7. The if condition checks the X value and decide whether it has to do edit of existing data or Add a new data. If X is greater than zero, then it selects the specified cell by row number (x) and replace the value. If X is not having any number, then it goes to one row after the last row (LR+1) and add the new data.
8. Then it popup a message "Record Saved"

Now we can add the following record to sub category. Select any one main category in top combo box, it fills the group and Mcode in sub category field. Add

Description and click save button. Then click Add new button, change the Description and click save button. Like add all sub category items related to main category. Then change main category and add its sub category.

| Group | Sub Category | Mcode | Scode | |
|---|---|---|---|---|
| Expenses | Rent / Loan Premium | 10 | 100 | |
| Expenses | Service Charges | 10 | 101 | |
| Expenses | Electric Charges | 10 | 102 | |
| Expenses | Water Charges | 10 | 103 | |
| Expenses | Sewage Charges | 10 | 104 | |
| Expenses | Property Tax | 10 | 105 | |
| Expenses | Water Tax | 10 | 106 | Auto Generated Number |
| Expenses | Home Article Repairs | 10 | 107 | |
| Expenses | Home Improvement | 10 | 108 | |
| Expenses | Land Line / Internet | 10 | 109 | |
| Expenses | Home Insurance | 10 | 110 | |
| Expenses | Groceries Food Items | 11 | 111 | |
| Expenses | Personel Items (Cosmatics) | 11 | 112 | |
| Expenses | House Maintenance Items | 11 | 113 | |
| Expenses | Milk | 11 | 114 | |

| Group | Sub Category | Mcode | Scode | |
|---|---|---|---|---|
| Expenses | Vegitables | 11 | 115 | |
| Expenses | Non-Veg items | 11 | 116 | |
| Expenses | Cloth Dry Cleaning / Ironing | 11 | 117 | |
| Expenses | Salon / SPA | 11 | 118 | |
| Expenses | Dining Out | 11 | 119 | |
| Expenses | Mobile Phone bills | 11 | 120 | |
| Expenses | Servent Maid Salory | 11 | 121 | |
| Expenses | Fuel | 12 | 122 | |
| Expenses | Car / Two wheeler Maintenance | 12 | 123 | |
| Expenses | Car wash / Detailing Service | 12 | 124 | Auto Generated Number |
| Expenses | Car / Two Wheeler Insurance | 12 | 125 | |
| Expenses | Driver Salory | 12 | 126 | |
| Expenses | Toll / Parking charges | 12 | 127 | |
| Expenses | Public Bus Transportion | 12 | 128 | |
| Expenses | Air / Train Transportion | 13 | 129 | |
| Expenses | Accomodation / Foods | 13 | 130 | |
| Expenses | Local Taxi | 13 | 131 | |
| Expenses | Enterance fee for Intersting Place | 13 | 132 | |

| Group | Sub Category | Mcode | Scode |
|---|---|---|---|
| Expenses | Helth Club / Zim | 14 | 133 |
| Expenses | Unexpected Doctor Expences | 14 | 134 |
| Expenses | Medical Check up | 14 | 135 |
| Expenses | Regular Drugs for family | 14 | 136 |
| Expenses | Mediclaim Insurance | 14 | 137 |
| Expenses | Pet animal Medical Expencess | 14 | 138 |
| Expenses | Cable / Sat TV subscription | 15 | 139 |
| Expenses | News paper / Magazines | 15 | 140 |
| Expenses | Movie / Play Theater | 15 | 141 |
| Expenses | Concerts / Clubs | 15 | 142 |
| Expenses | Books / DVD / CD | 15 | 143 |
| Expenses | Week end tour | 15 | 144 |
| Expenses | Birth day / Wedding day | 16 | 145 |
| Expenses | Deepawali /Pongal | 16 | 146 |
| Expenses | Personel Dress | 16 | 147 |
| Expenses | Jewels / Gifts | 16 | 148 |
| Expenses | Donation / Offerings | 16 | 149 |

*Auto Generated Number*

| Group | Sub Category | Mcode | Scode |
|---|---|---|---|
| Expenses | School / College Fees | 17 | 150 |
| Expenses | School / College Transports | 17 | 151 |
| Expenses | Extra Course | 17 | 152 |
| Expenses | Books / Notes / Stationary | 17 | 153 |
| Expenses | School uniform / Shoes | 17 | 154 |
| Expenses | Snacks | 17 | 155 |
| Expenses | Pet animal Foods | 18 | 156 |
| Expenses | Pet animal Doctor Expenses | 18 | 157 |
| Income | From Salary | 19 | 158 |
| Income | From Deposit Interest | 19 | 159 |
| Income | From Rental of Property | 19 | 160 |
| Income | From Trade | 19 | 161 |

*Auto Generated Number*

Now we completed the main and Sub category master and we have to create a navigation system to move the sub category record and allow user to edit the description. First step, whenever we select the main category it should filter the sub category data based on main category selected. Then it has to fill the first record description and SCode to field. Then by clicking Previous and Next button it should move the record on either side to park the decided Description for editing. For that we have to create two Text box and position it at either side of Previous and Next button. Rename the text box name to R1 and R2.

This will capture the record count and update based on every click of navigation button.

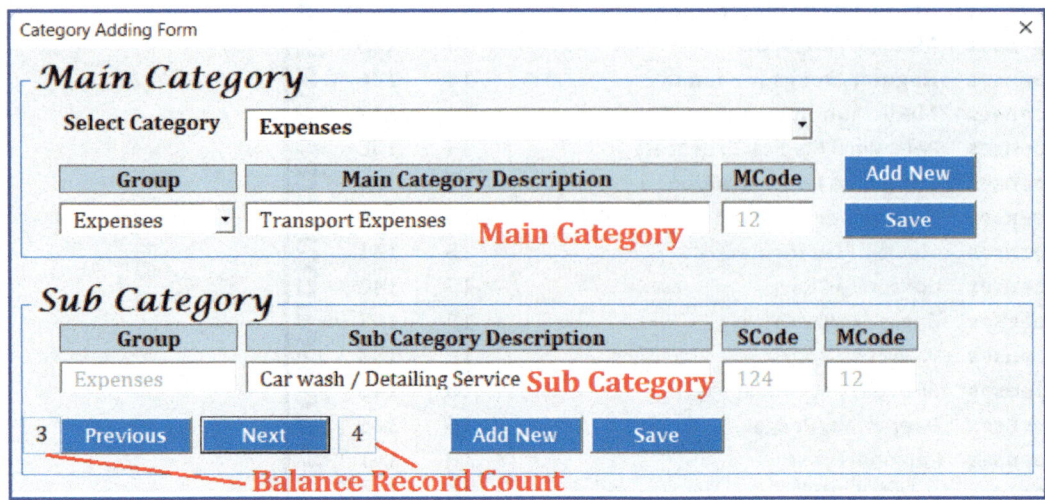

To extract data from sub category, we have to write a separate procedure by name "GetRec". Then to call that procedure, we have to add procedure calling statement in Mcat combo box event and Save2 button event procedure as shown below.

---------------------------Code Start----------------------------------
**Private Sub Mcat_Change()**
If Mcat.Value <> "" Then
'----------Main category
  Group.Value = Mcat.Column(0)
  TB1.Value = Mcat.Column(1)
  TB2.Value = Mcat.Column(2)
'---------Sub category
  TB3.Value = Mcat.Column(0)
  TB6.Value = Mcat.Column(2)
  Getrec       '--------Call GetRec sub procedure
End If
**End Sub**
-------------------------------------------------------------------
**Private Sub Save2_Click()**
'--------Validation check
....................
....................
....................
    ws.Cells(Lr + 1, 4) = TB5.Value
  End If
  MsgBox "Record Saved"
  Getrec       '--------Call GetRec sub procedure
**End Sub**

----------------------End code----------------------------------

Then create a GetRec procedure and add the code as shown below. This procedure sorts the Mcode and Scode column in Sub category sheet and filter the data to match the selected Main category in top combo box. Then the filtered rows are added to a Multi-dimensional variable and assign the first row value to Description and Scode field. The Multi-dimensional array value has to be used in different procedure, so it should be declared at module General section (At first line of Module).

Dim Data1() as variant

Here we declared the Data1 variable without size and will be changed by Rdim statement in the code.

---------------------Code start--------------------------------------

```vba
Private Sub Getrec()
  Dim wb As WorkBook
  Dim ws As Worksheet
On Error GoTo ErrorHandler
  Set wb = Workbooks("Home Budget-BE.xlsx")
  Set ws = wb.Sheets("Sub Category")
On Error Resume Next
  ws.ShowAllData
  ws.Sort.SortFields.Clear
  Lr = ws.Cells(ws.Rows.Count, "B").End(xlUp).Row   '-----Last row of sheet
'--------------Sorting
  ws.AutoFilter.Sort.SortFields.Add Key:=Range("C2:D" & Lr), _
    SortOn:=xlSortOnValues, Order:=xlAscending, DataOption:=xlSortNormal
  With ws.AutoFilter.Sort
       .Header = xlYes
        .MatchCase = False
        .Orientation = xlTopToBottom
        .SortMethod = xlPinYin
        .Apply
  End With
'--------------Filter
    ws.Range("A2:D" & Lr).AutoFilter Field:=3, Criteria1:=TB2.Value
        Set Rng = ws.Range("B3:B" & Lr).SpecialCells(xlCellTypeVisible)
        Rcnt = Rng.Count
        ReDim Data1(2, Rcnt)
        k = 1
```

```
        For Each Cel In Rng
            Data1(1, k) = Cel
            Data1(2, k) = Cel.Offset(, 2)
            k = k + 1
        Next

        TB4.Value = Data1(1, 1)
        TB5.Value = Data1(2, 1)
        R1.Value = 0
        R2.Value = Rcnt
    Exit Sub
    ErrorHandler:
        MsgBox Err.Description
    End Sub
```
---------------------------Code End------------------

**Code Explanation**

1. First step is declaring the object variable and assign the work book and sheet object to wb and ws.
2. We are continually using filters on Sub category sheet, so we have to reset the filter. show all and sorting clear method will clear sorting and show all records in the sheet.
3. Next line is to find the last line of sheet which has data and assign to Lr variable.
4. Next line is sorting the Sheet by column C and D which has the Main category and sub category code.
5. Next line is filter the sheet with Mcode field(3) with the TB2 value.
6. Next line is creating a range with special cells function which assign only the visible cells (xlCellTypeVisible) to that range variable Rng. Here we consider only "B" column as reference range.
7. Next line counts the Rng data and assign to Rcnt variable.
8. Then the data1 array is re dimensioned with Redim function and assign the size 2 as lower bound and Rcnt as Upper bound.
9. Then by For each loop statement, we are running the data one by one from Rng range and which will assign to Cel variable. We can specify any name to this variable. Since we referred only 'B' column in range setting, it considers only the cells in "B" columns and assign the value to Cel variable. The Cel is cell reference, so it value is transferred to Data1 array variable to first column. The Data1 second column value will be assigned

by Cel.offset(,2) method which move two columns from "B" column and get the value from "D" column in same row. Here k is used to as an increment variable to specify the Data1 position.
10. Then the first record value of Description (Date1(1,1)) and Scode (Date1(2,1)) is assigned to the form text fields.
11. Data1 is multi-dimensional array has two columns and **n** numbers of Rows. The row number is taken from the Range count(Rcnt). So the first column is used to store the Description value and second column will be used to store the Scode value. If the Range has 6 rows, then it stores six set of data in Data1 array.
12. Same time it adds zero to R1 text box and the total count of Data1 array(Rcnt) value to R2 text box.

Test the code by Debugging mode and check.


## Navigation Controls

Next we have to write event procedure for Previous and Next Button. This event will change the Description and Scode field value based on the number displayed in the R1 Text box.

```
--------------------------Code Start----------------------------
Private Sub PreRec_Click()
    If R1.Value = "" Then MsgBox "First Select the Main Category": Exit Sub
    If R1.Value = 0 Then MsgBox "First Record": Exit Sub
    R1.Value = R1.Value - 1
    R2.Value = R2.Value + 1
    If R1.Value = 0 Then TB4.Value = Data1(1, 1) Else TB4.Value = Data1(1, R1.Value)
    If R1.Value = 0 Then TB5.Value = Data1(2, 1) Else TB5.Value = Data1(2, R1.Value)
End Sub
--------------------------------------------------------------------------------
Private Sub NextRec_Click()
    If R2.Value = "" Then MsgBox "First Select the Main Category": Exit Sub
    If Int(R2.Value) = 0 Then MsgBox "Last Record": Exit Sub
    X = WorksheetFunction.Count(Data1)
    If Int(R2.Value) <= X Then R2.Value = R2.Value - 1
    R1.Value = R1.Value + 1
    TB4.Value = Data1(1, R1.Value)
    TB5.Value = Data1(2, R1.Value)
End Sub
```

---------------------Code End----------------------------------

**Code Explanation**

1. The first two statement in both event is for validation check. The R1 text box will receive value 0 after selection of main category in Mcat combo box otherwise it will be empty string. Same way if R1 and R2 text box has a value 0 then the navigation is in first row or last row. So once it reaches zero value it Pop up a message "First Record" or "Last Record".
2. For every click of Previous button, it subtracts one increment from R2 text box and Add one increment to R1 Text box.
3. Then it executes two If condition, if R1 value is zero then it assign Data1(1,1) that is first row data to TB4 text box and Data1(2,1) value to TB5 text box. If value is not zero, then it assign Data1(1, R1 value) to TB4 text box and Data1(2,R1 value) to TB5 text box.
4. In Next button code, it counts the number of item in Data1 array by worksheet function Count and assign to X variable.
5. It compare the R2 value to X variable, if it is less or equal to X, then it subtracts one from R2 value and increase one increment to R1 text box.
6. It replace the TB4 and TB5 text value by Data1(1,R1 value) and Data1(2,R1 value).

Now the entire process of Category adding form is completed. Test it in debug mode and ensure for proper result.

## Data Adding Form

We use another sheet to build data adding form. Rename the Sheet2 as "Expenses" and add the following controls and text as shown below. The first row will be form Heading and 2nd row will hold all our control elements. The third row is the Column header to display the data below that.

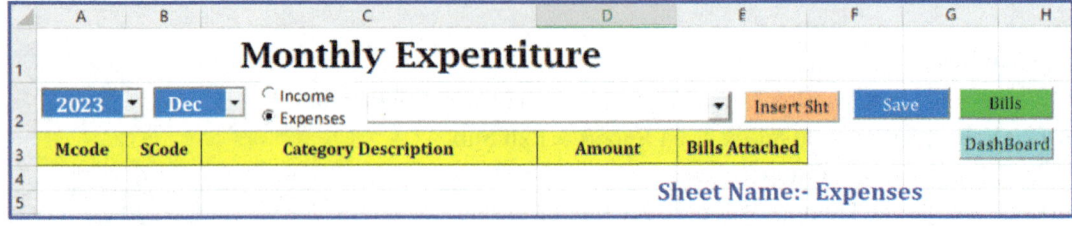

First you have to add two Drop down list to show the Year and month and name it **Years** and **Mon**. You can format the font size and back ground and fore ground colors as you like and place it in same line. We have to add the Item filling

141

script in worksheet_Activate event, so that whenever the sheet is activating, it fills the item in both drop down list.

---------------------Code Start-------------------------------
```vba
Private Sub Worksheet_Activate()
'---------Fill Year drop down
   yr = Year(Date) - 2
   Years.Clear
   For k = 1 To 5
      Years.AddItem yr + k
   Next
   Years.Value = yr + 2
'--------fill Month drop down
   Dim Months As Variant
   Months = Array("Jan", "Feb", "Mar", "Apr", "May", "Jun", "Jul", "Aug", "Sep", "Oct",
                  "Nov", "Dec")
   Mon.Clear
   Mon.List = Months
   Mon.Text = MonthName(Month(Date), True)   '---refer Date in-build function
End Sub
```
---------------------Code End-------------------------------

**Code Explanation**

1. First line getting the current year from current date and subtract two and assign the value to yr variable. So the drop down list starts from two year earlier.
2. Next clearing all old items in Years drop down list
3. The for loop statement additem to years drop down. Here it assigns the first value as one year back(yr+1) and add another 5 years.
4. The next line set or select the current year from the list
5. To show months, we created an Array in the name of Months and assigned short description of all month name.
6. Next clearing all old items in Mon drop down list
7. Next line adds the items to Mon from the Array elements by list method.
8. Next line gets the current month name in short description and set or select it in Mon drop down.

Test the code by activating the Sheet and verify whether the Years and Mon drop down list showing the current year and month.

Next we have to add two radio button and one Drop down list. The radio button is used to select the different Group : Income and Expenses. Name the income radio button as Sel1 and expenses radio button as Sel2. The drop down list will show the main category item based on Group selection. Name the drop down control as MainCat and format as you like. Now we have to add change event for radio button, which will update the MainCat drop down list.

------------------------Code start--------------------------------

```
Private Sub Sel1_Click()
  GroupSel (1)
End Sub
---------------------------------------------------------------------
Private Sub Sel2_Click()
  GroupSel (2)
End Sub
---------------------------------------------------------------------
Public Sub GroupSel(X As Integer)
'----Load list to MainCat combo box
  Set wb = Workbooks("Home Budget-BE.xlsx")
  Set ws = wb.Sheets("Main Category")
  Set ws1 = Sheets("Expenses")
  ws1.Range("A4:D100").Clear
  ws1.MainCat.Clear
  Lr = ws.Cells(ws.Rows.Count, "C").End(xlUp).Row
  ws.Range("A3:D" & Lr).Sort Key1:=ws.Range("B3:B" & Lr), Order1:=xlAscending, _
      Header:=xlNo
'---------Set combo box properties
  ws1.MainCat.ColumnCount = 2
  ws1.MainCat.ColumnWidths = "160 pt; 40Pt"
  k = 0: k1 = 0
For M = 3 To Lr           '—The data start from 3th row in Main category sheet
'-----------For Option Income
    If X = 1 Then
      If ws.Cells(M, 1) = "Income" Then
        ws1.MainCat.AddItem
        ws1.MainCat.List(k, 0) = ws.Cells(M, 2).Value
        ws1.MainCat.List(k, 1) = ws.Cells(M, 3).Value
        k = k + 1
      End If
    End If
'-----------For Option Expenses
    If X = 2 Then
      If ws.Cells(M, 1) = "Expenses" Then
        ws1.MainCat.AddItem
        ws1.MainCat.List(k, 0) = ws.Cells(M, 2).Value
```

```
        ws1.MainCat.List(k, 1) = ws.Cells(M, 3).Value
        k = k + 1
      End If
    End If
  Next
End Sub
```
---------------------Code end---------------------------------------

**Code Explanation**

1. While click of any one option in radio button, it simply call a GroupSel() procedure by sending a parameter value. If the selection is Income, it sends 1 as parameter value and if selection is Expenses, then it sends value 2.
2. The groupSel() procedure is mainly used to load item list to MainCat combo box. The first three lines are used to set object variables.
3. Next it clears all the old data below 4$^{th}$ row and clear the old list item in MainCat combo box.
4. Find the last record row in main category sheet and assign to Lr.
5. Next line sort the main category sheet by Mcode column.
6. Set the MainCat control properties of ColumnCount and ColumnWidths. These properties can be set in control property dialogue box. For learning purpose its added to understant, how to set properties by VBA code.
7. Two counter K and K1 is added with Initial value of Zero
8. The for loop repeat the cycle from 4 to Last row of sheet
9. Under the for loop we written code for two option. The parameter passed by radio button is assigned to X as argument value. So we checking the X value by If statement. If the Value is 1 then it executes first option code otherwise it executes second option code.
10. The second If condition statement, check the Group value is whether income or Expenses. Then it adds the Main category item to MainCat combo box. It repeat the cycle up to last row and add all the relevant main category item to combo box.
11. The list option of combo box, add the Category description value to first column of combo box and Mcode value to second column of combo box.

Test the code by Debugging tool and check it loading correct main category item in list for different selection of Radio button.

**Expenses Data Sheet**

The plan to save the expenses data for each year is in separate sheet and it contain the expenses for all months. So for every year we have to insert a new sheet with the name of the selected year. So without corresponding year sheet in Back end excel file, we can't retrieve the data or save the data. So we have to add an event to Years combo box to verify the availability of sheet.

------------------Code start--------------------------------
```vba
Private Sub Years_Change()
    Dim wb As Workbook
    Dim ws As Worksheet
'--------Find work sheet
    Set wb = Workbooks("Home Budget-BE.xlsx")

    If Years <> "" Then
        For Each sht In wb.Worksheets
            If sht.Name = Years.Value Then Exit Sub
        Next
        MsgBox "For this year Sheet is not available in Back End Excel" & Chr(13) & _
                "Create the Sheet By Clicking Insert Sheet button"
End If
'-------Clear Sheet data
    Sheets("Expenses").Range("A4:D100").Clear
End Sub
----------------------------------------------------------------------------
Private Sub Mon_Change()
 '-------Clear Sheet data
    Dim wb As Workbook
    Dim ws As Worksheet
    Set wb = Workbooks("Home Budget-FE.xlsm")
    Set ws = wb.Sheets("Expenses")
    ws.Range("A4:D100").Clear
    MainCat = ""
End Sub
```
---------------------------Code End------------------------------------

**Code Explanation**

1. First step, we have to check whether the Years combo box has a value. If it has a value, then it executes the Sheet checking process.
2. Here we used For Each statement, which will loop all the worksheets name in Back end excel file and assign to sht variable.
3. Next the sht name is checked with Years combo box selected value by If condition.

145

4. If it found match, then it exit from the for loop, otherwise it continue the cycle.
5. If no match found, then go to next line of for loop statement and Pop up a message. Here Chr(13) is added to create second line.
6. Also it clear the old data populated after 4th row in expenses sheet.

By this it indicates to user there is no sheet is available for this year. So user has to create a New sheet. The mon_change event will just empty out the data in expenses from 4th row to 100 the row.

## Insert New Sheet

We have to create a new sheet for each year. To make a new sheet by easily and make all format as uniform, we have to write a procedure to Insert Sheet. Insert a command Button in expenses Sheet and name it as IYear. Add the following code to insert a new sheet in back end file.

```
-----------------------------Code Start-----------------------------
Private Sub Iyear_Click()
    Dim wb As Workbook
    Dim ws As Worksheet
'--------Find work sheet
    Set wb = Workbooks("Home Budget-BE.xlsx")
'--------Check the sheet avilablity
    If Years = "" Then MsgBox "Select Year": Exit Sub
    For Each sht In wb.Worksheets
        If sht.Name = Years.Value Then
            MsgBox "Already Work sheet is Available for this year"
            Exit Sub
        End If
    Next

'---------Create a Sheet with format
    wb.Sheets.Add(After:=wb.Sheets(wb.Sheets.Count)).Name = Years.Value
    Set ws = wb.Sheets(Years.Value)
    ws.Activate
'---------Adding Column Heading
    ws.Range("A1").Value = "MID"
    ws.Range("B1").Value = "SID"
    ws.Range("C1").Value = "Description"
    ws.Range("D1").Value = "Jan"
    ws.Range("E1").Value = "Feb"
```

```vba
    ws.Range("F1").Value = "Mar"
    ws.Range("G1").Value = "Apr"
    ws.Range("H1").Value = "May"
    ws.Range("I1").Value = "Jun"
    ws.Range("J1").Value = "Jul"
    ws.Range("K1").Value = "Aug"
    ws.Range("L1").Value = "Sep"
    ws.Range("M1").Value = "Oct"
    ws.Range("N1").Value = "Nov"
    ws.Range("O1").Value = "Dec"
    ws.Range("P1").Value = "Total"
    ws.Range("Q1").Value = "Group"
'----------Format columns
    ws.Columns("A:B").ColumnWidth = 10
    ws.Columns("C:C").ColumnWidth = 50
    ws.Columns("D:Q").ColumnWidth = 10

    ws.Range("A1:Q1").Select
    With Selection.Font
        .Name = "Cambria"
        .Size = 14
        .Bold = True
    End With
    With Selection
        .HorizontalAlignment = xlCenter
        .VerticalAlignment = xlCenter
    End With
    With Selection.Interior
        .Pattern = xlSolid
        .PatternColorIndex = xlAutomatic
        .Color = RGB(254, 246, 91)
    End With

    ws.Range("A1:Q1").Borders.LineStyle = xlContinuous
    ActiveWindow.WindowState = xlMinimized
End Sub
```
-------------------------------Code End-------------------------------

**Code Explanation**

1. First step is to check whether the year sheet is available in the back end file to avoid duplicate insert. The procedure is same like as explained in Years change event.

2. Next step is adding sheet to back end work book(wb). The wb.sheets.count, counts the number of sheets available in work book and the function sheets.add, add the new sheet after the last sheet by the name of years combo box value (like 2023).
3. Next step is to set the newly added sheet as current active sheet.
4. Next step is it add the column heading in first row of each column.
5. Next three lines, format the column width of each column
6. Next it selects a range from A1:Q1, that is entire column of first row.
7. With that selection it changes the font style, size and boldness, text alignment, fill the cell with yellow color and make the border all around cell.
8. The last line minimizes the back end work book.

**Output in Back end excel file**

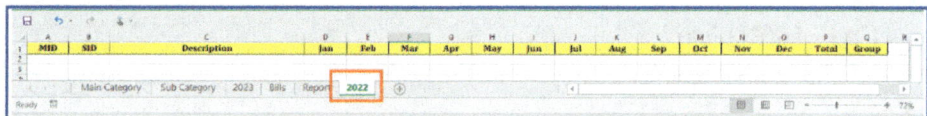

## Extract Expenses Data

It is planned to attach a bill in the form of PDF or Image file to each expenditure. For that we have to create a separate sheet in the name of Bills in back end excel file as shown below. This sheet hold all bill reference for all year and all months. So one sheet will handle the total bill attachment.

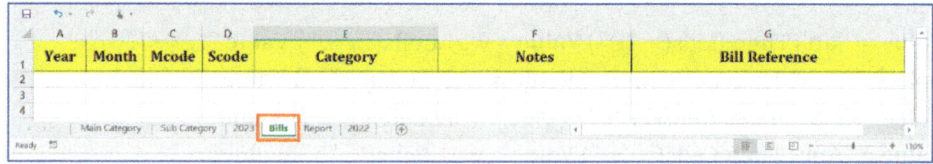

Now we created the sheet for a specific year and Bills, the next step is to add monthly expenses and attach relevant bills. We have already filled the item list in MainCat combo box and now we have to add the event procedure to MainCat to execute data extraction process.

-----------------------------Code Start-------------------------------
```
Private Sub MainCat_Change()
    Dim wb As Workbook
    Dim ws As Worksheet
If MainCat.Value <> "" Then
    Set wb = Workbooks("Home Budget-BE.xlsx")
    Set ws = wb.Sheets("Sub Category")
```

148

```vba
    Set ws1 = wb.Sheets(Years.Value)
    Set ws2 = wb.Sheets("Bills")
    '----------Extract data from Sub category
    On Error Resume Next
    ws.ShowAllData
    ws.Sort.SortFields.Clear
    Lr = ws.Cells(ws.Rows.Count, "C").End(xlUp).Row
    Set Rng = ws.Range("A2:C" & Lr)
    '--------------Sorting
    Rng.Sort Key1:=Range("C2"), Key2:=Range("D2"), Header:=xlYes, _
            Order1:=xlAscending, Order2:=xlAscending
    '--------------Filter
    ws.Range("A2:C" & Lr).AutoFilter Field:=3, Criteria1:=MainCat.Value
    Set Rng = ws.Range("B3:B" & Lr).SpecialCells(xlCellTypeVisible)
    Rcnt = Rng.Count
'------Add Sub Category to sheet
    ActiveSheet.Range("A4:E100").Clear
    k = 4
    For Each Cel In Rng
        Cells(k, 3) = Cel
        Cells(k, 1) = Cel.Offset(, 1)
        Cells(k, 2) = Cel.Offset(, 2)
        X = 0
        '-----month Cost working
        On Error Resume Next
        X = ws1.Range("B:B").Cells.Find(Cells(k, "B").Value).Row
        If X > 0 Then
            If Mon.Value = "Jan" Then Cells(k, "D").Value = ws1.Cells(X, "D").Value
            If Mon.Value = "Feb" Then Cells(k, "D").Value = ws1.Cells(X, "E").Value
            If Mon.Value = "Mar" Then Cells(k, "D").Value = ws1.Cells(X, "F").Value
            If Mon.Value = "Apr" Then Cells(k, "D").Value = ws1.Cells(X, "G").Value
            If Mon.Value = "May" Then Cells(k, "D").Value = ws1.Cells(X, "H").Value
            If Mon.Value = "Jun" Then Cells(k, "D").Value = ws1.Cells(X, "I").Value
            If Mon.Value = "Jul" Then Cells(k, "D").Value = ws1.Cells(X, "J").Value
            If Mon.Value = "Aug" Then Cells(k, "D").Value = ws1.Cells(X, "K").Value
            If Mon.Value = "Sep" Then Cells(k, "D").Value = ws1.Cells(X, "L").Value
            If Mon.Value = "Oct" Then Cells(k, "D").Value = ws1.Cells(X, "M").Value
            If Mon.Value = "Nov" Then Cells(k, "D").Value = ws1.Cells(X, "N").Value
            If Mon.Value = "Dec" Then Cells(k, "D").Value = ws1.Cells(X, "O").Value
        End If
        '-----Bills attached count
        Lr1 = ws2.Cells(ws2.Rows.Count, "D").End(xlUp).Row
        Z = WorksheetFunction.CountIfs(ws2.Range("A2:A" & Lr1), Years.Value,
```

```
            ws2.Range("B2:B" & Lr1), Mon.Value, ws2.Range("D2:D" & Lr1),
        Cells(k, "B").Value)
      If Z > 0 Then Cells(k, "E").Value = Z
    k = k + 1
  Next
End If
End Sub
```
----------------------------Code End--------------------------------

**Code Explanation**

1. First step assigning three sheet object to variable ws, ws1, ws2
2. Next step is extract data from sub category, for that first clear all filter and get last row number.
3. Then set the data range and assign to Rng variable and sort the data by C and D columns.
4. Then Apply a filter for column "C" match the value of MainCat selected value. For example, if we selected "Daily Living expenses" (Mcode=11) in MainCat drop down, then it sorts and filter the sub category sheet as shown below

| 1 | Sub Category | | | |
|---|---|---|---|---|
| 2 | Group | Sub Category | Mcode | Scode |
| 14 | Expenses | Groceries Food Items | 11 | 111 |
| 15 | Expenses | Personel Items (Cosmatics) | 11 | 112 |
| 16 | Expenses | House Maintenance Items | 11 | 113 |
| 17 | Expenses | Milk | 11 | 114 |
| 18 | Expenses | Vegitables | 11 | 115 |
| 19 | Expenses | Non-Veg items | 11 | 116 |
| 20 | Expenses | Cloth Dry Cleaning / Ironing | 11 | 117 |
| 21 | Expenses | Salon / SPA | 11 | 118 |
| 22 | Expenses | Dining Out | 11 | 119 |
| 23 | Expenses | Mobile Phone bills | 11 | 120 |
| 24 | Expenses | Servent Maid Salory | 11 | 121 |

5. Next step is it store the "B" column value of each Visible record to Rng variable by SpecialCells(xlCellTypeVisible) function.
6. Next step it clears the old data after 3$^{rd}$ row in Expenses Sheet
7. Using for each loop it gets data from Rng variable and assign to Cel variable. We set an increment variable k with value 4 which is meant hear the 4$^{th}$ row of Expenses sheet.
8. Then it writes the Cel value(B column of Sub category) to Expenses sheet in "C" column. By cell offset function, we get "C" and "D" column value from sub

category and write to "D" and "E" column of expenses sheet. Like it populates all relevant record in expenses sheet as shown below.

9. Next step extract the month cost data based on the Month selected in Mon drop down. In this the First step is to check whether the sub category (Scode) is available in the Year sheet by **find** function. If it found, then it assigns the record row number to X variable.
10. If the value of X is greater than zero, then it checks the value for a particular month. It is simple steps with 12 if condition statement. For example, the selected month is "Dec", then it gets the value of "o" column in year sheet and write to "D" column of expenses sheet.
11. Next step is find any bills are attached to any sub category. The **countIFs** function count number record with matching criteria. For detail please read the In-built function section. If count is greater than zero, then it writes that number in "E" column. The result is as shown below.

## Monthly Expentiture

| | Mcode | SCode | Category Description | Amount | Bills Attached |
|---|---|---|---|---|---|
| | 2023 | Dec | ○ Income ● Expenses  Daily Living expenses | Insert Sht | Save | Bills |
| | | | | | | DashBoard |
| 4 | 11 | 111 | Groceries Food Items | 1000 | |
| 5 | 11 | 112 | Personel Items (Cosmatics) | 2200 | |
| 6 | 11 | 113 | House Maintenance Items | 1853 | |
| 7 | 11 | 114 | Milk | 620 | |
| 8 | 11 | 115 | Vegitables | 2526 | 2 |
| 9 | 11 | 116 | Non-Veg items | 456 | |
| 10 | 11 | 117 | Cloth Dry Cleaning / Ironing | 280 | |
| 11 | 11 | 118 | Salon / SPA | 325 | |
| 12 | 11 | 119 | Dining Out | 200 | |
| 13 | 11 | 120 | Mobile Phone bills | | |
| 14 | 11 | 121 | Servent Maid Salory | 650 | |

Test it in Debug tool and achieve the results.

### Save Expenses

Whenever you select a New year or New month, it only shows Mcode, SCode and Description data and show blank value in Amount and Bill Attached columns. Please remember after selecting the main category in MainCat drop down, it always shows all sub category description in the Expenses sheet. It is not necessary to fill all rows of amount. Some category may occur rarely or occur once in three months, so value filling of Amount column is not mandatory. The Bills attached column is auto fill, so no need to enter any value for this column.

151

To save the expenses data we have to write the event for Save button as shown below.

---------------------------Code Start---------------------------------

```vba
Private Sub Save_Click()
   Dim wb As Workbook
   Dim ws As Worksheet
   Set wb = Workbooks("Home Budget-BE.xlsx")
   Set ws = wb.Sheets(Years.Value)
   Set ws1 = Sheets("Expenses")
   
   Lr1 = ws1.Cells(ws1.Rows.Count, "C").End(xlUp).Row
   
   For k = 4 To Lr1
      If ws1.Cells(k, "D").Value > 0 Then
         On Error Resume Next
         X = 0
         X = ws.Range("B:B").Cells.Find(ws1.Cells(k, "B").Value).Row
         If X > 0 Then
            Y=X
         Else
            Lr = ws.Cells(ws.Rows.Count, "C").End(xlUp).Row
            Y = Lr + 1
            ws.Cells(Y, 1) = ws1.Cells(k, 1)
            ws.Cells(Y, 2) = ws1.Cells(k, 2)
            ws.Cells(Y, 3) = ws1.Cells(k, 3)
            ws.Cells(Y, "P") = "=Sum(D" & Y & ":O" & Y & ")"
            If Sel1.Value = True Then ws.Cells(Y, "Q") = "Income"
            If Sel2.Value = True Then ws.Cells(Y, "Q") = "Expenses"
         End If
         '---------Month cost
         If Mon.Value = "Jan" Then ws.Cells(Y, "D").Value = ws1.Cells(K, "D").Value
         If Mon.Value = "Feb" Then ws.Cells(Y, "E").Value = ws1.Cells(K, "D").Value
         If Mon.Value = "Mar" Then ws.Cells(Y, "F").Value = ws1.Cells(K, "D").Value
         If Mon.Value = "Apr" Then ws.Cells(Y, "G").Value = ws1.Cells(K, "D").Value
         If Mon.Value = "May" Then ws.Cells(Y, "H").Value = ws1.Cells(K, "D").Value
         If Mon.Value = "Jun" Then ws.Cells(Y, "I").Value = ws1.Cells(K, "D").Value
         If Mon.Value = "Jul" Then ws.Cells(Y, "J").Value = ws1.Cells(K, "D").Value
         If Mon.Value = "Aug" Then ws.Cells(Y, "K").Value = ws1.Cells(K, "D").Value
         If Mon.Value = "Sep" Then ws.Cells(Y, "L").Value = ws1.Cells(K, "D").Value
         If Mon.Value = "Oct" Then ws.Cells(Y, "M").Value = ws1.Cells(K, "D").Value
         If Mon.Value = "Nov" Then ws.Cells(Y, "N").Value = ws1.Cells(K, "D").Value
         If Mon.Value = "Dec" Then ws.Cells(Y, "O").Value = ws1.Cells(K, "D").Value
```

        End If
    Next
End Sub
--------------------------Code End---------------------------------

**Code Explanation**

1. First step is declaring and assign the work book and work sheet object variable and find the Last row of sheet.
2. Then run a for loop from 4th row to Last row of sheet expenses.
3. If the Amount (D) column has a value, then only we will save that row in year sheet. For that the if condition check if the "D" column value is greater than zero, then it execute all code or just it reach next statement and return back to for loop line.
4. The next step is it check match record by SCode value in Year sheet by find function and return the row number to X variable. If it found it change the X value from zero to row number.
5. If X value is greater than zero, then the sub category item is available in that year sheet, so just we have to update the Amount value. So it just assigns the Row number (X) to Y variable.
6. If X value is zero, then we have to add a new record to Year sheet. So it calculates the last row of that sheet and add one and assign to Y variable.
7. Since it is new record, it adds Mcode, SCode, Sub Category Description to Year Sheet. Same time it add the Sum() formula and Category Group to "P" and "Q" columns. The Sum formula add all value from "Jan" to "Dec" months and indicate the year expenses of that sub category.
12. Then we have to add the Expenses amount from "D" column to corresponding selected Month column. For that we used 12 sets of If condition statement to find out the column number. For example, the selected month is "Dec", then it gets the value of "D" column in expenses sheet and write to "O" column in year sheet.

Test the code in debugging mode by adding one value in amount column. Repeat the step and fill the expenses value to all sub category. You can also repeat this process for another month.

**Bills Attachment**

    It is best practice to attach the Bills for high cost expenditure. It may be one or More bills for same category in a year. The bills may be in the form of PDF document or Image file. We have already created a separate worksheet in back end file to store bill reference. To upload the bills, we have to develop a user form as shown below.

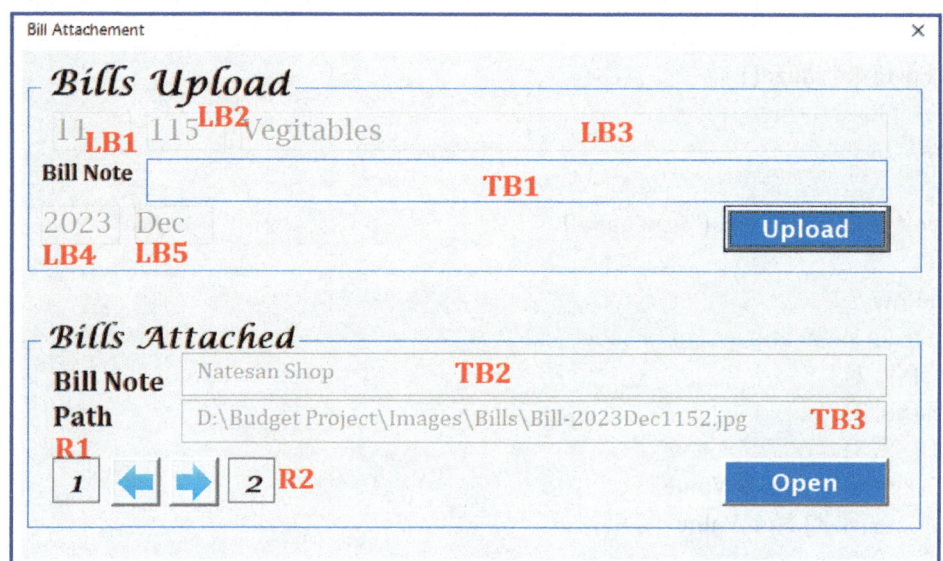

The form has two frame, one is for uploading new bills and another one is for show already attached bills. The form will be opened by Bills button click and while loading it get the MCode, SCode and Sub category description from selected row of expenses sheet and populate it in user form. Same time while opening it collect the details of already attached bills for that Sub category and list it in bottom frame.

To create new user form right click over Form module and select Insert->User form. It creates a new blank user form in form module. Rename the form name to "Bills" and caption to "Bill Attachment". Add two frame and change the caption as "Bills Upload" and Bills Attached". Add five labels and name it as LB1, LB2, LB3, LB4 and LB5. Add four text box and name it as TB1, TB2, TB3, R1 and R2. Add one button in each frame. Format and position all controls as shown in the above image.

Now we have to add event to Bills Button located in expenses sheet and in User form for Initialize event.

------------------------Code Start----------------------------
Private Sub Bill_Click()
    Set ws = ActiveWorkbook.Sheets("Expenses")
    Lr = ws.Cells(ws.Rows.Count, "C").End(xlUp).Row
    SR = ActiveCell.Row
    If SR > Lr +1 Then MsgBox "Select the Row Which Has Data": Exit Sub

```vba
    If SR < 4 Then MsgBox "Select the Row Which Has Data": Exit Sub
    Bills.Show
End Sub
-----------------------------------------------------------------------
'------Double click the Bills form and add the below code
Private Sub UserForm_Initialize()
    Dim wb As Workbook
    Dim ws, ws1 As Worksheet
    Dim SR As Integer
    Set ws1 = ActiveWorkbook.Sheets("Expenses")
    ws1.Select
    SR = ActiveCell.Row
    '--------Get value from sheet and assign to Label
    LB1 = ws1.Cells(SR, 1)
    LB2 = ws1.Cells(SR, 2)
    LB3 = ws1.Cells(SR, 3)
    LB4 = Sheets("Expenses").Years.Value
    LB5 = Sheets("Expenses").Mon.Value
    
    Set wb = Workbooks("Home Budget-BE.xlsx")
    Set ws = wb.Sheets("Bills")
    
    On Error Resume Next
    ws.ShowAllData
    ws.Sort.SortFields.Clear
    Lr = ws.Cells(ws.Rows.Count, "D").End(xlUp).Row
    Set Rng = ws.Range("A2:F" & Lr)
    
    '--------------Sorting
    Rng.Sort Key1:=Range("A1"), Key2:=Range("B1"), key3:=Range("D1"), _
            Header:=xlYes
    '--------------Filter
    ws.Range("A1:F" & Lr).AutoFilter Field:=1, Criteria1:=LB4.Caption
    ws.Range("A1:F" & Lr).AutoFilter Field:=2, Criteria1:=LB5.Caption
    ws.Range("A1:F" & Lr).AutoFilter Field:=4, Criteria1:=LB2.Caption
    
    Set Rng = ws.Range("F2:F" & Lr).SpecialCells(xlCellTypeVisible)
    Rcnt = Rng.Count
    ReDim Bdata(2, Rcnt)
    k = 1
    For Each Cel In Rng
        Bdata(1, k) = Cel
        Bdata(2, k) = Cel.Offset(, 1)
```

```
        k = k + 1
    Next

    TB2.Value = Bdata(1, 1)
    TB3.Value = Bdata(2, 1)
    R1.Value = 1
    R2.Value = Rcnt
End Sub
```
----------------------------------End Code----------------------------------

**Code Explanation**

1. After Bills Button click, it checks whether any row is selected in expenses sheet. For that it assigns the Active Cell row number to SR variable. Then it checks the SR value is Less than row number 4 or Greater than Last row number. If it is true, then it pops up a message and exit from the procedure. If the row number is within 4 to Lr value, then it open(Show) the Bills form.
2. While Opening of Bills form, it executes all code in form Initialize event. First step is it assigns the workbook and worksheet objects to variable and activate the expenses sheet. Then it finds the current cell row and assign to SR variable.
3. Then it extract the Mcode, SCode, Description value from the selected row and assign to LB1, LB2 and LB3 label in bills form.
4. Then it assigns the Selected Year and Month to LB4 and LB5 label.
5. Next step is assigning of Back end work book and Bills sheet to variable and Clear all old filter and sorting.
6. Then it sorts Year (A), Month (B) and Scode (D) columns in Bills sheet
7. Then it filters the record range by Year, Month and Scode by criteria value of LB5, LB4 and LB2.
8. Then it assigns the "F" columns value of all visible rows to Rng variable and assign its count to Rcnt variable.
9. Then we re-dimension the Bdata array to by Bdata(2, Rcnt).
10. Using For each loop, we extract data from Rng variable and assign to Cel variable. Then it assigns the Bill Notes (F) and Bill Reference(G) to Bdata array.
11. Next step it populate the Notes and path data to TB2 and TB3 textbox. Also it assign 1 to R1 and Rcnt value to R2 text Box.

Test the code, it opens the form with relevant data of selected row. Also it shows already attached bills in bottom frame, if exists.

## Upload Bills

Now we have to add event to upload the Bill to Upload button.

---------------------------Code start----------------------------

```vba
Private Sub Upd_Click()
  Dim sc, yr, mn, opt As Variant
  Dim wb As Workbook
  Dim ws As Worksheet
  If TB1.Value = "" Or IsEmpty(TB1.Value) Then MsgBox "Fill the Bill Note": Exit Sub

  Set wb = Workbooks("Home Budget-BE.xlsx")
  Set ws = wb.Sheets("Bills")
  Lr = ws.Cells(ws.Rows.Count, "C").End(xlUp).Row
  Y = Lr + 1
'------Call Image upload function
  sc = LB2.Caption
  yr = LB4.Caption
  mn = LB5.Caption
  opt = 2
  Rn = Y
  X = FileUpload(opt, sc, yr, mn, Rn)
'---Save record to Back end file
  ws.Cells(Y, 1) = LB4.Caption
  ws.Cells(Y, 2) = LB5.Caption
  ws.Cells(Y, 3) = LB1.Caption
  ws.Cells(Y, 4) = LB2.Caption
  ws.Cells(Y, 5) = LB3.Caption
  ws.Cells(Y, 6) = TB1.Value
  ws.Cells(Y, 7) = X

MsgBox "File Uploaded"
End Sub
```

---------------------------Code End----------------------------

### Code Explanation

1. For uploading bills, we have to call a common function FileUpload located in Module1. For that we have to supply 5 parameters like SCode(sc), Year(yr), Month(mn), Selection Obtion(opt) and Row number(Rn).
2. The sc, yr and mn value are get from the form label LB2, LB4 and LB5. For option value, we used one for Panel image upload and for bill upload we

assign a constant value of 2 to opt variable. The row number is Last row +one (Y) is assigned to Rn variable.

3. Now call FileUpload function supplying all the above parameter and assign the return result to X variable. It open file explorer dialogue box, for selecting the file. After selecting the file, it creates a new file name with the combination of Year, Month, Scode, Row number and upload it to Image/Bill folder

```
    If opt = 2 Then         '-------for Bill Image file
        Fname = "Bill-" & yr & mn & sc & Rn & "." & ext
        copyfile = "D:\Budget Project\Images\Bills\" & Fname
    end if
```

The folder path is constant and it return the result value of Copyfile to calling function.

4. Then it save the value as a new record to Bills sheet and pops up a message file uploaded.

Now we have to write the record navigation for frame 2 to naviagete the attached file list. Once we seen the desired bill, then we can open that file by clicking open command.

---------------------------------Code Start---------------------------

```
Private Sub Prev_Click()
    If R1.Value = "" Then MsgBox "First Select the Main Category": Exit Sub
    If R1.Value = 1 Then MsgBox "First Record": Exit Sub
    R1.Value = R1.Value - 1
    R2.Value = R2.Value + 1
    TB2.Value = Bdata(1, R1.Value)
    TB3.Value = Bdata(2, R1.Value)

End Sub
```
-------------------------------------------------------------------------------
```
Private Sub NextR_Click()
    If R2.Value = "" Then MsgBox "First Select the Main Category": Exit Sub
    If Int(R2.Value) = 1 Then MsgBox "Last Record": Exit Sub
    R2.Value = Int(R2.Value) - 1
    R1.Value = R1.Value + 1
    TB2.Value = Bdata(1, R1.Value)
    TB3.Value = Bdata(2, R1.Value)
End Sub
```
-------------------------------------------------------------------------------
```
Private Sub OpenBill_Click()
    Fpath = TB3.Value
```

```
    Shell "Explorer.exe " & Fpath, vbMaximizedFocus
End Sub
```
--------------------------------Code End--------------------------

**Code Explanation**
1. The Previous and Next commands are identical to Category adding form, so you can read that explanation to understand the code.
2. When click open command button, it gets the File full path from TB3 text box and assign to Fpath variable.
3. Then by Shell function it opens the file and focus it.

Test the code. Now we completed all the data entry for Home expenses application. Now we can add some hide function of sheet while changeover from one sheet to another sheet. This code has to be added for "Expenses" button in dashboard sheet and DashBoard button(Home) in Expenses sheet.

---------------Code Start------------------
```
Private Sub Expenses_Click()
'---Activate Expenses Sheet
   Set ws1 = Sheets("Expenses")
   ws1.Visible = True
   ws1.Activate
   ws1.Sel2.Value = True
   Sheets("DashBoard").Visible = False
End Sub
-----------------------------------------------------------------------------
Private Sub Home_Click()
   Sheets("DashBoard").Visible = True
   Sheets("DashBoard").Select
   ActiveWorkbook.Sheets("Expenses").Visible = False
End Sub
-----------------------------------------------------------------
Private Sub Quit_Click()
   Set wb = Workbooks("Home Budget-BE.xlsx")
   wb.Close savechanges:=True
   ThisWorkbook.Save
   Application.Quit
End Sub
```
--------------Code End--------------------

**Code Explanation**
1. Whenever we click Expenses button, it set the expenses sheet to variable ws1 and make it visible property to Ture and activate that sheet. Same time it

makes the visible property of Dashboard sheet to false which will hide the Dash board sheet.
2. Same way if you click dashboard button, it makes the visible property of Dash Board sheet to true and for Expenses sheet to false.
3. The quit button in Dash board will save and close both Back end and Front end excel file and close the Excel application

# Report

Finally, we have to generate a PDF report for our expenses. For that we have to create a new sheet in the name of "Report" as shown below and we have to add the following code to Report Button in Dash board sheet.

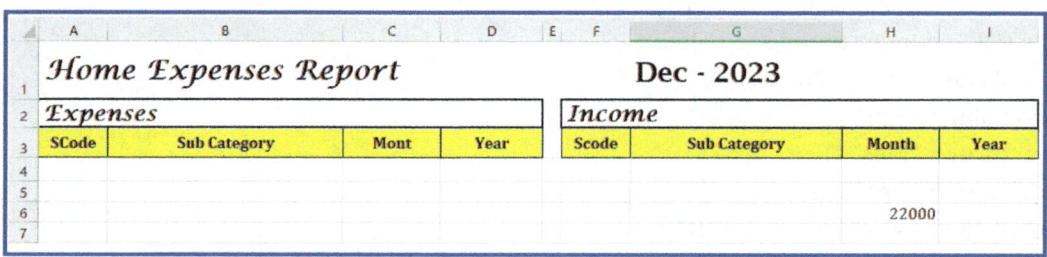

```
--------------------------Code Start------------------
Private Sub Report_Click()
    Dim wb As Workbook
    Dim ws As Worksheet
    Dim Rng As Range

On Error GoTo ErrorHandler
    Set wb = Workbooks("Home Budget-BE.xlsx")
'-------Checking Year sheet availability
    For M = 1 To wb.Worksheets.Count
        If wb.Worksheets(M).Name = Years.Value Then
        Set ws = wb.Sheets(Years.Value)
        Exit For
        End If
    Next M
If M > wb.Worksheets.Count Then MsgBox "For this year Sheet is not Created": Exit Sub
    Lr = ws.Cells(ws.Rows.Count, "B").End(xlUp).Row
'--------------Sorting
    On Error Resume Next
    ws.ShowAllData
    With ws.Sort
```

```vba
            .SortFields.Clear
            .SortFields.Add Key:=ws.Range("A1"), Order:=xlAscending
            .SortFields.Add Key:=ws.Range("B1"), Order:=xlAscending
            .SetRange ws.Range("A1:D" & Lr)
            .Header = xlYes
            .Apply
        End With
    '---------Format report contents
        Set ws1 = wb.Sheets("Report")
        Set ws2 = wb.Sheets("Main Category")
        Lr1 = ws1.Cells(ws1.Rows.Count, "B").End(xlUp).Row
        ws1.Range("A4:I200").Clear
        ws1.Range("A4:I200").Font.Name = "Cambria"
        ws1.Range("A4:I200").Font.Size = 12
    '-----Get Column Index by Selected Month
        If Mon.Value = "Jan" Then Col = "D"
        If Mon.Value = "Feb" Then Col = "E"
        If Mon.Value = "Mar" Then Col = "F"
        If Mon.Value = "Apr" Then Col = "G"
        If Mon.Value = "May" Then Col = "H"
        If Mon.Value = "Jun" Then Col = "I"
        If Mon.Value = "Jul" Then Col = "J"
        If Mon.Value = "Aug" Then Col = "K"
        If Mon.Value = "Sep" Then Col = "L"
        If Mon.Value = "Oct" Then Col = "M"
        If Mon.Value = "Nov" Then Col = "N"
        If Mon.Value = "Dec" Then Col = "O"
    '---------Write the Report
        ws1.Cells(1, "G") = Mon.Value & " - " & Years.Value
        Mcat = 0: R1 = 4: R2 = 4
        For k = 2 To Lr      '-----Report sheet starting row at 3
        '----Report of expenses Category
        If ws.Cells(k, 1) <> 19 Then
            If Mcat <> ws.Cells(k, 1) Then
                Mcat = ws.Cells(k, 1)
                X = ws2.Range("C:C").Cells.Find(Mcat).Row
                ws1.Cells(R1, 1).Value = ws2.Cells(X, 2).Value
                ws1.Cells(R1, 1).Font.Size = 14
                ws1.Cells(R1, 1).Font.Bold = True
                ws1.Cells(R1, 1).Font.Color = vbBlue
                R1 = R1 + 1
            End If
                ws1.Cells(R1, 1) = ws.Cells(k, 2)
```

```vba
            ws1.Cells(R1, 2) = ws.Cells(k, 3)
            ws1.Cells(R1, 3) = ws.Cells(k,Col)
            ws1.Cells(R1, 4) = ws.Cells(k, "P")
            R1 = R1 + 1
        End If
    '----Report of Income Category
        If ws.Cells(k, 1) = 19 Then
            If R2 = 4 Then
                ws1.Cells(R2, 6).Value = "Income"
                ws1.Cells(R2, 6).Font.Size = 14
                ws1.Cells(R2, 6).Font.Bold = True
                ws1.Cells(R2, 6).Font.Color = vbBlue
                R2 = R2 + 1
            End If
            ws1.Cells(R2, 6) = ws.Cells(k, 2)
            ws1.Cells(R2, 7) = ws.Cells(k, 3)
            ws1.Cells(R2, 8) = ws.Cells(k, Col)
            ws1.Cells(R2, 9) = ws.Cells(k, "P")
            R2 = R2 + 1
        End If
    Next
'----Sum of expenses Category
    Elr = ws1.Cells(ws1.Rows.Count, "A").End(xlUp).Row
    Elr2 = Elr + 2
    ws1.Cells(Elr2, 2) = "Total Expenses"
    ws1.Cells(Elr2, 3) = "=Sum(" & "C4:C" & Elr & ")"
    ws1.Cells(Elr2, 4) = "=Sum(" & "D4:D" & Elr & ")"
    ws1.Range("B" & Elr2 & ":D" & Elr2).Font.Size = 14
    ws1.Range("B" & Elr2 & ":D" & Elr2).Font.Bold = True
    ws1.Range("B" & Elr2 & ":D" & Elr2).Font.Color = vbRed
'----Sum of Income Category
    Ilr = ws1.Cells(ws1.Rows.Count, "F").End(xlUp).Row
    Ilr2 = Ilr + 2
    ws1.Cells(Ilr2, 7) = "Total Income"
    ws1.Cells(Ilr2, 8) = "=Sum(" & "H4:H" & Ilr & ")"
    ws1.Cells(Ilr2, 9) = "=Sum(" & "I4:I" & Ilr & ")"
    ws1.Range("G" & Ilr2 & ":I" & Ilr2).Font.Size = 14
    ws1.Range("G" & Ilr2 & ":I" & Ilr2).Font.Bold = True
    ws1.Range("G" & Ilr2 & ":I" & Ilr2).Font.Color = vbRed

'-----Balance on year
    Blr2 = Ilr2 + 2
    ws1.Cells(Blr2, 7) = "Balance Amount"
```

```vb
    ws1.Cells(Blr2, 9) = ws1.Cells(Ilr2, 9) - ws1.Cells(Elr2, 4)
    ws1.Range("G" & Blr2 & ":I" & Blr2).Font.Size = 14
    ws1.Range("G" & Blr2 & ":I" & Blr2).Font.Bold = True
    ws1.Range("G" & Blr2 & ":I" & Blr2).Font.Color = vbMagenta
'--------Print in to PDF
Fpath = "D:\Budget Project\Reports\Rpt-" & Mon.Value & "-" & Years.Value & ".PDF"
    ws1.Select
    ws1.ExportAsFixedFormat Type:=xlTypePDF, Filename:=Fpath, _
        Quality:=xlQualityStandard, IncludeDocProperties:=True, _
        IgnorePrintAreas:=False, OpenAfterPublish:=True

Exit Sub
ErrorHandler:
    MsgBox Err.Description
Resume Next
End Sub
```
--------------------------Code End-------------------------------------------------

**Code Explanation**

1. First step is to check whether the **Year** sheet is available in back end file. The for loop statement, compare the sheet name available in Back end file with the Selected Year and if it found, then assign to ws variable, otherwise it pops up a message "For this year Sheet is not Created"
2. Then it finds the Last row of **Year** sheet and clear all old sorting criteria.
3. Next step it clears the old contents of report sheet and format the report area with desired font name and font size.
4. Next step, a set of If condition statement compare the Selected month and get the column Index from Year sheet and assign to Col variable.
5. Next step it starts write the report content in **Report** Sheet and write the Month and Year in 1st row of "G" column.
6. The report has two section, at left it show all the expenses and at right it shows all the Income. Also the report sub divided in to main category section and list out all the sub category items with expenditure. The main category has two group Income and Expenses and the Mocde of Income category is 19 (Check your Main category), so it run the program in two section, like Mcode is not equal to 19 and equal to 19.
7. As a first run the Mcat value is zero and this will be compared to first record Mcode value. If it is not equal, then it run the code located in if conditions. It changes the Mcat value to Mcode value and get the Main Category Description

by find method. Then it writes that description in Report sheet and format it to bold, Blue color and higher font size.
8. Then it writes the Sub category code and description and month value in next line. Like that it continues and write all the expenses in the report sheet.
9. Same way it writes all the Income details in right side of report sheet
10. Next step, it find the last row of record in "A" column and add 2 to that and assign to Elr2 variable. Then it writes the "Total Expenses" text in "B" column and the Sum formula for Month and Year column. Then it formats that row with bold and Red color.
11. Same way it writes the total Income in right side income section.
12. Then it leaves two line and write the Balance amount by subtracting the Year expenses value from Year Income value.
13. Next step creating a file path by naming the folders and a file name with month and year and assign to Fpath variable.
14. Next step export the entire Report sheet to PDF format and show it window. That's all now our entire Application is completed. Here we may use some long route to utilize various function, that may be simplified after getting good experience.

# Annexure - Project Application Codes

## Dash Board Sheet

```
Private Sub AddPImage_Click()
   X = FileUpload(1, 0, 0, 0, 0)
   PanelImg.Picture = LoadPicture(X)
End Sub
------------------------------------------------------------------------
Private Sub CatFrm_Click()
   Category.Show
End Sub
------------------------------------------------------------------------
Private Sub Expenses_Click()
'---Activate Expenses Sheet
   Set ws1 = Sheets("Expenses")
   ws1.Visible = True
   ws1.Activate
   ws1.Sel2.Value = True
   Sheets("DashBoard").Visible = False
```

End Sub

---

Private Sub Quit_Click()
  Set wb = Workbooks("Home Budget-BE.xlsx")
  wb.Close savechanges:=True
  ThisWorkbook.Save
  Application.Quit
End Sub

---

Private Sub Refresh_Click()
  SummaryLoad   '-----Call function
End Sub

---

Private Sub Report_Click()
  Dim wb As Workbook
  Dim ws As Worksheet
  Dim Rng As Range

On Error GoTo ErrorHandler
  Set wb = Workbooks("Home Budget-BE.xlsx")
  For M = 1 To wb.Worksheets.Count
    If wb.Worksheets(M).Name = Years.Value Then
    Set ws = wb.Sheets(Years.Value)
    Exit For
  End If
  Next M

If i > wb.Worksheets.Count Then MsgBox "For this year Sheet is not Created": Exit Sub
Lr = ws.Cells(ws.Rows.Count, "B").End(xlUp).Row   '-----Last row of sheet
'--------------Sorting
On Error Resume Next
ws.ShowAllData
ws.Sort.SortFields.Clear
With ws.Sort
  .SortFields.Clear
  .SortFields.Add Key:=ws.Range("A1"), Order:=xlAscending
  .SortFields.Add Key:=ws.Range("B1"), Order:=xlAscending
  .SetRange ws.Range("A1:D" & Lr)
  .Header = xlYes
  .Apply
End With
Set ws1 = wb.Sheets("Report")
Set ws2 = wb.Sheets("Main Category")

```vba
Lr1 = ws1.Cells(ws1.Rows.Count, "B").End(xlUp).Row    '-----Last row of sheet
ws1.Range("A4:I200").Clear
ws1.Range("A4:I200").Font.Name = "Cambria"
ws1.Range("A4:I200").Font.Size = 12

'-----Month rabge
If Mon.Value = "Jan" Then Col = "D"
If Mon.Value = "Feb" Then Col = "E"
If Mon.Value = "Mar" Then Col = "F"
If Mon.Value = "Apr" Then Col = "G"
If Mon.Value = "May" Then Col = "H"
If Mon.Value = "Jun" Then Col = "I"
If Mon.Value = "Jul" Then Col = "J"
If Mon.Value = "Aug" Then Col = "K"
If Mon.Value = "Sep" Then Col = "L"
If Mon.Value = "Oct" Then Col = "M"
If Mon.Value = "Nov" Then Col = "N"
If Mon.Value = "Dec" Then Col = "O"

ws1.Cells(1, "G") = Mon.Value & " - " & Years.Value

Mcat = 0: R1 = 4: R2 = 4
For k = 2 To Lr    '-----Report sheet starting row at 3
If ws.Cells(k, 1) <> 19 Then
   If Mcat <> ws.Cells(k, 1) Then
      Mcat = ws.Cells(k, 1)
      X = ws2.Range("C:C").Cells.Find(Mcat).Row
      ws1.Cells(R1, 1).Value = ws2.Cells(X, 2).Value
      ws1.Cells(R1, 1).Font.Size = 14
      ws1.Cells(R1, 1).Font.Bold = True
      ws1.Cells(R1, 1).Font.Color = vbBlue
      R1 = R1 + 1
   End If

      ws1.Cells(R1, 1) = ws.Cells(k, 2)
      ws1.Cells(R1, 2) = ws.Cells(k, 3)
      ws1.Cells(R1, 3) = ws.Cells(k, Col)
      ws1.Cells(R1, 4) = ws.Cells(k, "P")
      R1 = R1 + 1
   End If

   If ws.Cells(k, 1) = 19 Then
```

```vb
      If R2 = 4 Then
        ws1.Cells(R2, 6).Value = "Income"
        ws1.Cells(R2, 6).Font.Size = 14
        ws1.Cells(R2, 6).Font.Bold = True
        ws1.Cells(R2, 6).Font.Color = vbBlue
        R2 = R2 + 1
      End If

      ws1.Cells(R2, 6) = ws.Cells(k, 2)
      ws1.Cells(R2, 7) = ws.Cells(k, 3)
      ws1.Cells(R2, 8) = ws.Cells(k, Col)
      ws1.Cells(R2, 9) = ws.Cells(k, "P")
      R2 = R2 + 1
    End If
  Next
'----Sum of expenses value
  Elr = ws1.Cells(ws1.Rows.Count, "A").End(xlUp).Row
  Elr2 = Elr + 2
  ws1.Cells(Elr2, 2) = "Total Expenses"
  ws1.Cells(Elr2, 3) = "=Sum(" & "C4:C" & Elr & ")"
  ws1.Cells(Elr2, 4) = "=Sum(" & "D4:D" & Elr & ")"
  ws1.Range("B" & Elr2 & ":D" & Elr2).Font.Size = 14
  ws1.Range("B" & Elr2 & ":D" & Elr2).Font.Bold = True
  ws1.Range("B" & Elr2 & ":D" & Elr2).Font.Color = vbRed
'----Sum of total value
  Ilr = ws1.Cells(ws1.Rows.Count, "F").End(xlUp).Row
  Ilr2 = Ilr + 2
  ws1.Cells(Ilr2, 7) = "Total Income"
  ws1.Cells(Ilr2, 8) = "=Sum(" & "H4:H" & Ilr & ")"
  ws1.Cells(Ilr2, 9) = "=Sum(" & "I4:I" & Ilr & ")"
  ws1.Range("G" & Ilr2 & ":I" & Ilr2).Font.Size = 14
  ws1.Range("G" & Ilr2 & ":I" & Ilr2).Font.Bold = True
  ws1.Range("G" & Ilr2 & ":I" & Ilr2).Font.Color = vbRed

'-----Balance on year
  Blr2 = Ilr2 + 2
  ws1.Cells(Blr2, 7) = "Balance Amount"
  ws1.Cells(Blr2, 9) = ws1.Cells(Ilr2, 9) - ws1.Cells(Elr2, 4)
  ws1.Range("G" & Blr2 & ":I" & Blr2).Font.Size = 14
  ws1.Range("G" & Blr2 & ":I" & Blr2).Font.Bold = True
  ws1.Range("G" & Blr2 & ":I" & Blr2).Font.Color = vbMagenta
'--------Print in to PDF
  Fpath = "D:\Budget Project\Reports\Rpt-" & Mon.Value & "-" & Years.Value & ".PDF"
```

```vb
    ws1.Select
    ws1.ExportAsFixedFormat Type:=xlTypePDF, Filename:=Fpath,_
        Quality:=xlQualityStandard, IncludeDocProperties:=True,_
        IgnorePrintAreas:=False, OpenAfterPublish:=True

Exit Sub
ErrorHandler:
    MsgBox Err.Description
Resume Next
End Sub
'----------------------------------------------------------------------------
Private Sub Worksheet_Activate()
    '---------Year
    yr = Year(Date) - 2
    Years.Clear
    For k = 1 To 5
        Years.AddItem yr + k
    Next
    Years.Value = yr + 2
    '--------Month
    Dim Months As Variant
    Months = Array("Jan", "Feb", "Mar", "Apr", "May", "Jun", "Jul", "Aug", "Sep", "Oct", "Nov", "Dec")
    Mon.Clear
    Mon.List = Months
    Mon.Text = MonthName(Month(Date), True)

    SummaryLoad    '-----Call function
End Sub
'----------------------------------------------------------------------------
Private Sub SummaryLoad()
    Dim wb As Workbook
    Dim ws As Worksheet
    Dim Rng As Range

On Error GoTo ErrorHandler
    Set wb = Workbooks("Home Budget-BE.xlsx")
    Set ws = wb.Sheets("Main Category")
    Set ws1 = Sheets("Dashboard")
    ' Set ws2 = wb.Sheets(Years.Value)
    For i = 1 To wb.Worksheets.Count
        If wb.Worksheets(i).Name = Years.Value Then
        Set ws2 = wb.Sheets(Years.Value)
        Exit For
```

```
        End If
    Next i
     If i > wb.Worksheets.Count Then MsgBox "For this year Sheet is not Created": Exit Sub


    Lr = ws.Cells(ws.Rows.Count, "B").End(xlUp).Row      '-----Last row of sheet
    Lr1 = ws2.Cells(ws2.Rows.Count, "B").End(xlUp).Row      '-----Last row of sheet

    On Error Resume Next
    ws.ShowAllData
    ws.Sort.SortFields.Clear

    '--------------Sorting
    ws.AutoFilter.Sort.SortFields.Add    Key:=Range("C2:C"    &    Lr),    SortOn:=xlSortOnValues,
Order:=xlAscending, DataOption:=xlSortNormal
    With ws.AutoFilter.Sort
        .Header = xlYes
        .MatchCase = False
        .Orientation = xlTopToBottom
        .SortMethod = xlPinYin
        .Apply
    End With


    ws1.Range("A5:D17").ClearContents
    '-----Month rabge
    If Mon.Value = "Jan" Then Set Rng = ws2.Range("D2:D" & Lr1)
    If Mon.Value = "Feb" Then Set Rng = ws2.Range("E2:E" & Lr1)
    If Mon.Value = "Mar" Then Set Rng = ws2.Range("F2:F" & Lr1)
    If Mon.Value = "Apr" Then Set Rng = ws2.Range("G2:G" & Lr1)
    If Mon.Value = "May" Then Set Rng = ws2.Range("H2:H" & Lr1)
    If Mon.Value = "Jun" Then Set Rng = ws2.Range("I2:I" & Lr1)
    If Mon.Value = "Jul" Then Set Rng = ws2.Range("J2:J" & Lr1)
    If Mon.Value = "Aug" Then Set Rng = ws2.Range("K2:K" & Lr1)
    If Mon.Value = "Sep" Then Set Rng = ws2.Range("L2:L" & Lr1)
    If Mon.Value = "Oct" Then Set Rng = ws2.Range("M2:M" & Lr1)
    If Mon.Value = "Nov" Then Set Rng = ws2.Range("N2:N" & Lr1)
    If Mon.Value = "Dec" Then Set Rng = ws2.Range("O2:O" & Lr1)


    For k = 3 To Lr     '-----MAin category Starting row at 4
        k1 = k + 2     '-----Dash board starting row
        If ws.Cells(k, "C").Value <> 19 Then
```

```
        ws1.Cells(k1, 2) = ws.Cells(k, 3)
        ws1.Cells(k1, 3) = ws.Cells(k, 2)
        ws1.Cells(k1, 4) = WorksheetFunction.SumIf(ws2.Range("A2:A" & Lr1), ws.Cells(k, 3), Rng)
        ws1.Cells(k1, 5) = WorksheetFunction.SumIf(ws2.Range("A2:A" & Lr1), ws.Cells(k, 3), ws2.Range("P2:P" & Lr1))
      End If
   Next

    ws1.Cells(18, 4) = WorksheetFunction.SumIf(ws2.Range("Q2:Q" & Lr1), "Income", ws2.Range("P2:P" & Lr1))



Exit Sub
ErrorHandler:
   MsgBox Err.Description
Resume Next
End Sub
```

---

# Expenses Sheet

```
Private Sub Bill_Click()
    Set ws = ActiveWorkbook.Sheets("Expenses")
    Lr = ws.Cells(ws.Rows.Count, "C").End(xlUp).Row
    SR = ActiveCell.Row
    If SR > Lr + 1 Then MsgBox "Select the Row Which Has Data": Exit Sub
    If SR < 4 Then MsgBox "Select the Row Which Has Data": Exit Sub
    Bills.Show
End Sub
```
---
```
Private Sub Home_Click()
   Sheets("DashBoard").Visible = True
   Sheets("DashBoard").Select
   ActiveWorkbook.Sheets("Expenses").Visible = False
End Sub
```
---
```
Private Sub MainCat_Change()
   Dim wb As Workbook
   Dim ws As Worksheet
If MainCat.Value <> "" Then
   Set wb = Workbooks("Home Budget-BE.xlsx")
   Set ws = wb.Sheets("Sub Category")
   Set ws1 = wb.Sheets(Years.Value)
```

```vba
    Set ws2 = wb.Sheets("Bills")
'----------Extract data from Sub category
    On Error Resume Next
    ws.ShowAllData
    ws.Sort.SortFields.Clear
    Lr = ws.Cells(ws.Rows.Count, "C").End(xlUp).Row
    Set Rng = ws.Range("A2:C" & Lr)

    '--------------Sorting
    Rng.Sort   Key1:=Range("C2"),   Key2:=Range("D2"),   Header:=xlYes,   Order1:=xlAscending, Order2:=xlAscending
    '--------------Filter
    ws.Range("A2:C" & Lr).AutoFilter Field:=3, Criteria1:=MainCat.Value
    Set Rng = ws.Range("B3:B" & Lr).SpecialCells(xlCellTypeVisible)
    Rcnt = Rng.Count
'------Add Sub Category to sheet
    ActiveSheet.Range("A4:E100").Clear
    k = 4
    For Each Cel In Rng
        Cells(k, 3) = Cel
        Cells(k, 1) = Cel.Offset(, 1)
        Cells(k, 2) = Cel.Offset(, 2)
        X = 0
        '-----Cost
          On Error Resume Next
          X = ws1.Range("B:B").Cells.Find(Cells(k, "B").Value).Row
          If X > 0 Then
            If Mon.Value = "Jan" Then Cells(k, "D").Value = ws1.Cells(X, "D").Value
            If Mon.Value = "Feb" Then Cells(k, "D").Value = ws1.Cells(X, "E").Value
            If Mon.Value = "Mar" Then Cells(k, "D").Value = ws1.Cells(X, "F").Value
            If Mon.Value = "Apr" Then Cells(k, "D").Value = ws1.Cells(X, "G").Value
            If Mon.Value = "May" Then Cells(k, "D").Value = ws1.Cells(X, "H").Value
            If Mon.Value = "Jun" Then Cells(k, "D").Value = ws1.Cells(X, "I").Value
            If Mon.Value = "Jul" Then Cells(k, "D").Value = ws1.Cells(X, "J").Value
            If Mon.Value = "Aug" Then Cells(k, "D").Value = ws1.Cells(X, "K").Value
            If Mon.Value = "Sep" Then Cells(k, "D").Value = ws1.Cells(X, "L").Value
            If Mon.Value = "Oct" Then Cells(k, "D").Value = ws1.Cells(X, "M").Value
            If Mon.Value = "Nov" Then Cells(k, "D").Value = ws1.Cells(X, "N").Value
            If Mon.Value = "Dec" Then Cells(k, "D").Value = ws1.Cells(X, "O").Value
          End If
          '-----Bills attached count
          Lr1 = ws2.Cells(ws2.Rows.Count, "D").End(xlUp).Row
```

```vb
        Z = WorksheetFunction.CountIfs(ws2.Range("A2:A" & Lr1), Years.Value, ws2.Range("B2:B" _
& Lr1), Mon.Value, ws2.Range("D2:D" & Lr1), Cells(k, "B").Value)
        If Z > 0 Then Cells(k, "E").Value = Z



    k = k + 1
  Next
End If
End Sub
-------------------------------------------------------------------------------------------
Private Sub Mon_Change()
  '-------Clear Sheet data
  Dim wb As Workbook
  Dim ws As Worksheet
  Set wb = Workbooks("Home Budget-FE.xlsm")
  Set ws = wb.Sheets("Expenses")
  ws.Range("A4:D100").Clear
  MainCat = ""
End Sub
-------------------------------------------------------------------------------------------
Private Sub Save_Click()
  Dim wb As Workbook
  Dim ws As Worksheet
  Set wb = Workbooks("Home Budget-BE.xlsx")
  Set ws = wb.Sheets(Years.Value)
  Set ws1 = Sheets("Expenses")
  Lr1 = ws1.Cells(ws1.Rows.Count, "C").End(xlUp).Row
  For k = 4 To Lr1
    If ws1.Cells(k, "D").Value > 0 Then
      On Error Resume Next
      X = 0
      X = ws.Range("B:B").Cells.Find(ws1.Cells(k, "B").Value).Row
      If X > 0 Then
        Y = X
      Else
        Lr = ws.Cells(ws.Rows.Count, "C").End(xlUp).Row
        Y = Lr + 1
        ws.Cells(Y, 1) = ws1.Cells(k, 1)
        ws.Cells(Y, 2) = ws1.Cells(k, 2)
        ws.Cells(Y, 3) = ws1.Cells(k, 3)
        ws.Cells(Y, "P") = "=Sum(D" & Y & ":O" & Y & ")"
        If Sel1.Value = True Then ws.Cells(Y, "Q") = "Income"
        If Sel2.Value = True Then ws.Cells(Y, "Q") = "Expenses"
```

```vb
            End If
        
            '---------Month cost
                If Mon.Value = "Jan" Then ws.Cells(Y, "D").Value = ws1.Cells(k, "D").Value
                If Mon.Value = "Feb" Then ws.Cells(Y, "E").Value = ws1.Cells(k, "D").Value
                If Mon.Value = "Mar" Then ws.Cells(Y, "F").Value = ws1.Cells(k, "D").Value
                If Mon.Value = "Apr" Then ws.Cells(Y, "G").Value = ws1.Cells(k, "D").Value
                If Mon.Value = "May" Then ws.Cells(Y, "H").Value = ws1.Cells(k, "D").Value
                If Mon.Value = "Jun" Then ws.Cells(Y, "I").Value = ws1.Cells(k, "D").Value
                If Mon.Value = "Jul" Then ws.Cells(Y, "J").Value = ws1.Cells(k, "D").Value
                If Mon.Value = "Aug" Then ws.Cells(Y, "K").Value = ws1.Cells(k, "D").Value
                If Mon.Value = "Sep" Then ws.Cells(Y, "L").Value = ws1.Cells(k, "D").Value
                If Mon.Value = "Oct" Then ws.Cells(Y, "M").Value = ws1.Cells(k, "D").Value
                If Mon.Value = "Nov" Then ws.Cells(Y, "N").Value = ws1.Cells(k, "D").Value
                If Mon.Value = "Dec" Then ws.Cells(Y, "O").Value = ws1.Cells(k, "D").Value
    
        End If
    Next
End Sub
'---------------------------------------------------------------------------------------
Private Sub Sel1_Click()
    GroupSel (1)
End Sub
'---------------------------------------------------------------------------------------
Private Sub Sel2_Click()
    GroupSel (2)
End Sub
'---------------------------------------------------------------------------------------
Private Sub Worksheet_Activate()
'---------Year
    yr = Year(Date) - 2
    Years.Clear
    For k = 1 To 5
        Years.AddItem yr + k
    Next
    Years.Value = yr + 2
    '--------Month
    Dim Months As Variant
    Months = Array("Jan", "Feb", "Mar", "Apr", "May", "Jun", "Jul", "Aug", "Sep", "Oct", "Nov", "Dec")
    Mon.Clear
    Mon.List = Months
    Mon.Text = MonthName(Month(Date), True)
    GroupSel (2) '---Calling Function
```

```vba
End Sub
Private Sub Iyear_Click()
    Dim wb As Workbook
    Dim ws As Worksheet
'--------Find work sheet
    Set wb = Workbooks("Home Budget-BE.xlsx")

    If Years = "" Then MsgBox "Select Year": Exit Sub
    For Each sht In wb.Worksheets
        If sht.Name = Years.Value Then
            MsgBox "Already Work sheet is Avilable for this year"
            Exit Sub
        End If
    Next

'---------Create a Sheet with format
    wb.Sheets.Add(After:=wb.Sheets(wb.Sheets.Count)).Name = Years.Value
    Set ws = wb.Sheets(Years.Value)
    ws.Activate
    ws.Range("A1").Value = "MID"
    ws.Range("B1").Value = "SID"
    ws.Range("C1").Value = "Description"
    ws.Range("D1").Value = "Jan"
    ws.Range("E1").Value = "Feb"
    ws.Range("F1").Value = "Mar"
    ws.Range("G1").Value = "Apr"
    ws.Range("H1").Value = "May"
    ws.Range("I1").Value = "Jun"
    ws.Range("J1").Value = "Jul"
    ws.Range("K1").Value = "Aug"
    ws.Range("L1").Value = "Sep"
    ws.Range("M1").Value = "Oct"
    ws.Range("N1").Value = "Nov"
    ws.Range("O1").Value = "Dec"
    ws.Range("P1").Value = "Total"
    ws.Range("Q1").Value = "Group"
    ws.Columns("A:B").ColumnWidth = 10
    ws.Columns("C:C").ColumnWidth = 50
    ws.Columns("D:Q").ColumnWidth = 10

    ws.Range("A1:Q1").Select
    With Selection.Font
        .Name = "Cambria"
```

```
      .Size = 14
      .Bold = True
   End With
   With Selection
      .HorizontalAlignment = xlCenter
      .VerticalAlignment = xlCenter
   End With
   With Selection.Interior
      .Pattern = xlSolid
      .PatternColorIndex = xlAutomatic
      .Color = RGB(254, 246, 91)
   End With
   ws.Range("A1:Q1").Borders.LineStyle = xlContinuous

   ActiveWindow.WindowState = xlMinimized
End Sub
------------------------------------------------------------------------------
Private Sub Years_Change()
Dim wb As Workbook
   Dim ws As Worksheet
'--------Find work sheet
   Set wb = Workbooks("Home Budget-BE.xlsx")
   If Years <> "" Then
      For Each sht In wb.Worksheets
         If sht.Name = Years.Value Then Exit Sub
      Next

   MsgBox "For this year Sheet is not avilable in Back End Excel" & Chr(13) & "Create the Sheet By Clicking Insert Sheet button"
   End If
   '-------Clear Sheet data
   Sheets("Expenses").Range("A4:D100").Clear
End Sub
------------------------------------------------------------------------------
Public Sub GroupSel(X As Integer)
'----Load list to MainCat combo box
   Set wb = Workbooks("Home Budget-BE.xlsx")
   Set ws = wb.Sheets("Main Category")
   Set ws1 = Sheets("Expenses")
   ws1.Range("A4:D100").Clear
   ws1.MainCat.Clear
   Lr = ws.Cells(ws.Rows.Count, "C").End(xlUp).Row
   ws.Range("A3:D" & Lr).Sort Key1:=ws.Range("B3:B" & Lr), Order1:=xlAscending, Header:=xlNo
```

```
    ws1.MainCat.ColumnCount = 2
    ws1.MainCat.ColumnWidths = "160 pt; 40Pt"
    k = 0: k1 = 0
    For M = 3 To Lr
        If X = 1 Then
            If ws.Cells(M, 1) = "Income" Then
                ws1.MainCat.AddItem
                ws1.MainCat.List(k, 0) = ws.Cells(M, 2).Value
                ws1.MainCat.List(k, 1) = ws.Cells(M, 3).Value
                k = k + 1
            End If
        End If

        If X = 2 Then
            If ws.Cells(M, 1) = "Expenses" Then
                ws1.MainCat.AddItem
                ws1.MainCat.List(k, 0) = ws.Cells(M, 2).Value
                ws1.MainCat.List(k, 1) = ws.Cells(M, 3).Value
                k = k + 1
            End If
        End If
    Next
End Sub
```

---

# This Work Book

```
Dim wb As Workbook
```
---
```
Private Sub Workbook_Open()
    ActiveWorkbook.Sheets("Dashboard").Activate
'------------Open Database file
    Dim wb As Workbook
    Fpath = "D:\Budget Project\Application File\Home Budget-BE.xlsx"
    Set wb = Workbooks.Open(Fpath)
    ActiveWindow.WindowState = xlMinimized
End Sub
```

---

# Forms

## Bills

```
Dim Bdata() As Variant
```
---

```vb
Private Sub NextR_Click()
    If R2.Value = "" Then MsgBox "First Select the Main Category": Exit Sub
    If Int(R2.Value) = 1 Then MsgBox "Last Record": Exit Sub
    R2.Value = Int(R2.Value) - 1
    R1.Value = R1.Value + 1
    TB2.Value = Bdata(1, R1.Value)
    TB3.Value = Bdata(2, R1.Value)
End Sub
'--------------------------------------------------------------------------------
Private Sub OpenBill_Click()
    Fpath = TB3.Value
    Shell "Explorer.exe " & Fpath, vbMaximizedFocus
End Sub
'--------------------------------------------------------------------------------
Private Sub Prev_Click()
    If R1.Value = "" Then MsgBox "First Select the Main Category": Exit Sub
    If R1.Value = 1 Then MsgBox "First Record": Exit Sub
    R1.Value = R1.Value - 1
    R2.Value = R2.Value + 1
    TB2.Value = Bdata(1, R1.Value)
    TB3.Value = Bdata(2, R1.Value)
End Sub
'--------------------------------------------------------------------------------
Private Sub Upd_Click()
    Dim sc, yr, mn, opt As Variant
    Dim wb As Workbook
    Dim ws As Worksheet
    If TB1.Value = "" Or IsEmpty(TB1.Value) Then MsgBox "Fill the Bill Note": Exit Sub
    Set wb = Workbooks("Home Budget-BE.xlsx")
    Set ws = wb.Sheets("Bills")
    Lr = ws.Cells(ws.Rows.Count, "C").End(xlUp).Row
    Y = Lr + 1
'------Call Image upload function
    sc = LB2.Caption
    yr = LB4.Caption
    mn = LB5.Caption
    opt = 2
    Rn = Y
    X = FileUpload(opt, sc, yr, mn, Rn)
'---Save record to Back end file
    ws.Cells(Y, 1) = LB4.Caption
    ws.Cells(Y, 2) = LB5.Caption
    ws.Cells(Y, 3) = LB1.Caption
```

```vba
        ws.Cells(Y, 4) = LB2.Caption
        ws.Cells(Y, 5) = LB3.Caption
        ws.Cells(Y, 6) = TB1.Value
        ws.Cells(Y, 7) = X
        
        MsgBox "File Uploaded"
End Sub
'--------------------------------------------------------------------------------
Private Sub UserForm_Initialize()
    Dim wb As Workbook
    Dim ws, ws1 As Worksheet
    Dim SR As Integer
    Set ws1 = ActiveWorkbook.Sheets("Expenses")
    ws1.Select
    SR = ActiveCell.Row
    '--------Get value from sheet and assign to Label
    LB1 = ws1.Cells(SR, 1)
    LB2 = ws1.Cells(SR, 2)
    LB3 = ws1.Cells(SR, 3)
    LB4 = Sheets("Expenses").Years.Value
    LB5 = Sheets("Expenses").Mon.Value
    Set wb = Workbooks("Home Budget-BE.xlsx")
    Set ws = wb.Sheets("Bills")
    On Error Resume Next
    ws.ShowAllData
    ws.Sort.SortFields.Clear
    Lr = ws.Cells(ws.Rows.Count, "D").End(xlUp).Row
    Set Rng = ws.Range("A2:F" & Lr)
    '--------------Sorting
    Rng.Sort Key1:=Range("A1"), Key2:=Range("B1"), key3:=Range("D1"), Header:=xlYes
    '--------------Filter
    ws.Range("A1:F" & Lr).AutoFilter Field:=1, Criteria1:=LB4.Caption
    ws.Range("A1:F" & Lr).AutoFilter Field:=2, Criteria1:=LB5.Caption
    ws.Range("A1:F" & Lr).AutoFilter Field:=4, Criteria1:=LB2.Caption
    
    Set Rng = ws.Range("F2:F" & Lr).SpecialCells(xlCellTypeVisible)
    Rcnt = Rng.Count
    ReDim Bdata(2, Rcnt)
    k = 1
    For Each Cel In Rng
        Bdata(1, k) = Cel
        Bdata(2, k) = Cel.Offset(, 1)
        k = k + 1
```

```
    Next

    TB2.Value = Bdata(1, 1)
    TB3.Value = Bdata(2, 1)
    R1.Value = 1
    R2.Value = Rcnt
End Sub
```
---

## Category form

```
Dim Data1() As Variant
```
---
```
Private Sub Add_Click()
    Group.Value = ""
    TB1.Value = ""
    TB2.Value = ""
End Sub
```
---
```
Private Sub AddNew_Click()
    TB3.Value = Group.Value
    TB4.Value = ""
    TB5.Value = ""
    TB6.Value = TB2.Value
End Sub
```
---
```
Private Sub Group_Change()
If TB2.Value = "" Then
    '----Find last number of Code
    Set wb = Workbooks("Home Budget-BE.xlsx")
    Set ws = wb.Sheets("Main Category")
    X = Application.WorksheetFunction.Max(ws.Range("C:C"))
    If IsNull(X) = True Or X = 0 Then Y = 10
    If X > 1 Then Y = X + 1
    TB2.Value = Y
End If

End Sub
```
---
```
Private Sub Mcat_Change()
If Mcat.Value <> "" Then
'----------Main category
    Group.Value = Mcat.Column(0)
    TB1.Value = Mcat.Column(1)
```

```vb
    TB2.Value = Mcat.Column(2)
'---------Sub category
    TB3.Value = Mcat.Column(0)
    TB6.Value = Mcat.Column(2)
'--------Call GetRec sub procedure
    Getrec
End If
End Sub
'----------------------------------------------------------------------
Private Sub Getrec()
Dim ws As Worksheet
On Error GoTo ErrorHandler
    Set wb = Workbooks("Home Budget-BE.xlsx")
    Set ws = wb.Sheets("Sub Category")
On Error Resume Next
    ws.ShowAllData
    ws.Sort.SortFields.Clear
    Lr = ws.Cells(ws.Rows.Count, "B").End(xlUp).Row    '-----Last row of sheet

    '--------------Sorting
    ws.AutoFilter.Sort.SortFields.Add   Key:=Range("C2:D"   &   Lr),   SortOn:=xlSortOnValues, Order:=xlAscending, DataOption:=xlSortNormal
    With ws.AutoFilter.Sort
        .Header = xlYes
        .MatchCase = False
        .Orientation = xlTopToBottom
        .SortMethod = xlPinYin
        .Apply
    End With
    '--------------Filter
    ws.Range("A2:D" & Lr).AutoFilter Field:=3, Criteria1:=TB2.Value
    Set Rng = ws.Range("B3:B" & Lr).SpecialCells(xlCellTypeVisible)
    Rcnt = Rng.Count
    ReDim Data1(2, Rcnt)
    k = 1
    For Each Cel In Rng
        Data1(1, k) = Cel
        Data1(2, k) = Cel.Offset(, 2)
        k = k + 1
    Next

    TB4.Value = Data1(1, 1)
    TB5.Value = Data1(2, 1)
```

```vb
    R1.Value = 0
    R2.Value = Rcnt

Exit Sub
ErrorHandler:
   MsgBox Err.Description
Resume Next
End Sub
'--------------------------------------------------------------------------
Private Sub NextRec_Click()
  If R2.Value = "" Then MsgBox "First Select the Main Category": Exit Sub
  If Int(R2.Value) = 0 Then MsgBox "Last Record": Exit Sub
  X = WorksheetFunction.Count(Data1)
  If Int(R2.Value) <= X Then R2.Value = Int(R2.Value) - 1

  R1.Value = R1.Value + 1
  TB4.Value = Data1(1, R1.Value)
  TB5.Value = Data1(2, R1.Value)
End Sub
'--------------------------------------------------------------------------
Private Sub PreRec_Click()
   If R1.Value = "" Then MsgBox "First Select the Main Category": Exit Sub
   If R1.Value = 0 Then MsgBox "First Record": Exit Sub
   R1.Value = R1.Value - 1
   R2.Value = R2.Value + 1
   If R1.Value = 0 Then TB4.Value = Data1(1, 1) Else TB4.Value = Data1(1, R1.Value)
   If R1.Value = 0 Then TB5.Value = Data1(2, 1) Else TB5.Value = Data1(2, R1.Value)
End Sub
'--------------------------------------------------------------------------
Private Sub Save1_Click()
'--------Validation check
   If Group.Value = "" Then MsgBox "Enter Group fieled": Exit Sub
   If TB1.Value = "" Then MsgBox "Enter Data to Description fieled": Exit Sub
   If TB2.Value = "" Then MsgBox "Enter Data to MCode fieled": Exit Sub
   Set wb = Workbooks("Home Budget-BE.xlsx")
   Set ws = wb.Sheets("Main Category")
   Lr = ws.Cells(ws.Rows.Count, "C").End(xlUp).Row
   X = 0
   On Error Resume Next
   X = ws.Range("C:C").Cells.Find(TB2.Value).Row

   If X > 0 Then
    ws.Cells(X, 1) = Group.Value
```

```vba
      ws.Cells(X, 2) = TB1.Value
   Else
      ws.Cells(Lr + 1, 1) = Group.Value
      ws.Cells(Lr + 1, 2) = TB1.Value
      ws.Cells(Lr + 1, 3) = TB2.Value
   End If
   MsgBox "Record Saved"
End Sub
```
---
```vba
Private Sub Save2_Click()
'--------Validation check
   If TB3.Value = "" Then MsgBox "First select the Main category": Exit Sub
   If TB4.Value = "" Then MsgBox "Enter Data to Description fieled": Exit Sub

   Set wb = Workbooks("Home Budget-BE.xlsx")
   Set ws = wb.Sheets("Sub Category")
   Lr = ws.Cells(ws.Rows.Count, "C").End(xlUp).Row
   X = 0
   On Error Resume Next
   X = ws.Range("D:D").Cells.Find(TB5.Value).Row

   If X > 0 Then
      ws.Cells(X, 2) = TB4.Value
   Else
      ws.Cells(Lr + 1, 1) = TB3.Value
      ws.Cells(Lr + 1, 2) = TB4.Value
      ws.Cells(Lr + 1, 3) = TB6.Value
      ws.Cells(Lr + 1, 4) = TB5.Value

   End If
   MsgBox "Record Saved"
   Getrec   '---Call procedure
End Sub
```
---
```vba
Private Sub TB4_Change()
   If TB5.Value = "" Then
   '----Find last number of Code
   Set wb = Workbooks("Home Budget-BE.xlsx")
   Set ws = wb.Sheets("Sub Category")
   X = Application.WorksheetFunction.Max(ws.Range("D:D"))
   If IsNull(X) = True Or X = 0 Then Y = 100
   If X > 1 Then Y = X + 1
   TB5.Value = Y
```

```vba
    End If
End Sub
-------------------------------------------------------------------------
Private Sub UserForm_Initialize()
    Dim wb As Workbook
    Dim ws As Worksheet
    '----Fill category Drop down list
    Set wb = Workbooks("Home Budget-BE.xlsx")
    Set ws = wb.Sheets("Main Category")
    Lr = ws.Cells(ws.Rows.Count, "C").End(xlUp).Row
    ws.Range("A2:D" & Lr).Sort Key1:=ws.Range("B2:B" & Lr), Order1:=xlAscending, Header:=xlNo
    Mcat.Clear
    Mcat.List = ws.Range("A3:C100").Value
    
    '----Fill list to Group
    Group.AddItem "Income"
    Group.AddItem "Expenses"
End Sub
-------------------------------------------------------------------------
```

## Module1

```vba
Public Function FileUpload(opt, sc, yr, mn, Rn As Variant)
    Dim fDialog As Office.FileDialog
    Dim varFile As Variant
    Dim strPath, copyfile As String

On Error GoTo HandleError
    Set fDialog = Application.FileDialog(msoFileDialogFilePicker) 'Set File Dialogue box.
    With fDialog
        .AllowMultiSelect = False    '---Not allow multiple selections in the  dialog box.
        .Title = "Select Image File to Upload"  '--- Set the title of the dialog box.
        .Filters.Clear         '--- Clear out the current filters, and then add your own.
        .Filters.Add "Image Files", "*.JPG; *.JPEG; *.PNG; *.PDF"
        '-Filter setting will filter the file in the selected folder to our desired file type by
        '-extension we mentioned in that line. Also it shows the Heading as Image files
        '-as specified in the code.
        If .Show = True Then
            For Each varFile In .SelectedItems
                strPath = varFile
            Next
        Else
            MsgBox "You Have not selected any File Process Canceled."
            Exit Function
```

```
        End If
    End With
    ext = Right(strPath, Len(strPath) - InStrRev(strPath, "."))   '---Get file extension
    '-------Store the file based on option parameter passed to this procedure
    If opt = 1 Then         '-------for Panel Image file Option
        copyfile = "D:\Budget Project\Images\General\Panel-Img." & ext
    End If
    If opt = 2 Then         '-------for Bill file
        Fname = "Bill-" & yr & mn & sc & Rn & "." & ext
        copyfile = "D:\Budget Project\Images\Bills\" & Fname
    End If
'----------Copy file to folder
    FileCopy strPath, copyfile
    FileUpload = copyfile
Exit Function
HandleError:
    MsgBox Err.Description
End Function
```
-------------------------------------------------------------------------

# Annexure – VBA Inbuilt function List

| In-Built Function | Pupose |
|---|---|
| **Lookup/Ref Functions** | |
| ADDRESS (WS) | Returns a text representation of a cell address |
| AREAS (WS) | Returns the number of ranges in a reference |
| CHOOSE (WS, VBA) | Returns a value from a list of values based on a given position |
| COLUMN (WS) | Returns the column number of a cell reference |
| COLUMNS (WS) | Returns the number of columns in a cell reference |
| HLOOKUP (WS) | Performs a horizontal lookup by searching for a value in the top row of the table and returning the value in the same column based on the index_number |
| HYPERLINK (WS) | Creates a shortcut to a file or Internet address |
| INDEX (WS) | Returns either the value or the reference to a value from a table or range |
| INDIRECT (WS) | Returns the reference to a cell based on its string representation |
| LOOKUP (WS) | Returns a value from a range (one row or one column) or from an array |
| MATCH (WS) | Searches for a value in an array and returns the relative position of that item |
| OFFSET (WS) | Returns a reference to a range that is offset a number of rows and columns |
| ROW (WS) | Returns the row number of a cell reference |
| ROWS (WS) | Returns the number of rows in a cell reference |
| TRANSPOSE (WS) | Returns a transposed range of cells |
| VLOOKUP (WS) | Performs a vertical lookup by searching for a value in the first column of a table and returning the value in the same row in the index_number position |
| XLOOKUP (WS) | Performs a lookup (either vertical or horizontal) |

| | |
|---|---|
| **String/Text Functions** | |
| ASC (VBA) | Returns ASCII value of a character |
| BAHTTEXT (WS) | Returns the number in Thai text |
| CHAR (WS) | Returns the character based on the ASCII |

| | |
|---|---|
| | value |
| CHR (VBA) | Returns the character based on the ASCII value |
| CLEAN (WS) | Removes all nonprintable characters from a string |
| CODE (WS) | Returns the ASCII value of a character or the first character in a cell |
| CONCAT (WS) | Used to join 2 or more strings together |
| CONCATENATE (WS) | Used to join 2 or more strings together (replaced by CONCAT Function) |
| CONCATENATE with & (WS, VBA) | Used to join 2 or more strings together using the & operator |
| DOLLAR (WS) | Converts a number to text, using a currency format |
| EXACT (WS) | Compares two strings and returns TRUE if both values are the same |
| FIND (WS) | Returns the location of a substring in a string (case-sensitive) |
| FIXED (WS) | Returns a text representation of a number rounded to a specified number of decimal places |
| FORMAT STRINGS (VBA) | Takes a string expression and returns it as a formatted string |
| INSTR (VBA) | Returns the position of the first occurrence of a substring in a string |
| INSTRREV (VBA) | Returns the position of the first occurrence of a string in another string, starting from the end of the string |
| LCASE (VBA) | Converts a string to lowercase |
| LEFT (WS, VBA) | Extract a substring from a string, starting from the left-most character |
| LEN (WS, VBA) | Returns the length of the specified string |
| LOWER (WS) | Converts all letters in the specified string to lowercase |
| LTRIM (VBA) | Removes leading spaces from a string |
| MID (WS, VBA) | Extracts a substring from a string (starting at any position) |
| NUMBERVALUE (WS) | Returns a text to a number specifying the decimal and group separators |
| PROPER (WS) | Sets the first character in each word to uppercase and the rest to lowercase |
| REPLACE (WS) | Replaces a sequence of characters in a string with another set of characters |
| REPLACE (VBA) | Replaces a sequence of characters in a string with another set of characters |

| Function | Description |
|---|---|
| REPT (WS) | Returns a repeated text value a specified number of times |
| RIGHT (WS, VBA) | Extracts a substring from a string starting from the right-most character |
| RTRIM (VBA) | Removes trailing spaces from a string |
| SEARCH (WS) | Returns the location of a substring in a string |
| SPACE (VBA) | Returns a string with a specified number of spaces |
| SPLIT (VBA) | Used to split a string into substrings based on a delimiter |
| STR (VBA) | Returns a string representation of a number |
| STRCOMP (VBA) | Returns an integer value representing the result of a string comparison |
| STRCONV (VBA) | Returns a string converted to uppercase, lowercase, proper case or Unicode |
| STRREVERSE (VBA) | Returns a string whose characters are in reverse order |
| SUBSTITUTE (WS) | Replaces a set of characters with another |
| T (WS) | Returns the text referred to by a value |
| TEXT (WS) | Returns a value converted to text with a specified format |
| TEXTJOIN (WS) | Used to join 2 or more strings together separated by a delimiter |
| TRIM (WS, VBA) | Returns a text value with the leading and trailing spaces removed |
| UCASE (VBA) | Converts a string to all uppercase |
| UNICHAR (WS) | Returns the Unicode character based on the Unicode number provided |
| UNICODE (WS) | Returns the Unicode number of a character or the first character in a string |
| UPPER (WS) | Convert text to all uppercase |
| VAL (VBA) | Returns the numbers found in a string |
| VALUE (WS) | Converts a text value that represents a number to a number |

| Date/Time Functions | |
|---|---|
| DATE (WS) | Returns the serial date value for a date |
| DATE (VBA) | Returns the current system date |
| DATEADD (VBA) | Returns a date after which a certain time/date interval has been added |
| DATEDIF (WS) | Returns the difference between two date values, based on the interval specified |

| | |
|---|---|
| DATEDIFF (VBA) | Returns the difference between two date values, based on the interval specified |
| DATEPART (VBA) | Returns a specified part of a given date |
| DATESERIAL (VBA) | Returns a date given a year, month, and day value |
| DATEVALUE (WS, VBA) | Returns the serial number of a date |
| DAY (WS, VBA) | Returns the day of the month (a number from 1 to 31) given a date value |
| DAYS (WS) | Returns the number of days between 2 dates |
| DAYS360 (WS) | Returns the number of days between two dates based on a 360-day year |
| EDATE (WS) | Adds a specified number of months to a date and returns the result as a serial date |
| EOMONTH (WS) | Calculates the last day of the month after adding a specified number of months to a date |
| FORMAT DATES (VBA) | Takes a date expression and returns it as a formatted string |
| HOUR (WS, VBA) | Returns the hours (a number from 0 to 23) from a time value |
| ISOWEEKNUM (WS) | Returns the ISO week number for a date |
| MINUTE (WS, VBA) | Returns the minutes (a number from 0 to 59) from a time value |
| MONTH (WS, VBA) | Returns the month (a number from 1 to 12) given a date value |
| MONTHNAME (VBA) | Returns a string representing the month given a number from 1 to 12 |
| NETWORKDAYS (WS) | Returns the number of work days between 2 dates, excluding weekends and holidays |
| NETWORKDAYS.INTL (WS) | Returns the number of work days between 2 dates, excluding weekends and holidays |
| NOW (WS, VBA) | Returns the current system date and time |
| SECOND (WS) | Returns the seconds (a number from 0 to 59) from a time value |
| TIME (WS) | Returns a decimal number given an hour, minute and second value |
| TIMESERIAL (VBA) | Returns a time given an hour, minute, and second value |
| TIMEVALUE (WS, VBA) | Returns the serial number of a time |
| TODAY (WS) | Returns the current system date |
| WEEKDAY (WS, VBA) | Returns a number representing the day of the week, given a date value |
| WEEKDAYNAME (VBA) | Returns a string representing the day of the week given a number from 1 to 7 |

| | |
|---|---|
| WEEKNUM (WS) | Returns the week number for a date |
| WORKDAY (WS) | Adds a specified number of work days to a date and returns the result as a serial date |
| WORKDAY.INTL (WS) | Adds a specified number of work days to a date and returns the result as a serial date (customizable weekends) |
| YEAR (WS, VBA) | Returns a four-digit year (a number from 1900 to 9999) given a date value |
| YEARFRAC (WS) | Returns the number of days between 2 dates as a year fraction |

| Math/Trig Functions | |
|---|---|
| ABS (WS, VBA) | Returns the absolute value of a number |
| ACOS (WS) | Returns the arccosine (in radians) of a number |
| ACOSH (WS) | Returns the inverse hyperbolic cosine of a number |
| AGGREGATE (WS) | Apply functions such AVERAGE, SUM, COUNT, MAX or MIN and ignore errors or hidden rows |
| ASIN (WS) | Returns the arcsine (in radians) of a number |
| ASINH (WS) | Returns the inverse hyperbolic sine of a number |
| ATAN (WS) | Returns the arctangent (in radians) of a number |
| ATAN2 (WS) | Returns the arctangent (in radians) of (x,y) coordinates |
| ATANH (WS) | Returns the inverse hyperbolic tangent of a number |
| ATN (VBA) | Returns the arctangent of a number |
| CEILING (WS) | Returns a number rounded up based on a multiple of significance |
| CEILING.PRECISE (WS) | Returns a number rounded up to the nearest integer or to the nearest multiple of significance |
| COMBIN (WS) | Returns the number of combinations for a specified number of items |
| COMBINA (WS) | Returns the number of combinations for a specified number of items and includes repetitions |
| COS (WS, VBA) | Returns the cosine of an angle |
| COSH (WS) | Returns the hyperbolic cosine of a number |
| DEGREES (WS) | Converts radians into degrees |
| EVEN (WS) | Rounds a number up to the nearest even integer |

| | |
|---|---|
| EXP (WS, VBA) | Returns e raised to the nth power |
| FACT (WS) | Returns the factorial of a number |
| FIX (VBA) | Returns the integer portion of a number |
| FLOOR (WS) | Returns a number rounded down based on a multiple of significance |
| FORMAT NUMBERS (VBA) | Takes a numeric expression and returns it as a formatted string |
| INT (WS, VBA) | Returns the integer portion of a number |
| LN (WS) | Returns the natural logarithm of a number |
| LOG (WS) | Returns the logarithm of a number to a specified base |
| LOG (VBA) | Returns the natural logarithm of a number |
| LOG10 (WS) | Returns the base-10 logarithm of a number |
| MDETERM (WS) | Returns the matrix determinant of an array |
| MINVERSE (WS) | Returns the inverse matrix for a given matrix |
| MMULT (WS) | Returns the matrix product of two arrays |
| MOD (WS) | Returns the remainder after a number is divided by a divisor |
| MOD (VBA) | Returns the remainder after a number is divided by a divisor |
| ODD (WS) | Rounds a number up to the nearest odd integer |
| PI (WS) | Returns the mathematical constant called pi |
| POWER (WS) | Returns the result of a number raised to a given power |
| PRODUCT (WS) | Multiplies the numbers and returns the product |
| RADIANS (WS) | Converts degrees into radians |
| RAND (WS) | Returns a random number that is greater than or equal to 0 and less than 1 |
| RANDBETWEEN (WS) | Returns a random number that is between a bottom and top range |
| RANDOMIZE (VBA) | Used to change the seed value used by the random number generator for the RND function |
| RND (VBA) | Used to generate a random number (integer value) |
| ROMAN (WS) | Converts a number to roman numeral |
| ROUND (WS) | Returns a number rounded to a specified number of digits |
| ROUND (VBA) | Returns a number rounded to a specified number of digits |

| | | |
|---|---|---|
| ROUNDDOWN (WS) | | Returns a number rounded down to a specified number of digits |
| ROUNDUP (WS) | | Returns a number rounded up to a specified number of digits |
| SGN (VBA) | | Returns the sign of a number |
| SIGN (WS) | | Returns the sign of a number |
| SIN (WS, VBA) | | Returns the sine of an angle |
| SINH (WS) | | Returns the hyperbolic sine of a number |
| SQR (VBA) | | Returns the square root of a number |
| SQRT (WS) | | Returns the square root of a number |
| SUBTOTAL (WS) | | Returns the subtotal of the numbers in a column in a list or database |
| SUM (WS) | | Adds all numbers in a range of cells |
| SUMIF (WS) | | Adds all numbers in a range of cells based on one criteria |
| SUMIFS (WS) | | Adds all numbers in a range of cells, based on a single or multiple criteria |
| SUMPRODUCT (WS) | | Multiplies the corresponding items in the arrays and returns the sum of the results |
| SUMSQ (WS) | | Returns the sum of the squares of a series of values |
| SUMX2MY2 (WS) | | Returns the sum of the difference of squares between two arrays |
| SUMX2PY2 (WS) | | Returns the sum of the squares of corresponding items in the arrays |
| SUMXMY2 (WS) | | Returns the sum of the squares of the differences between corresponding items in the arrays |
| TAN (WS, VBA) | | Returns the tangent of an angle |
| TANH (WS) | | Returns the hyperbolic tangent of a number |
| TRUNC (WS) | | Returns a number truncated to a specified number of digits |

| | |
|---|---|
| **Statistical Functions** | |
| AVEDEV (WS) | Returns the average of the absolute deviations of the numbers provided |
| AVERAGE (WS) | Returns the average of the numbers provided |
| AVERAGEA (WS) | Returns the average of the numbers provided and treats TRUE as 1 and FALSE as 0 |
| AVERAGEIF (WS) | Returns the average of all numbers in a range of cells, based on a given criteria |

| | |
|---|---|
| AVERAGEIFS (WS) | Returns the average of all numbers in a range of cells, based on multiple criteria |
| BETA.DIST (WS) | Returns the beta distribution |
| BETA.INV (WS) | Returns the inverse of the cumulative beta probability density function |
| BETADIST (WS) | Returns the cumulative beta probability density function |
| BETAINV (WS) | Returns the inverse of the cumulative beta probability density function |
| BINOM.DIST (WS) | Returns the individual term binomial distribution probability |
| BINOM.INV (WS) | Returns the smallest value for which the cumulative binomial distribution is greater than or equal to a criterion |
| BINOMDIST (WS) | Returns the individual term binomial distribution probability |
| CHIDIST (WS) | Returns the one-tailed probability of the chi-squared distribution |
| CHIINV (WS) | Returns the inverse of the one-tailed probability of the chi-squared distribution |
| CHITEST (WS) | Returns the value from the chi-squared distribution |
| COUNT (WS) | Counts the number of cells that contain numbers as well as the number of arguments that contain numbers |
| COUNTA (WS) | Counts the number of cells that are not empty as well as the number of value arguments provided |
| COUNTBLANK (WS) | Counts the number of empty cells in a range |
| COUNTIF (WS) | Counts the number of cells in a range, that meets a given criteria |
| COUNTIFS (WS) | Counts the number of cells in a range, that meets a single or multiple criteria |
| COVAR (WS) | Returns the covariance, the average of the products of deviations for two data sets |
| FORECAST (WS) | Returns a prediction of a future value based on existing values provided |
| FREQUENCY (WS) | Returns how often values occur within a set of data. It returns a vertical array of numbers |
| GROWTH (WS) | Returns the predicted exponential growth based on existing values provided |
| INTERCEPT (WS) | Returns the y-axis intersection point of a line using x-axis values and y-axis values |
| LARGE (WS) | Returns the nth largest value from a set of values |

192

| | |
|---|---|
| LINEST (WS) | Uses the least squares method to calculate the statistics for a straight line and returns an array describing that line |
| MAX (WS) | Returns the largest value from the numbers provided |
| MAXA (WS) | Returns the largest value from the values provided (numbers, text and logical values) |
| MAXIFS (WS) | Returns the largest value in a range, that meets a single or multiple criteria |
| MEDIAN (WS) | Returns the median of the numbers provided |
| MIN (WS) | Returns the smallest value from the numbers provided |
| MINA (WS) | Returns the smallest value from the values provided (numbers, text and logical values) |
| MINIFS (WS) | Returns the smallest value in a range, that meets a single or multiple criteria |
| MODE (WS) | Returns most frequently occurring number |
| MODE.MULT (WS) | Returns a vertical array of the most frequently occurring numbers |
| MODE.SNGL (WS) | Returns most frequently occurring number |
| PERCENTILE (WS) | Returns the nth percentile from a set of values |
| PERCENTRANK (WS) | Returns the nth percentile from a set of values |
| PERMUT (WS) | Returns the number of permutations for a specified number of items |
| QUARTILE (WS) | Returns the quartile from a set of values |
| RANK (WS) | Returns the rank of a number within a set of numbers |
| SLOPE (WS) | Returns the slope of a regression line based on the data points identified by known_y_values and known_x_values |
| SMALL (WS) | Returns the nth smallest value from a set of values |
| STDEV (WS) | Returns the standard deviation of a population based on a sample of numbers |
| STDEVA (WS) | Returns the standard deviation of a population based on a sample of numbers, text, and logical values |
| STDEVP (WS) | Returns the standard deviation of a population based on an entire population of numbers |

| | |
|---|---|
| STDEVPA (WS) | Returns the standard deviation of a population based on an entire population of numbers, text, and logical values |
| VAR (WS) | Returns the variance of a population based on a sample of numbers |
| VARA (WS) | Returns the variance of a population based on a sample of numbers, text, and logical values |
| VARP (WS) | Returns the variance of a population based on an entire population of numbers |
| VARPA (WS) | Returns the variance of a population based on an entire population of numbers, text, and logical values |

| Logical Functions | |
|---|---|
| AND (WS) | Returns TRUE if all conditions are TRUE |
| AND (VBA) | Returns TRUE if all conditions are TRUE |
| CASE (VBA) | Has the functionality of an IF-THEN-ELSE statement |
| FALSE (WS) | Returns a logical value of FALSE |
| FOR...NEXT (VBA) | Used to create a FOR LOOP |
| IF (WS) | Returns one value if the condition is TRUE or another value if the condition is FALSE |
| IF (more than 7) (WS) | Nest more than 7 IF functions |
| IF (up to 7) (WS) | Nest up to 7 IF functions |
| IF-THEN-ELSE (VBA) | Returns a value if a specified condition evaluates to TRUE or another value if it evaluates to FALSE |
| IFERROR (WS) | Used to return an alternate value if a formula results in an error |
| IFNA (WS) | Used to return an alternate value if a formula results in #N/A error |
| IFS (WS) | Specify multiple IF conditions within 1 function |
| NOT (WS) | Returns the reversed logical value |
| OR (WS) | Returns TRUE if any of the conditions are TRUE |
| OR (VBA) | Returns TRUE if any of the conditions are TRUE |
| SWITCH (WS) | Compares an expression to a list of values and returns the corresponding result |
| SWITCH (VBA) | Evaluates a list of expressions and returns the corresponding value for the first expression in the list that is TRUE |
| TRUE (WS) | Returns a logical value of TRUE |
| WHILE...WEND (VBA) | Used to create a WHILE LOOP |

| Information Functions | |
|---|---|
| CELL (WS) | Used to retrieve information about a cell such as contents, formatting, size, etc. |
| ENVIRON (VBA) | Returns the value of an operating system environment variable |
| ERROR.TYPE (WS) | Returns the numeric representation of an Excel error |
| INFO (WS) | Returns information about the operating environment |
| ISBLANK (WS) | Used to check for blank or null values |
| ISDATE (VBA) | Returns TRUE if the expression is a valid date |
| ISEMPTY (VBA) | Used to check for blank cells or uninitialized variables |
| ISERR (WS) | Used to check for error values except #N/A |
| ISERROR (WS, VBA) | Used to check for error values |
| ISLOGICAL (WS) | Used to check for a logical value (TRUE or FALSE) |
| ISNA (WS) | Used to check for #N/A error |
| ISNONTEXT (WS) | Used to check for a value that is not text |
| ISNULL (VBA) | Used to check for a NULL value |
| ISNUMBER (WS) | Used to check for a numeric value |
| ISNUMERIC (VBA) | Used to check for a numeric value |
| ISREF (WS) | Used to check for a reference |
| ISTEXT (WS) | Used to check for a text value |
| N (WS) | Converts a value to a number |
| NA (WS) | Returns the #N/A error value |
| TYPE (WS) | Returns the type of a value |

| Financial Functions | |
|---|---|
| ACCRINT (WS) | Returns the accrued interest for a security that pays interest on a periodic basis |
| ACCRINTM (WS) | Returns the accrued interest for a security that pays interest at maturity |
| AMORDEGRC (WS) | Returns the linear depreciation of an asset for each accounting period, on a prorated basis |
| AMORLINC (WS) | Returns the depreciation of an asset for each accounting period, on a prorated basis |
| DB (WS) | Returns the depreciation of an asset based on the fixed-declining balance method |

| | |
|---|---|
| DDB (WS, VBA) | Returns the depreciation of an asset based on the double-declining balance method |
| FV (WS, VBA) | Returns the future value of an investment |
| IPMT (WS, VBA) | Returns the interest payment for an investment |
| IRR (WS, VBA) | Returns the internal rate of return for a series of cash flows |
| ISPMT (WS) | Returns the interest payment for an investment |
| MIRR (WS, VBA) | Returns the modified internal rate of return for a series of cash flows |
| NPER (WS, VBA) | Returns the number of periods for an investment |
| NPV (WS, VBA) | Returns the net present value of an investment |
| PMT (WS, VBA) | Returns the payment amount for a loan |
| PPMT (WS, VBA) | Returns the payment on the principal for a particular payment |
| PV (WS, VBA) | Returns the present value of an investment |
| RATE (WS, VBA) | Returns the interest rate for an annuity |
| SLN (WS, VBA) | Returns the depreciation of an asset based on the straight-line depreciation method |
| SYD (WS, VBA) | Returns the depreciation of an asset based on the sum-of-years' digits depreciation method |
| VDB (WS) | Returns the depreciation of an asset based on a variable declining balance depreciation method |
| XIRR (WS) | Returns the internal rate of return for a series of cash flows that may not be periodic |
| **Database Functions** | |
| DAVERAGE (WS) | Averages all numbers in a column in a list or database, based on a given criteria |
| DCOUNT (WS) | Returns the number of cells in a column or database that contains numeric values and meets a given criteria |
| DCOUNTA (WS) | Returns the number of cells in a column or database that contains nonblank values and meets a given criteria |
| DGET (WS) | Retrieves from a database a single record that matches a given criteria |
| DMAX (WS) | Returns the largest number in a column in a list or database, based on a given criteria |
| DMIN (WS) | Returns the smallest number in a column in a list or database, based on a given criteria |

| | |
|---|---|
| DPRODUCT (WS) | Returns the product of the numbers in a column in a list or database, based on a given criteria |
| DSTDEV (WS) | Returns the standard deviation of a population based on a sample of numbers |
| DSTDEVP (WS) | Returns the standard deviation of a population based on the entire population of numbers |
| DSUM (WS) | Sums the numbers in a column or database that meets a given criteria |
| DVAR (WS) | Returns the variance of a population based on a sample of numbers |
| DVARP (WS) | Returns the variance of a population based on the entire population of numbers |

| Engineering Functions | |
|---|---|
| BIN2DEC (WS) | Converts a binary number to a decimal number |
| BIN2HEX (WS) | Converts a binary number to a hexadecimal number |
| BIN2OCT (WS) | Converts a binary number to an octal number |
| COMPLEX (WS) | Converts coefficients (real and imaginary) into a complex number |
| CONVERT (WS) | Convert a number from one measurement unit to another measurement unit |

| File/Directory Functions | |
|---|---|
| CHDIR (VBA) | Used to change the current directory or folder |
| CHDRIVE (VBA) | Used to change the current drive |
| CURDIR (VBA) | Returns the current path |
| DIR (VBA) | Returns the first filename that matches the pathname and attributes specified |
| FILEDATETIME (VBA) | Returns the date and time of when a file was created or last modified |
| FILELEN (VBA) | Returns the size of a file in bytes |
| GETATTR (VBA) | Returns an integer that represents the attributes of a file, folder, or directory |
| MKDIR (VBA) | Used to create a new folder or directory |
| SETATTR (VBA) | Used to set the attributes of a file |

| Data Type Conv. Functions | |
|---|---|
| CBOOL (VBA) | Converts a value to a boolean |

| | |
|---|---|
| CBYTE (VBA) | Converts a value to a byte (ie: number between 0 and 255) |
| CCUR (VBA) | Converts a value to currency |
| CDATE (VBA) | Converts a value to a date |
| CDBL (VBA) | Converts a value to a double |
| CDEC (VBA) | Converts a value to a decimal number |
| CINT (VBA) | Converts a value to an integer |
| CLNG (VBA) | Converts a value to a long integer |
| CSNG (VBA) | Converts a value to a single-precision number |
| CSTR (VBA) | Converts a value to a string |
| CVAR (VBA) | Converts a value to a variant |

# The End

Made in the USA
Las Vegas, NV
10 February 2024